# Spectatorship and the Real in French Contemporary Theatre

**Methuen Drama Engage** offers original reflections about key practitioners, movements and genres in the fields of modern theatre and performance. Each volume in the series seeks to challenge mainstream critical thought through original and interdisciplinary perspectives on the body of work under examination. By questioning existing critical paradigms, it is hoped that each volume will open up fresh approaches and suggest avenues for further exploration.

### Series Editors

*Mark Taylor-Batty*
University of Leeds, UK
*Enoch Brater*
University of Michigan, USA

### Titles in the series include:

*Contemporary Drag Practices and Performers: Drag in a Changing Scene Volume 1*
Edited by Mark Edward and Stephen Farrier
ISBN 978-1-3500-8294-6

*Performing the Unstageable: Success, Imagination, Failure*
Karen Quigley
ISBN 978-1-3500-5545-2

*Drama and Digital Arts Cultures*
David Cameron, Michael Anderson and Rebecca Wotzko
ISBN 978-1–472-59219–4

*Social and Political Theatre in 21st-Century Britain: Staging Crisis*
Vicky Angelaki
ISBN 978-1–474-21316–5

*Watching War on the Twenty-First-Century Stage: Spectacles of Conflict*
Clare Finburgh
ISBN 978-1-472-59866-0

*Fiery Temporalities in Theatre and Performance: The Initiation of History*
Maurya Wickstrom
ISBN 978-1-4742-8169-0

*Ecologies of Precarity in Twenty-First Century Theatre: Politics, Affect, Responsibility*
Marissia Fragkou
ISBN 978-1-4742-6714-4

*Robert Lepage/Ex Machina: Revolutions in Theatrical Space*
James Reynolds
ISBN 978-1-4742-7609-2

*Social Housing in Performance: The English Council Estate on and off Stage*
Katie Beswick
ISBN 978-1-4742-8521-6

*Postdramatic Theatre and Form*
Edited by Michael Shane Boyle, Matt Cornish and Brandon Woolf
ISBN 978-1-3500-4316-9

*Sarah Kane's Theatre of Psychic Life: Theatre, Thought and Mental Suffering*
Leah Sidi
ISBN 978-1-3502-8312-1

For a complete listing, please visit
https://www.bloomsbury.com/series/methuen-drama-engage/

# Spectatorship and the Real in French Contemporary Theatre

Amélie Mons

Series Editors:
Mark Taylor-Batty and Enoch Brater

methuen | drama
LONDON • NEW YORK • OXFORD • NEW DELHI • SYDNEY

METHUEN DRAMA
Bloomsbury Publishing Plc
Bloomsbury Publishing Plc, 50 Bedford Square, London, WC1B 3DP, UK
Bloomsbury Publishing Inc, 1385 Broadway, New York, NY 10018, USA
Bloomsbury Publishing Ireland, 29 Earlsfort Terrace, Dublin 2, D02 AY28, Ireland

BLOOMSBURY, METHUEN DRAMA and the Methuen Drama logo are
trademarks of Bloomsbury Publishing Plc

First published in Great Britain 2024
This paperback edition published 2025

Copyright © Amélie Mons, 2024

Amélie Mons has asserted her right under the Copyright, Designs and Patents
Act, 1988, to be identified as author of this work.

Cover image: Close-Up of woman veiled hand (© Rieko Honma / Getty Images)

All rights reserved. No part of this publication may be: i) reproduced or transmitted in
any form, electronic or mechanical, including photocopying, recording or by means of
any information storage or retrieval system without prior permission in writing from the
publishers; or ii) used or reproduced in any way for the training, development or operation
of artificial intelligence (AI) technologies, including generative AI technologies. The rights
holders expressly reserve this publication from the text and data mining exception as per
Article 4(3) of the Digital Single Market Directive (EU) 2019/790.

Bloomsbury Publishing Plc does not have any control over, or responsibility for,
any third-party websites referred to or in this book. All internet addresses given
in this book were correct at the time of going to press. The author and publisher
regret any inconvenience caused if addresses have changed or sites have ceased
to exist, but can accept no responsibility for any such changes.

A catalogue record for this book is available from the British Library.

Library of Congress Cataloging-in-Publication Data
Names: Mons, Amélie, author.
Title: Spectatorship and the real in French contemporary theatre / Amélie Mons.
Description: London ; New York : Methuen Drama, 2024. | Series: Methuen
drama engage | Includes bibliographical references.
Identifiers: LCCN 2023030917 (print) | LCCN 2023030918 (ebook) | ISBN
9781350300835 (hardback) | ISBN 9781350300873 (paperback) | ISBN
9781350300842 (epub) | ISBN 9781350300859 (pdf)
Subjects: LCSH: Experimental theater–France–History–21st century. |
Experimental drama, French–21st century–History and criticism. |
Theater–Production and direction–France–History–21st century.
Classification: LCC PN2635.2 .M66 2024 (print) | LCC PN2635.2 (ebook) |
DDC 792.0944–dc23/eng/20230927
LC record available at https://lccn.loc.gov/2023030917
LC ebook record available at https://lccn.loc.gov/2023030918

ISBN: HB: 978-1-3503-0083-5
PB: 978-1-3503-0087-3
ePDF: 978-1-3503-0085-9
eBook: 978-1-3503-0084-2

Series: Methuen Drama Engage

Typeset by Deanta Global Publishing Services, Chennai, India

For product safety related questions contact productsafety@bloomsbury.com.

To find out more about our authors and books visit www.bloomsbury.com and
sign up for our newsletters.

*To Rob.*

I know a state beyond thought, conscience, being, one which has neither words or letters, but into which you enter through screams and swipes. And it is no longer sound or sense that escapes, nor words, just bodies *(Artaud 2004: 1351).*[1]

# Contents

Introduction ..... 1
   The real on stage ..... 3
   Contemporary practices and reactions ..... 8
   The real as an enigma ..... 14
   The encounter with 'the real thing' ..... 18
   A theatre for spectators ..... 24
   All the world's a stage . . . ..... 28

I  In the audience: Miscomprehension of contemporary theatre in France ..... 31
   1.1. Lack of pleasure, lack of meaning ..... 31
      1.1.1. Avignon 2005 ..... 31
      1.1.2. Power relationships between spectators and directors ..... 38
   1.2. The French political problem ..... 44
      1.2.1. Public funding and elitist theatre ..... 44
      1.2.2. Contemporary practices in conventional spaces ..... 52

II  On stage: Strategies to challenge perception ..... 61
   2.1. Our processes of recognition ..... 61
      2.1.1. Why do we need to recognize our surroundings? ..... 61
      2.1.2. The difficulty in apprehending shows that challenge processes of recognition ..... 64
   2.2. Strategies to thwart processes of recognition ..... 72
      2.2.1. Duration and exhaustion of the signs ..... 72
      2.2.2. The unfamiliar ..... 85
      2.2.3. Children and animals ..... 96

III  Spectatorship as a philosophical practice ..... 109
   3.1. Do we really want to encounter the real? ..... 109
      3.1.1. A cruel world ..... 109
      3.1.2. *Terra incognita* ..... 125

|   |        |                               |     |
|---|--------|-------------------------------|-----|
|   | 3.2.   | Becoming masters of our gaze  | 146 |
|   |        | 3.2.1. Accepting simplicity   | 146 |
|   |        | 3.2.2. Peace of mind          | 153 |

Conclusion   171

Notes   175
Works cited   195
Index   203

# Introduction

Sitting quietly in the dark I observe nine actors, in underwear, performing a task. They are walking, but only very slowly because their bodies are violently shaking. They seem to be nervously paralysed. Their breath begins to shorten, their skin reddens and their bodies start sweating. They have signed up for one of Jan Fabre's teaching groups. A few minutes earlier, Cédric Charron and Annabelle Chambon, two experienced performers who worked for the Flemish director for years, asked them to cross the rehearsal room while contracting every single muscle they could feel. They formed a line, their backs against a wall, and, once the signal was given, mutated into these shivering, exposed bodies. Now they are only focused on one single task: to reach the other side of the room before the fatigue makes them fall. I watch them, first impressed by the intense physical effort their bodies are producing. I root for them. I want to see them successfully complete the task. They are telling me a story; perhaps it is the story of an impossible race, or perhaps it is a metaphor for life and the ageing process. Or maybe it represents a tragic battle between humans and the physical world. There I am, sitting quietly in the dark, thinking, reflecting on what this action means, what it is telling me. And while I am trying to decide which of my theories is the most convincing, the actors are still shaking, and they are still sweating, and they are still panting. After a little while I see it. I stop elaborating an image, I stop projecting my own elucubrations onto their bodies and their actions. I see that what they do is nothing more than what they do. The sound of their breathing is nothing more than the sound of their breathing. Their shaking and redness are nothing more than shaking and redness, simple involuntary reactions to physical stimuli. Them crossing the room is really nothing more than them crossing the room. This exercise lasted almost thirty minutes. It took me half of this time to stop trying to understand, and to fully open my perception to what was being done. For a few precious minutes, I became a humble guest in a world of mere bodies performing a task. This experience was intellectually disturbing. Strangely, it was also very emotional. To this day, I am still struck by how this level of perception is complex to reach, and yet feels so simple when experienced.

In one of his meditations, Marcus Aurelius talks about the perception of the 'real thing' (as translated by Martin Hammond). In order to see the real thing, a shift in perception must occur. The causes of this shift remain mysterious, but it certainly leads to many discoveries. A delicious roast meat will thus reveal the *dead body* of a fish, a bird or a pig. The Falernian wine will give way to 'the mere juice of grapes', the purple robe will become 'the hair of a sheep soaked in shell-fish blood'. Similarly, sexual intercourse will be considered as nothing more than 'the friction of a membrane and a spurt of mucus ejected'. These perceptions are to be valued says Marcus Aurelius. In fact, they should constitute a 'practice throughout all your life' (Marcus Aurelius 2006: 47). When we see things as they appear to us, our vanity is defeated. We may then realize that the world exists on its own terms and no longer belongs to us. This practice also allows us, as spectators, to extend our field of perception of the stage, or indeed, of the world. Refraining ourselves from projecting our own representations means looking beyond our own interests; the world is no longer how we want it to be. It just is. By doing so, we can enhance our empathy towards others and, in fact, towards ourselves. These perceptions reveal a world that we inhabit not as secluded individuals but as humanity. However, it seems that these valuable discoveries can only be experienced in fleeting moments. Constantly perceiving the things insofar as they appear to us would be extremely challenging, if not impossible. We will always need to recognize and understand our surroundings in order to evolve and communicate. Yet, if we are aware that such perceptions are possible, and if we know what can potentially trigger them, it may impact some of our responses in daily life for the better.

## The real on stage

The encounter that took place in that rehearsing room is not a unique example, nor was it accidental. Some contemporary theatre practices invite their spectators to forego their own process of projection onto the stage in order to see *only* what stands before them. In Fabre's theatre for instance, repetition and duration are two important strategies. They give enough time for the spectators to exhaust their attempts to grasp, to understand. After witnessing the same action on repeat for ten, fifteen, twenty minutes, some spectators will eventually let 'their guard down' and experience the raw, unvarnished reality of what they are facing. These strategies cause controversy, partly because they question the common assumption that theatre is a cultural place based on collective processes of recognition.

This book argues that the theatre can be the best place for one to experience the real. Here, the real is understood as the things as they first appear to us. It does not refer to the objective world or to the world as it is (since, unsurprisingly, we do not have access to it). The real describes the world as it hits us before we process it through cultural assimilation. The modalities of such an encounter in a theatre are complex; more complex than in everyday life. The reason for this is that on stage, a chair is hardly *just* a chair, a crown *just* a crown, a tree *just* a tree and so on. As a meaningful space, the stage provides inevitably a double to every object. Tadeusz Kowzan pointed out that the first reality of any theatrical objects is the one given by the stage, that is, their representation (1992).[1] They exist first and foremost as signs. Their physical reality is not always clearly acknowledged. To explain this further let me provide a personal example. In 2012, in Lyon (France), I went to see *Le Goret* by Johanny Bert at the Théâtre des Célestins. I was sitting in the front row. The actor on stage was playing with a high heel shoe, symbolizing the woman that his character was in love with. At some point, the character became angry and threw the shoe away, so far that it landed off the stage and at my feet. I was now looking at this shoe which a minute ago was the image of a woman. Something was not quite right about it; it was suddenly a shoe, *just* a shoe. My attention was drawn towards its physical presence: the irregularities in the material, the slightly damaged heel and the shoe's vibrant colour. The object struck me in its material reality. I was paying attention to this object as never before. There was something mysterious in the presence of this shoe. This mystery, I think, came from the fact that the shoe had been stripped of its initial meaning. The shoe became an intruder, not only in my spectator's space but also in my own perception, preventing me from recognizing it, disturbing my gaze. 'How did I not realize it was real?' Suddenly, the shoe showed me that it exists, too, not as an image, but as a real object.[2] In a theatre, the perception of material realities is rarely predominant. The stage should therefore be the place where the 'real thing' cannot appear.

We may think that the real is the opposite of theatricality. William Egginton defines theatricality as 'the capacity to experience meaning as [...] occupying another spatial realm existing in a mimetic relationship to the real, substantial one' (2003: 86). Theatricality refers to the ability to project meaning onto the stage; to turn the stage into a mental double constructed thanks to a pre-established set of tools (representations, references, concepts, desires, and so forth). It refers to the ability to *recognize* the actions and objects on stage. The theatre is thus the place of recognition *par excellence*. In 2012, I went to see *An Enemy of the People* directed by German director Thomas Ostermeier in Lyon. After a change of scene, a prop, originally used as a lectern, was turned into a fridge. A few days later, during a meeting with the director at the Goethe Institute, a spectator asked him whether this double use was a symbol of our consumer society, in which political ideas are increasingly standardized. Ostermeier seemed amused and replied that the reason for using the same prop to represent two very different objects was simply because it was the most practical solution. Said plainly, he was just killing two birds with one stone. Over-interpreting the actions and objects on stage is a common pitfall for anyone used to going to the theatre; we have, after all, been taught that the stage is a meaningful space. But the theatrical stage is not the only place where people are invited to perceive through doubles. This perception also defines our modern relationship with the world. Theatre, in a sense, is only the consecration of such a worldview. According to Gumbrecht, humans began to perceive the world as a 'hermeneutic field' (i.e. as an object to decipher, analyse, interpret) many centuries ago. He identifies meaning as interpretation:

> To interpret the world means to go beyond its material surface or to penetrate that surface in order to identify a meaning (i.e., something spiritual) that is supposed to lie behind or beneath it. Conversely, it also becomes more and more conventional to think of the world of objects and of the human body as surfaces that 'express' deeper meanings. (2004: 25–6)

Interpretation became the 'exclusive paradigm that Western culture made available for those who wanted to think the relationship of humans to their world' (28). Following a similar approach, Egginton argues that humans began to consider the world as detached from themselves (hence as a space of projection) from the sixteenth century, along with advances in science and the rise of individualism (2003). Theatricality is thus not only to be found in theatres, but also in our everyday relationship to the world. The world became a stage, and the stage withdrew a little further from the world.

Yet it is precisely because of this apparent incompatibility between the real and theatricality that theatre makers can trigger encounters with the world. Many directors who perform regularly in France invite the experience of the real back on stage. These include Fabre, Romeo Castellucci, Rodrigo García, Jan Lauwers and Gisèle Vienne. They show that the theatrical can give rise to such encounters. Spectators who expect to perceive the world on stage as they imagined it can be struck by a sudden apparition of the 'real' world. For once, they may no longer be able to mentally recreate what they are watching. This is reminiscent of what Lehmann explains regarding the postdramatic spectator: 'The task of the spectators is no longer the neutral reconstruction, the re-creation and patient retracing of the fixed image but rather the mobilization of their own ability to react and experience in order to realize their participation in the process that is offered to them' (2006: 134–5). Directors play with the expectations of spectators who assume they will see something they can recognize. They develop strategies that use these very expectations and representations to better thwart them and provoke shock. In this regard, it is hardly surprising that a certain distrust between them and the audience has developed. As interesting as these strategies are, they nonetheless demonstrate a form of manipulation. Nevertheless, these theatres are far from being free from theatricality. They do contain signs – references, symbols and so on – easy for a spectator to recognize and appropriate. But they often use these signs to better distance themselves from them.

Here, I will examine the possibilities of an encounter with the 'real thing' (to quote Marcus Aurelius) in contemporary French theatre and will explore how some strategies implemented on stage have contributed to a growing sense of mistrust between directors and their audiences. This book is not a study on presence in postdramatic theatre. Although some of our cited authors do discuss the concept of presence (Gumbrecht, Egginton, Jean-Luc Nancy), this study primarily focuses on experiences of the real. Presence has been widely discussed in theatre studies. It has often been considered as opposed to another notion. In *Liveness, Performance in a Mediatized Culture*, Philip Auslander considers presence through the opposition between live (theatre) and recorded (mass media). Presence is thus explored as liveness, as *hic et nunc*. In *Critique du théâtre*, Jean-Pierre Sarrazac argues that postdramatic theatre 'is a theatre which would require a theatrical event that would be such a pure presentification of theatre that it will remove any idea of reproduction and repetition of the real' (2000: 63).[3] Similarly, Jean-François Lyotard defines the postdramatic theatre of 'forces, intensities, present affects' (quoted by Lehmann 2006: 37). In his influential essay *Postdramatic theatre*, Hans-Thies Lehmann discusses presence thus:

> As long as signs, as discussed above, still include some material 'content' (references) – even if they no longer offer a synthesis – they

can still be assimilated through labyrinthine associative work. If, however, these references cease almost entirely, then reception faces an even more radical refusal: the confrontation with a figuratively 'silent' and dense presence of bodies, materials and forms. The sign merely communicates itself, or more precisely: its presence. Perception finds itself thrown back onto the perception of structures. [...] Actors, lights, dancers, etc. are given over to a purely formal observation; the gaze finds no occasion to detect a depth of symbolic significance beyond the given, but instead – either with pleasure or boredom – remains stuck within the activity of seeing the 'surface' itself. (2006: 98–9)

Presence in theatre is here understood as opposed to meaning. The spectator's gaze is suddenly immobilized. 'Perception of structures', 'purely formal observation', 'gaze [. . .] stuck' are all expressions that emphasize the spectators' passivity. While facing presence, the audience is intellectually freezing, stuck in a superficial observation of the things on stage. For Lehmann, the immediate confrontation with the stage is thus an experience in which something is missing, hence risky, as it can easily fail and bore the audience. Lehmann does not develop his argument further. He neither addresses nor explores the experience any further. Later in the essay, he does mention examples of performances in which the real suddenly appears on stage, but he does not analyse the impact of such enterprises on the spectators. For many authors, presence is defined as non-representation and nowness. 'It is the idea that theatre needs to abolish representation and become monstration,' underlines Alain Badiou (2013: 22).[4] Lauwers himself explains that 'we have to destroy the idea of representation in the theatre and replace it with presentation' (Lauwers 2010: 453). Postdramatic theatre often tries to be as close in its relationship to the present world as possible. For this purpose, it suspends the effects of representation by different means. Lehmann provides a useful example regarding acting: 'For performance, just as for postdramatic theatre, "liveness" comes to the fore, highlighting the provocative presence of the human being rather than the embodiment of a figure' (2006: 135). However, the fact that most postdramatic performances take place on a stage (traditional space of illusions) is a paradox that is often ignored. To understand presence as mere here and now leads to simplifications if we are analysing shows that maintain physical distance between the stage and the audience. In productions by directors such as Vienne, Fabre, Castellucci, García or Lauwers, the 'real thing' usually appears thanks to a complex entanglement of presence and representations.

In Fabre's theatre, for instance, performers might perform dangerous or exhausting acts; but they are *also* characters. Thus, the stage remains a space of illusion, even though the presence of the actions is emphasized. In *Le Metope del Partenone* (2015), Castellucci does not establish a physical distance between the actors and the audience and invites the spectators to move freely around the action (this absence of physical distance remains extremely rare in his theatre). Yet the actors do not interact with them and remain mysteriously distant. In *4* by García (2015), the presence of animals and children on stage reminds the audience of the 'real world'. However, their presence is caught up in a complex system of representations. These directors create a space on stage where actions appear both fictitious and hyper-present. This practice is not new, but it conveys an aspect which is not often discussed: the idea that presence on stage becomes mysterious.[5] While presence as nowness does not appear to be satisfactory in studies of these performances, the notion of 'the real' as developed by contemporary French philosopher Clément Rosset can bring some new insights into the understanding of these contemporary practices. In Rosset's philosophy, the encounter with the real does not banish meaning as the experience of presence often does. There is meaning in the encounter with the real, says Rosset. This meaning is simply more complex because it does not primarily rely on processes of recognition. I will come back to this later in the introduction.

## Contemporary practices and reactions

This book focuses on theatre makers who are particularly well known in France. Although I explore various works, some directors will be consistently discussed throughout the reflection: Jan Fabre, Romeo Castellucci, Gisèle Vienne, Rodrigo García and, to a lesser extent, Jan Lauwers. Particular attention will be paid to Fabre's and Castellucci's productions, as the two directors count among the most famous (and controversial) directors still actively performing in France. Their practice is particularly misapprehended by French audiences. Analysing some of their productions in great details will help us better understand how experiences of the real can arise in a theatre and why they can trigger controversies.

Since the 1990s, these directors' productions have been both vehemently rejected and rapturously received by different audiences across Europe. French audiences have been the most divided. France enjoys one of the liveliest and most international theatre scenes in Europe. Yet French audiences are often openly opposed to contemporary directors' works. At the 2005 Avignon festival, numerous spectators and critics labelled their works as 'obscene', 'pretentious', 'demagogic' and 'provocative'. Vienne (Franco-Austrian), Lauwers (Belgian), García (Argentinian), Fabre (Belgian) and Castellucci (Italian) often access French funding and regularly present their work in France. These artists are, mostly, involved in transdisciplinary work in addition to their work for performance, and their practice of theatre diverges strongly from the dominant modes and expectations of French audiences. In their productions, the stage is indeed no longer a space of projection and identification for audiences but a space in which the reality of perception itself becomes ambiguous and unstable. To understand to what extent these practices are not always fully appreciated by various audiences for what they have to offer, one can provide a recent example. When García took charge of the national theatre of Montpellier in 2014 (being appointed by Aurélie Filippetti, who was then the culture minister), he invited many contemporary artists to perform such as Fabre, Philippe Quesne, Lauwers and Tiago Rodrigues. He also presented some of his own work. However, he made the decision in September 2016 to leave his post by the end of 2018. In a letter dated October 2016, he explained that his decision was partly motivated by the 'incomprehension' he faced from the population of Montpellier and the lack of support from his economic partners. He also underlined that the theatre of Montpellier has one of the smallest budgets, and that since he took office, the city decided to withdraw 100,000 euros from the initial budget of 450,000 euros per year. During García's direction, the theatre lost 10,000 spectators over the course of a year (a third of its audience). García's experience in Montpellier is one of the most glaring examples of the persistence of specific spectators' habits and preferences that remain irreconcilable with more contemporary practices. A significant difference between audience expectations and these directorial projects persists. As soon as performances depart from familiarly codified aesthetics, the act of spectating itself becomes accordingly complex and leaves audiences confused (if not frustrated), doubtful of the codes and practices of spectatorship. In fact, contradictory discourses from critics, researchers and directors have blurred established knowledge of the nature and function of spectatorship. Audiences are being encouraged to engage with these directors' projects while also to resist reductive responses which privilege rational understanding. It appears that new approaches to contemporary theatre are needed so that avant-garde theatre retains a meaningful place in France and in Europe more generally.

These directors' productions could be categorized as predominantly visual and physical, even though their actors commonly use scripts. Although their aesthetics differ, these directors are particularly interested in the materiality of the bodies and actions on stage. Lauwers and Fabre first started as visual artists and Vienne as a puppeteer. Castellucci has defined himself as a pilgrim of matter, and García's company is eloquently named 'La Carniceria Teatro' ('Butcher Shop Theatre' – García's father was a butcher). Admittedly, it is not easy to categorize these directors' shows as belonging to a specific practice of theatre or genre as they engage with many different traditions. Yet they all have been significantly influenced by various forms of physical theatre (García, Vienne, Fabre and Lauwers arguably more than Castellucci). Physical forms of theatre often demonstrate an absence of clear narrative and focus mainly on the actors' physical movements. In *Through The Body: A Practical Guide to Physical Theatre*, Dymphna Callery provides a useful insight on how physical theatre could be approached:

> Physical theatre is not codifiable. The term is applied to such a diverse range of work that it has become virtually undefinable. Yet some significant parallels emerge [. . .]: the emphasis is on the actor-as-creator rather than the actor-as-interpreter; the working process is collaborative; the working practice is somatic; the stage-spectator relationship is open; the live-ness of the theatre medium is paramount. The method of working is based on the idea that theatre is about craft, celebration and play, rooted in collaboration, and made by an ensemble dedicated to discovering a collective imagination. (2005: 5)

Physical theatre questions the validity of categorising different practices of theatre because it is influenced by various fields of art. Vienne appeared particularly annoyed during an interview in 2021 when Fabienne Pascaud (famous theatre critic for left-wing journal *Télérama*) insisted on the fact that her productions were mixing theatre, dance, puppets and music. Vienne replied: 'Since Bob Wilson, Pina Bausch and Kantor, there is no need for these categories to exist. I am surprised that in 2021 we are still asking this question' (Vienne 2021).[6] Similarly, Lauwers does not consider himself as a director only but 'as an artist who among other things also happens to make theatre' (Lehmann 2006: 107). During an interview in 2010, replying to a question asking him to describe himself, he says: 'Not as a director, painter, writer or filmmaker. I am just an artist who tries to use all those different media. Isn't that the only way to survive? Why should I restrict myself? Art should not specialize' (Lauwers 2010: 449). Additionally, these directors' productions borrow from endurance art, including the performance of some dangerous or very demanding actions. For instance, in *Snakesong Trilogy III* by Lauwers, a young woman builds an unstable and dangerous looking pyramid made of pieces of glass. The possibility of injury is certainly present. In fact, endurance arts can involve pain or exhaustion for the performers. It includes durational art, largely present in Fabre's theatre, with actors repeating the same action until they reach physical exhaustion. Fabre has, for instance, collaborated with performance artist Marina Abramović on *Virgin Warrior – Two Hearts* in 2004. Fabre and García often work with animals, and Castellucci and García occasionally work with children. One of the main similarities between these artists is their great affinity with Antonin Artaud's theatre of cruelty. This does not mean that their shows are systematically physically violent. Artaud himself explained several times that the theatre of cruelty was not necessarily violent: 'as soon as I said "cruelty" everyone took it to mean "blood". But a *"theatre of cruelty"* means theatre that is difficult and cruel for myself first of all' (1970: 60). In accordance with Artaud's definition, their theatres invite the spectators to explore their 'nervous sensibility' (66), while rejecting what Artaud called 'psychological theatre' (64). Artaud's reflections upon theatre offered to reconsider the place of the spectator in theatre. He explored the potential of an audience's responses to the actions taking place on a stage. In their own ways, these directors perpetuate these considerations. They aim to disturb their spectators in order to extend their fields of perception.

Fabre's and Castellucci's theatres have interested many scholars. The following list is non-exhaustive and only includes the most influential references. As early as 1994, Hugo De Greef and Jan Hoet published *Jan Fabre, le guerrier de la beauté*, in which they transcribed a series of interviews with Fabre. We owe the main study of Jan Fabre's theatre to Luk Van Den Dries, who in 2005 published *Jan Fabre, observations sur un processus de creation*. In this essay, Van Den Dries details rehearsal processes (which he attended) and provides interviews with Fabre and some of his actors. He works closely with Jan Fabre and his company and is probably the scholar who has the closest relationship with the Flemish director. In 2013, he edited *Jan Fabre, Esthétique du paradoxe* with Marianne Beauviche, following a conference held in 2011. The book mainly focuses on the representations of bodies on stage and Fabre's dramaturgy. Romeo Castellucci has attracted more academic attention, partly because he has himself published essays on his theatre and therefore established a theoretical frame to help audiences approach his productions. In 2000, he published an article on the presence of animals on stage, 'The Animal Being on Stage' in *Performance Research*. With his sister, the philosopher Claudia Castellucci, he published *Les Pèlerins de la matière* in 2001. He is arguably more willing to participate in interviews than Fabre and has published books in collaboration with scholars, such as *The Theatre of Societas Raffaello Sanzio*, with Joe Kelleher and Nicholas Ridout in 2007. In 2005, Bruno Tackels published *Les Castellucci*, in which he gathered several interviews that he had conducted with Castellucci, as well as reports on rehearsals, which he had followed. Several others have more recently focused on the actual experience of the spectators when attending specific shows by Castellucci, sometimes detailing their own personal experience as spectators. This is the case in *Stage Fright, Animals and Other Theatrical Problems*, by Ridout, in 2006, *After Live, Possibility, Potentiality, and the Future of Performance*, by Daniel Sack in 2015 and *The Theatre of Death – The Uncanny Mimesis* by Mischa Twitchin in 2016. These essays are not entirely dedicated to Castellucci's theatre, yet they discuss his performances from the spectator's perspective. Rodrigo García, Gisèle Vienne and Jan Lauwers have attracted less critical attention, especially in the UK. We owe one of the major studies of García's work to Bruno Tackels, with his essay *Rodrigo García*, published in 2007 in his series 'Ecrivains de plateau' which reviews several major European theatre makers (including Castellucci). García's theatre has been discussed in a few academic papers (mainly in French and Spanish), as well as briefly in *Practising the Real on the Contemporary Stage* by José A. Sánchez (2014). Bryan Reynolds has more recently – and extensively – analysed the aesthetics of his theatre in *Intermedial Theatre: Performance Philosophy, Transversal Poetics, and the Future of Affect* (2017), as well as Lauwers's work. Vienne's work has mainly been discussed in the UK thanks to Julia Dobson, who published, for instance, in 2013, 'Troublantes matières: des corps (in)habités dans l'œuvre de Gisèle Vienne', in *Surmarionnettes et mannequins: Craig, Kantor et leurs héritages contemporains*. In 2017, Anna Gallagher-Ross published an article in *Theater* entitled *Uncanny Landscapes: Gisèle Vienne*. Overall, Vienne's work has been predominantly analysed through her use of puppets on stage. Finally, Jan Lauwers's processes of creation are mentioned a few times in *Postdramatic Theatre* by Hans-Thies Lehmann (2006, first published in German in 1999). His theatre has often been put in parallel with Fabre's one, for instance, in the article co-written by Van Den Dries, Timmy De Laet and Edith Cassiers 'Creating by Annotating: the director's notebooks of Jan Fabre and Jan Lauwers' in *Performance Research*, published online in 2015. *No Beauty for Me There Where Human Life is Rare*, published in 2007, explores in detail his approach to theatre and his aesthetics.

## The real as an enigma

I have argued that the notion of presence is not entirely satisfactory for this study of theatrical encounters, because it does not consider the fact that the stage is paradoxically a space of illusions. Yet, one author has explained particularly well how *presence* on stage can also appear mysterious. For Denis Guénoun, theatrical presence is 'a very singular and enigmatic manifestation' that only shows itself as a pure phenomenon (2014: 94). Manifestation comes from the Latin *manifestare* which means 'to show' but also 'to discover, to reveal', hence the connotations of mystery. Guénoun argues that the spectators' perception entangles two dimensions: the face and the profile. The predominant one is the profile: 'this is the dimension that is presented to the audience, not directly addressed to them, but presented as configuring an image, a drawing; presented as a profile for them to observe' (2014: 92). The profile thus refers to the imaginary world represented on stage, the image, the double that the spectators create in their mind. The face, on the other hand, constitutes the second dimension of every spectator's perception. It characterizes the physical presence of the play, yet not simply as here and now. Theatrical presence remains enigmatic, inexplicable:

> Presence is the naked act of manifesting on stage, *thanks* to the stage. [. . .] Everyone knows and every actor experiences how presence involves and requires an element of reservation of withdrawal, of sobriety or discretion as much as it may also be exuberance and projection towards the audience. Anecdotes abound amongst actors about situations in which one of them may have little or nothing to do or say on stage, being perhaps in a secondary or minor role, and yet all eyes are upon him or her. This is because he or she 'has presence', whereas a 'gesticulator' may wear himself out trying to attract people's attention. [. . .] Presence is therefore by no means equivalent to addressing. (2014: 94)

The expression 'all eyes are upon him or her' is particularly interesting (the literal translation is in fact 'we see only him or her'). Theatrical presence can *invade* the spectators' perceptual fields. The presence of certain actors can make us oblivious of anything else. Moreover, the fact that Guénoun writes he or she 'has presence' instead of he or she 'is present' is relevant. Theatrical presence is presence *in* someone (or something), rather than presence *of* someone. The stage appears for Guénoun as a privileged space for this phenomenon to occur. Indeed, while the stage is commonly seen as a space that conveys meaning to everything, it is also a space that provides a certain greater force to what it hosts. An actor might be fascinating on stage, have a mysterious presence, but might appear very ordinary once seen walking in the streets. In this sense, the stage appears as a space of revelation.

The experience of the real in theatre can bring along this sense of revelation. Castellucci has clearly expressed this idea. For him, the stage is capable of making pure fiction 'real'. Conversely, the 'real' elements on stage would appear less real. Therefore, using real blood on stage makes the action 'necessarily false', explains Castellucci in an interview (2007: 217). Perhaps the reason for this is that, on Castellucci's stage, things do not tend to refer to something else.

Instead, they are unduplicable. The stage gives its objects and actions freedom. It is precisely because they are on stage that they can be perceived free from any systems of representation. In other words, the objects and actions owe their existence to the mere existence of the stage, and the only purpose of the stage is to be observed (the old Greek *théatron* means a place for viewing). Therefore, what happens on stage will always have the possibility to happen only for the sake of it. The purpose of things can be as little as being their mere presence. For instance, an actor walking on stage might be perceived as more real than a pedestrian crossing a road, because his action only addresses the necessity to walk on the stage while the pedestrian crossing the road is doing so for a particular purpose, in order to go somewhere. On stage, the action can also be the intention. On this matter, Artaud famously defined theatre as 'momentary pointlessness which drives [people] to useless acts without immediate profit' (1970: 15). The real in theatre can be thus more powerful than the everyday reality. '*It is the real* against reality. [. . .] It is firstly an unknown energy, and energy from the unknown,' affirms Castellucci (Banu and Tackels 2005: 256).[7]

In November 2015, I went to see a production by Castellucci, *Le Metope del Partenone*, which was performed in the Grande Halle de la Villette in Paris.[8] The space in which the production took place was vast and did not feature any specific reserved space for the audience. We spectators therefore wandered around the place, waiting for the performance to begin while wondering where exactly the action might take place. Without any warning (such as a change of light or a particular sound), an actor arrived in the middle of the space and started to pretend that he was choking. He was so physically involved in this simulation that his face turned red and one wondered whether he was now choking for real. Antonin Artaud wanted the actors as well as the spectators to enter 'a state that one enters into through screams and swipes'. This sentence was particularly relevant for the action we witnessed. The choking character finally hit the ground, his body contorted with pain. His life appeared to be in danger when, from the back of the Halle, an ambulance arrived. It made its way through the spectators to reach the injured character. The rescue team tried to save him, but the character eventually died. In silence, the team tidied up their equipment, got back in the ambulance and left. The corpse of the character stayed there for several long minutes before the actor stood up and solemnly left the space. This scene was repeated six times with different characters and accidents: amputation, allergic reaction, disembowelment and so on. They all died. The representations of the physical injuries were extremely realistic.

In between each accident, the spectators were walking around, waiting for another catastrophe to happen. During these few minutes where time felt like it was suspended, an enigma was projected on a screen on one of the walls, questioning the reality of what we had just perceived. I remember how surprising it was to see a new actor entering the space, as the majority of us identified them rather late and therefore did not always spot where they were coming from. Yet, nothing looked more real than these fake accidents and deaths. It did not look real in the sense that it looked like actors were 'really' injured and about to 'really' die. Instead, it looked real because the mere presence of the actors justified their actions and, conversely, their actions justified their presence. In other words, everything that occurred was intentional, meant to happen. This might sound obvious, but in Castellucci's productions, this conveys a certain gravity to the actions. The characters and actors are sometimes taken as being the same because the person on stage seems to know how it will end; there is no pretending in this sense. Nicholas Ridout has said that '[he] had never seen anyone else [than Castellucci] taking the imitation game so seriously' (2007: 13). In the street, a passer-by witnessing an accident might try to understand how the person injured themselves, how bad the injury is, what to do to help them. In this performance, none of these preoccupations matter. The action did not have to be explained. It was meant to be watched. Paradoxically, the stage in these directors' theatres is a place where one can experience what philosopher Clément Rosset named the '*idiocy*' of the real.

## The encounter with 'the real thing'

French philosopher Clément Rosset refers to the world as it first appears to us as 'the real'. The real is *idiotic*, he argues in *Le Réel, traité de l'idiotie*. From the Latin *idiotès*, something idiotic is without reflection, without doubles (Rosset 2014: 7).[9] The real is idiotic because it is simple, unique and unduplicable. In modern use, the term 'idiot' labels a person who may not be able to see beyond the mere appearance of things. An idiot's mind is thus considered without depth. Interestingly, in Rosset's philosophy, the idiot is more likely to encounter with the real than anyone else. Since they are less inclined to interpret the world, to double it with complex representations, the real appears to them more easily. The image of the idiot is the personification of a certain experience; it is, of course, not to be taken literally. In fact, for most of us, the encounter with the real will only occur if there is a temporary confusion between our representations and reality. Rosset is one the most innovative philosophers of the real and has analysed with great detail how, and in which circumstances, such an experience can be triggered.[10] His philosophy conveys complex ideas and analyses unusual experiences while always remaining extremely accessible. Most of his reflections are thus inserted into the context of everyday life. As a result, philosophy becomes a playful activity, inviting the reader to seek and enact the described experiences. His philosophy has not been discussed in relation to theatre yet. However, our understanding of the spectators' encounter with the real in a theatre would strongly benefit from his ludic approach to perceptive experiences. Theatre may be considered as a microcosm where such experiences are triggered, whether on purpose, accidentally, or as the result of the spectator's will to perceive in a certain way. Inspired by Rosset's approach to philosophy, I want to consider the possibility for spectatorship to be a playful philosophical activity.

Among Rosset's practical examples, two are particularly useful to understand how an encounter with the real can be triggered. The first one is called the anticipated representation ('la représentation anticipée';

2014: 163–5). It is based on the idea that the real commonly precedes its representation. In theatre for instance, a play will be the representation of individuals' social bonds, of historical events, of pre-established stories and so on. Yet to truly encounter with the real, one may want to follow the converse pattern. The anticipated representation defines an experience where the real is experienced *after* its representation. Rosset mentions a passage of *The Future of an Illusion* by Freud. In this book, Freud reports his journey to Athens and describes the shock he felt in front of the old city. As a child, he explains, he was taught about Athens's history, its architecture and its geography. But looking now at the temples, the old ruins, the blue sea, he cannot help but be surprised. Things were not so different from what he had imagined and yet they appear to him with an unexpected strength. For Rosset, this confirms the fact that the real is indeed idiotic; no representation can prepare us for it. What struck Freud is the uniqueness of the real. This is obvious one may argue; but these powerful connections with the world are nonetheless rarely experienced. The real is unique but spectating its uniqueness is far from being an obvious and easy process. Yet the anticipated representation is a helpful example that demonstrates how the real can appear into our lives. Experiencing the representation of the object before experiencing the object itself is an anecdote that helps us to understand how processes of recognition work and how they can be frustrated to give rise to the real. The anticipated representation can also help us understand some strategies used by theatre makers, and how they can impact upon us as spectators. When reading Rosset's example, I found myself recalling a puppet show that I saw years ago. During the first half of the performance, the only actor on stage was constantly playing with a life-size puppet. The puppet was realistic. It did not look alive, but it certainly looked like a human being with its own specific facial traits. It was thus easy for us as spectators to imagine the presence of a tall, old man, as represented by the puppet. And then, suddenly, another actor made his entrance. He *was* the puppet; more specifically, he was the one who served as the model for the puppet. The puppet was his representation. His sudden presence appeared mysterious and uncanny, and irradiated the whole theatre. In some ways, he was almost scary, as his presence was threatening our reality as an assembly of quiet and docile representations. He was *there*, looking at the audience, looking at us.

The second experience described by Rosset is called the panic representation ('la représentation panique'; 2014: 165–8). For Rosset, the panic representation occurs when the real and its representation are perceived at the very same time. He takes the example of a film by Steven Spielberg called *Duel*, in which a car driver is pursued by a truck for a whole day. No reason is given. Nothing explains the action. The truck, says Rosset, is a *signifiant* without a *signifié*. There is no meaning to be found in this chase; no explanation that would help the spectator (or the car driver) understand the situation. 'It is what it is and that's all, it's unbelievable, but there's nothing else to find,' states Rosset (2004: 168).[11] The action and its representation therefore exist at the same time. Indeed, the chase *also* seems to be represented. From the spectator's point of view, this representation is easy to understand. A game of lights and shadows as well as different camera angles *mettent en scène* the chase. The spectator is confronted with a chase starting *in medias res*, with no landmark, yet staged. But according to Rosset, the car driver, the main character in the film, also seems to perceive the chase as a representation. The character feels like he recognizes something in the event, even though he is experiencing this situation for the very first time. Perhaps he understands that this chase *has* to happen? Maybe what he recognizes is the tragic of the situation? Here, the meaning of the chase is to be found in its presence itself, in the simple fact that it takes place. The car driver panics because he does not have time to process the situation, yet he understands that it is happening. He does not have time to attribute a meaning to it himself; his own meaning. While the car driver and the spectator may not understand the situation, they may appreciate its inevitability. The action and its meaning overlap each other. The real has thus a chance to strike all at once. Like the anticipated representation, the panic representation highlights our need to attribute meaning to things, and our potential distress (or wonder) when we fail to do so. This strategy is used by Fabre in some of his shows. *L'Histoire des larmes*, for instance, plays on the same confusion between action and representation. The spectator is confronted with an opening scene starting *in medias res*, without any points of reference, yet staged. The performance starts with nine actresses on stage, on the floor, screaming and crying like babies. The play was first performed at the Cour d'honneur during the Festival of Avignon in 2005. This first scene lasts for sixteen minutes, offering no possible escape for the spectator (about 2,000 spectators fit in the Cour d'honneur, it is thus rather unlikely to be seated near an exit). The performance was not well received by the public, and this opening section was sometimes met by booing from the audience.[12] It is easy enough to understand why the audience may reject such a start to the performance. The scene was disturbing because it could not be grasped, nor could it be stopped. Its meaning was seemingly to be found in its presence itself; in the simple fact that it occurred on stage, that it was staged. Of course, some spectators may feel irritated when faced with a scene that does not provide any key to decipher it. If we really want to, we can still interpret retrospectively and find some deeper meaning. Where there is a path, a will can always be found, claims Rosset.[13] But at the very instant audiences of *Duel* or *L'Histoire des larmes* are spectating the actions, nothing makes sense. Yet something is happening. Processes of recognition are simply failing to identify what it is.

These two experiences, the anticipated representation and the panic representation, can lead to an unbiased experience of the world. In both cases, this experience occurs because the subjects fail to fully recognize what stands before them. This can also be related to Deleuze's concept of the encounter. According to Deleuze, the experience of an encounter is only possible if the subject does not recognize what they are facing. It is only possible if what they perceive remains a *terra incognita*, neither recognized nor recognizable (2001: 136). To experience an encounter is unusual as recognition remains the main mode of our perceptive faculties. For the philosopher, everyday objects (or concepts) are assimilated thanks to a pre-existing set of intellectual tools: identity, opposition, analogy and so on. The perception of an object is in fact a more or less complex entanglement of many things already known (memories) articulated by the intellect (concepts). There are thus two different kinds of object which lead to two different perceptions: the objects of recognition and the objects of encounter. The objects of recognition only let the thoughts refer to themselves: 'thought is thereby filled with no more than an image of itself' (138). In contrast, the objects of encounter force us to *think*. For Deleuze, one must be unable to recognize the objects to produce real thoughts. In Deleuzian philosophy, the objects of encounter provide a thought without image. The absence of recognition is particularly difficult to experience because it coerces the subject to think, that is, to create.[14]

The real can therefore be experienced if there is a failure of recognition. Furthermore, I make the hypothesis that the encounter with the real, in life or on stage, may in fact be generated by a constant oscillation between *attempts* at recognition and *failures* to do so. In other words, the real can only be experienced if the subject fails to recognize and not if they simply do not recognize. Attempts must be made. To clarify this idea, Jean-Luc Nancy's definition of presence may be useful. For him, presence is 'the coming that effaces itself and brings itself back' (1994: 5). Consequently, being is 'is not yet to have been, and already to have been' (2). The encounter with the real (or 'presence' in Nancy's vocabulary) is generated by a perpetual movement between what is about to be perceived and that which has already been perceived. Hans Ulrich Gumbrecht offers an enlightening explanation of Nancy's approach:

> Being, I think, refers to the things of the world before they become part of a culture (or, using the rhetorical figure of the paradox, the concept refers to the things of the world before they become part of the world) [. . .] Again, in order to be experienced, Being would have to become part of a culture. As soon, however, as Being crosses this threshold, it is, of course, no longer Being. (2004: 70)

Such encounter with the world may thus happen in this fragile moment made of thwarted attempts at recognition. It is in this very moment, before cultural assimilation, that the real can appear. It is in this very moment that it may suddenly display its uniqueness. The encounter with the real coexists with the incapacity to recreate what is perceived. The failure in being able to grasp is important because it makes the subject realize that the existence of the world precedes their gaze. The present study does not seek to discuss trances or pure sensory experiences, but rather to analyse how an encounter with the real can be triggered. What the subjects lose in this experience is not their ability to *think*, as Deleuze defines it, but to recognize.

It is important to repeat at this stage that the real here does not refer to the objective world or to the world as it is. Rosset himself has repeatedly argued that any perceptions of the world is necessary partly a sensory experience.[15] Going even further, Deleuze explains that the object of encounter 'gives rise to sensibility with regard to a given sense' (2001: 139). The world is understood by the senses yet remains unintelligible: 'that which can only be sensed (the *sentiendum* or the being of the sensible) moves the soul, "perplexes" it – in other words, forces it to pose a problem' (140; original emphasis). This (in) comprehension via the senses is accentuated by the fact that meaning here seems extra-verbal. In other words, thoughts are not shaped by language but are rather triggered by 'something in the world that presents itself to sensations', as Laura Cull puts it (2012a).[16] The 'real thing' opens the door to an uninterpretable world, refusing our intellect and our control. To encounter it, the subject must abandon their doubles (representations) that parasite perception. Such an experience welcomes our senses but prevent our 'anti-perception' (a term used by Clément Rosset in *Tropiques* and *L'invisible*). For Rosset, to anti-perceive means not to perceive but also to perceive what one believes to perceive. This faculty enables humans to transform what they see in order to reconcile their expectations with their relationship to the world. Perhaps this proves to be a downside to human intelligence. We are capable to understand as well as capable to believe we understand. We are capable to persuade ourselves that we perceive something that we actually do not see. In order to encounter with the real, one must refrain oneself from this tendency. Our contemporary directors aim to challenge spectators' habits of 'anti-perception' along with their interpretative grasp of the world. These directors offer, in this way, the possibility to learn to unlearn.

## A theatre for spectators

To be able to get rid of our preconceived ideas, we need to know that we are indeed invited to do so, and that we may and can. In the conclusion to his essay on presence and theatricality, Egginton rightly pointed out that it is by knowing how our perception of the stage works that we 'can facilitate the effort to work effectively within it, and, if so desired, to effectuate change' (2003: 168). The present book does not claim that change necessarily needs to happen nor that these theatre makers are misunderstood geniuses. It is an attempt to produce an alternative approach to some forms of contemporary practice, which explores non-verbal meaning and its impact on the spectators. Its ambition is to clarify how an encounter with the real can occur and how such experiences may open the field of our possibilities as spectators.

The directors under scrutiny are questioning the spectators' sense of reality. I examine how they implement strategies on stage that aim to frustrate processes of recognition and, eventually, to trigger an unveiling of the 'real thing'. Actively engaging with Rosset's philosophy will allow me to refocus on the spectators' experience. His philosophy could be seen as overly simple, and yet it can be challenging to apply. Indeed, to be appreciated, his readers must abandon their tendency towards recurrent interpretation. However, while this study proposes a new approach to appreciate what these performances can offer, it does not question the fact that these performances are not to everybody's liking. It does not provide a strict methodology on how to be 'the ideal spectator' and does not seek to establish evaluation criteria. Instead, I propose an enrichment of spectatorship and a set of strategies to see these works in a new and more fruitful way – I do not cast judgement on reactions. Similarly, Rosset's philosophy does not establish a strict system of thought but, rather, through a series of reflections on the real, invites the reader to experience new ways of engaging with the world. Here, I simply want to open new paths, examine some possibilities, and the reader may find that some analyses echo with their sensibility more than others. Besides Rosset's concept of the real, other compatible philosophical perspectives are combined to support an articulation of how such an encounter might take place. They include Deleuze's concept of difference and repetition, Giorgio Agamben's concept of profanation and Viktor Shklovsky's defamiliarization. An original mixed methodology is constructed: close analysis of productions and the reactions they triggered from the audience, observation of methods employed in actor training sessions, examination of the practitioners' philosophies (disseminated in interviews, essays, statements) and analyses of the data from audience testimonies. These theatres offer new kinds of meaning; new kinds of perception should be thus explored.[17] There is, of course, something contradictory in trying to analyse non-verbal meaning. Yet, as Deleuze argued, philosophical thoughts, to truly be formed, need to be disrupted by the unthinkable.

As stated previously, the encounter with the real does not refer to the experience of the 'objective' world. While it asks its subject to partially get rid of social and cultural representations, it remains, partly, a sensory experience. Anyone will experience this encounter according to their own sensitivity. In this sense, the book does not seek to apply pre-existing concepts to performances. Philosophy is not to be treated as a master-code that would help us discover the truth. Instead, it is *from* these encounters that a range of new concepts can be developed. I will thus explore philosophy-as-performance and performance-as-philosophy. In this regard, this study is partly influenced by the Performance Philosophy field. Laura Cull points out in *Encounter in Performance Philosophy* that 'Performance Philosophy should strive to decrease the tendency to merely *apply* extant philosophy to performance' and should instead 'tend more towards addressing the extent to which performance might be considered a philosophical activity in its own right' (2014: 15; original emphasis). Similarly, David Krasner and David Saltz have clarified that 'using' and 'doing' philosophy are two distinct practices (2006: 7–8). 'Using' philosophy to apprehend theatre, that is, to apply pre-existing concepts in performances appears unsatisfactory in many ways. Daniel Johnston underlines:

> Many scholars analyse performance by invoking theories developed in literary theory and cultural studies, for example 'using' Judith Butler, Jean Baudrillard, and Pierre Bourdieu to analyse a particular production or practice. The validity of such arguments may well stand or fall depending on each 'theory' rather than in the scholar's own argument. (2017: 6)

Cull expresses the same concern and argues that even though a 'critical turning point has been reached' in the relationship between philosophy and performance, many scholars still tend to adopt a certain philosophy as their 'guiding methodology for performance analysis' (2012b: 20). To explore the relationship between performance and philosophy itself would thus enable one 'to value the seemingly ineffable or even superficial or "meaningless" aspects of performance practice (from the point of view of linguistically, semiotically, representationally focused modes of analysis)' (2012b: 20–1). Johnston argues thus:

> Yet performance philosophy can also be studied in its own right despite drawing on previous theorists. The analyses of performance philosophy are therefore distinct from critical studies and prescriptive manifestos in that they see theatre as a *philosophical practice*. (2017: 6; original emphasis)

Following this statement, the present study analyses performances from a philosophical perspective, rather than a critical one. Krasner and Saltz explain that critical studies 'interpret' specific elements from performances while philosophical studies advance 'new approaches' to discuss 'the nature' of theatre (2006: 2). Here, I want to question *how* these theatres can be approached and *which* experience their productions can offer to the spectators.

I will explore how spectatorship itself can be a philosophical practice. Spectatorship is something we perform: it is an experience created from incomprehension, questions, sensations and emotions. I argue that spectatorship is a form of philosophical practice and should be investigated as such. By identifying various spectators' perceptual and sensory experiences, I hope to demonstrate that audiences are themselves active philosophers and that the meaning of a play is co-created or indeed belongs to them rather than to the directors (following Jacques Rancière's thoughts on the emancipated spectator). The book will develop philosophical tools not to help understand the stage, but to help spectators identify and understand their own processes of perception. Eva Schuermann explains that philosophy 'has been primarily interested in vision as a means of obtaining knowledge' (2019: 1), but here philosophy will be treated as a practice that does not seek to obtain knowledge but rather helps to extend our fields of perception. Moreover, and due to the diversity of the spectators' experience, philosophy will be treated as an ongoing and creative process, constantly redefining its approach. These innovative directors offer theatre the opportunity to become a playground for the mind; there is perhaps nothing to decipher yet everything to explore. The book will open the door to a creative and productive understanding of spectatorship that conciliates spectators' expectations and directors' projects.

The first chapter explores the cultural and historical context of the critical rejection of these directors' theatres. It examines the reasons behind a contemporary disregard for some contemporary theatrical practices, especially in France, and draws on the political problems that the performances engender. The second chapter explores strategies implemented on stage by the directors to thwart their spectators' processes of recognition, leading them to thus encounter with the real forcefully and surprisingly. Finally, the third chapter investigates how spectators can partially take back control of their own perceptions in a theatre.

I may sometimes refer to the spectator as an individual. I do not intend to generalize and am aware that audience members as individuals may well react differently from one another. When I mention a specific reaction, I do so with the support of other scholars, or in accordance with the director's project (how audiences might be encouraged to respond), or within the framework of my own experience as a spectator. The possibility of an unbiased encounter with the world is, of course, a subjective and intimate experience. Each spectator has not only their own sensitivity, but different groups of spectators can be identified with their own expectations, cultural, social, and intellectual habits: the traditional bourgeois ticket-buyer, the established critic, the mostly white audience, the culturally marginalized, the experienced theatregoer, the highly educated attendee and so on. Reception is cultural, social and situational. Shows are discussed and transmitted by people who are willing to speak and share their experiences. I am aware that, sadly, we tend to hear more from the educated and privileged cast than others.[18] Inevitably, most experiences will be kept quiet and locked in each individual's memories. I analyse reactions to better understand how those shows are perceived by some and what they can trigger in certain spectators; never to homogenize an audience's response.

## All the world's a stage . . .

In his last essay, *Eye and Mind*, Maurice Merleau-Ponty compares the surveyor ('le géomètre') with the geographer ('le géographe'). The geographer walks through specific environments, landscapes, while the surveyor manipulates objects; maps, compasses, rulers.[19] The surveyor is a scientist, because they make a distinction between the sensitive and the intelligible world. The geographer is an explorer; they aim to maintain a close relationship with the physical world and produce a knowledge that emanates from a sensitive experience. For Merleau-Ponty, one feels the world before one knows it. This book navigates through theatrical experiences, attempts to explore that which has no name, and argues that spectators should not have to remain surveyors and can instead become their own geographers.

When I saw *Le Goret* by Johanny Bert in 2012, the presence of the shoe that had fallen onto the floor next to my seat was surprising because it appeared before I had time to think about it. The shoe was no longer on stage, which means that it was no longer inserted into a system of signs that I could analyse. It landed in my landscape. I no longer recognized it because it was now *with* me. From being the surveyor I became the geographer. As Egginton has pointed out, we tend now to perceive the whole world as a stage; a space to decipher and where everything refers to something else. But if we focus on the theatrical stage, where indeed everything *should* refer to something else, perhaps we can understand how to cease distancing ourselves from the world. By exploring the stage like the geographer explores the land (or like our directors explore matter), we may reconnect with theatre as a practice, a celebration; *une fête*.

Johnston provides the example of an exercise he gives to his students that is comparable to the philosophical process spectators may go through:

> I usually ask my students to describe what a shoelace is and how to tie it. But then I add in that they need to do so as if they were talking to an alien [...] [who has] no understanding of anything that is familiar to our environment. [...] the students explain what a shoe is, what its parts are, what it is for, the activity of walking, what it means to protect a foot, what a foot is, what material the lace is made of, and so on. [...] All of these elements are important to what a shoelace is, but none of them individually encapsulates the matter. [...] The exercise emphasises the idea that the world 'hits us all at once' rather than as discrete properties of an object, qualities of an action, or words and phrases with intrinsic meaning. (2017: 27–8)

In many ways, contemporary directors question their spectators the same way that Johnston questions his students. Different elements on stage can be analysed, such as the decor, the costumes, the style of acting and the script. But what happens when the performances deconstruct these landmarks? When the decor is a mixture of familiar and non-familiar elements, when the costumes are inexistent, when the acting is not an act per se, when the script does not seem to make sense? The stage may then 'hits us all at once' and with any luck the world may reveal itself.

*What* is it that we see?

# I

# In the audience

## Miscomprehension of contemporary theatre in France

## 1.1. Lack of pleasure, lack of meaning

### 1.1.1. Avignon 2005

In July 2005, many spectators and critics raised their voices in the warm southern city of Avignon, to express their frustration, indignation, and anger at what they were spectating on the festival stages. In many ways, the highly controversial 2005 Avignon festival clarified what the expectations of some French audiences were. Founded in 1947 by actor and director Jean Vilar, the festival is renowned for inviting avant-garde international directors to present their work each summer. In 2005, numerous spectators and critics categorized some of these works as 'obscene', 'pretentious', 'demagogic' and 'provocative'. The festival revealed an important gap between many contemporary artists and an audience who conceptualized theatre in different and seemingly non-reconcilable ways. For French scholar Florence Dupont, 2005 broke significantly with the festival's traditions:

> For everyone, the 2005 festival broke with the tradition established by Jean Vilar. The Cour d'honneur did not host, as main performance, a text-based play, old or contemporary, written by an acclaimed playwright, directed by a prestigious director (2007: 17)[1]

By promoting a non-text-based theatre, avant-garde practitioners were accused, more or less explicitly, of betraying the spirit of Avignon and, by extension, of theatre itself: 'no theatre this year in Avignon' proclaimed some spectators that year (Banu and Tackels 2005: 11).² Jan Fabre was the invited artist; a Flemish playwright, performance artist, stage director and choreographer, rather than 'just' a *metteur en scène*. His show *Histoire des larmes* was presented in the Cour d'honneur. The Cour d'honneur is the most prestigious place in which an artist might hope to perform during the festival. It is located within the courtyard of the Palace of the Popes (Avignon was the residence of popes during the fourteenth century). Among the directors presenting their work this year were also Romeo Castellucci (presenting *B.#03 Berlin* and *BR.#04 Bruxelles)*, Thomas Ostermeier (*Anéantis* by Sarah Kane), Jacques Delcuvellerie (*Anathème*), Marina Abramović and Michael Laub (*The Biography remix*), Gisèle Vienne and Denis Cooper (*Une belle enfant blonde*), Jan Lauwers (*Needlapb 10*), Mathilde Monnier (*Frère&Soeur*) and Pascal Rambert (*AFTER/BEFORE*). These artists are Italian, German, Belgian, Serbian, American, Franco-Austrian, French. Most of them were, and still are, involved in plastic arts as well as being stage directors. Their practice of theatre is different from the dominant modes expected by French audiences. They offer a unique experience to their spectators with shows centred on the materiality of bodies, objects and movements. Spectators are not invited to identify with characters and engage with a narrative story but, instead, to let objects, bodies and actions on stage disturb their sense of reality and challenge their processes of perception.

Shows were controversial that year. But is theatre not necessarily a controversial activity? To what extent was Avignon 2005 more than a mere re-enactment of old debates around what theatre 'is'? As French writer Émile Zola famously wrote: 'Theatre does not exist, there are theatres, and I'm looking for my own' (1881: 388).³ Theatre is primarily a practice and certainly not an ideology. Performances can take different shapes from one culture to another. Performances can even follow different trends and belong to different art movements within one culture. Nevertheless, the history of theatre has been punctuated with scandals, in France and elsewhere, and spectators have always made claims over what theatre 'should' be. French modern history saw each century experiencing its own controversies.[4] Such scandals usually occur when long-established trends are widely criticized or simply not followed. Theatre scandals are very useful to study because they help us to understand what the audience's expectations were in a given cultural environment at a certain time. They also indicate how these expectations evolve throughout history. Not only can they trigger societal change, they also reveal the way people articulate theatre as both a political and cultural practice.

Avignon 2005 attracted a lot of critical attention because it was rapidly categorized as a contemporary theatre scandal. Books from critics and researchers were published the same year, trying to make sense of spectators' indignation and anger. The reported reactions were indeed unusually strong and aggressive. 'What have we done to you? Why have you made us suffer like this for an hour and a half?' yelled, for instance, a distressed spectator at the end of *AFTER/BEFORE* by Rambert, presented in the 'in' category (Talon-Hugon 2006: 24).[5] Directors were directly accused of provoking pain, suffering. Referring to that specific spectator, French scholar Carole Talon-Hugon argues that their reaction became emblematic of the spectators' profound mistrust in the shows that year in Avignon: 'Soon becoming the opponents' rallying cry, this phrase testifies to the refusal and incomprehension of their aesthetical experience, which, according to them, is one of suffering' (2006: 25–6).[6] Many of the 2005 shows were not well received because of their emotional intensity. Brigitte Salino, a journalist for *Le Monde* (one of the most widely read newspaper in France, alongside *Libération* and *Le Figaro*), claimed that the performances were leaving the spectators 'in a passive shock, up against an intense production which left no room for reflection' (2005).[7] The journalist Jean Claude Raspiengeas argued in *La Croix* (a Catholic newspaper) that the spectators 'were receiving a continuous stream of electric shocks' (Talon-Hugon 2006: 23).[8] Spectators appeared to have perceived themselves as victims, unfairly 'attacked' by avant-garde directors. The philosopher and journalist Régis Debray referred to them thus: 'an audience who considered themselves, no doubt incorrectly, as punished and blameless' (2005: 95).[9] Similarly, the journalist Didier Mereuze (*La Croix*) considered the festival this year as 'one of provocation and contempt' (2005),[10] and theatre director René Gonzales (in *L'Humanité*, previously an organ of the French Communist party) referred to it as 'an institutionalized lie, stated and cynically imposed to an audience ultimately taken hostage by veritable attacks on the truth, intelligence, modesty, humility; on their very dignity' (Herzberg et al. 2005).[11] Spectators from all political sides (from the left to the right wing), from various religious and moral backgrounds, were attacking the productions together. In some ways, the criticism that these directors attracted was arguably just as violent as some of their own shows. For actor George Bibille, who performed in *AFTER/BEFORE*, violence was primarily emanating from the audience, not from the stage (Banu and Tackels 2005: 31). Many spectators' reactions were indeed unequivocal. Jean-Marc Adolphe (founder of the bimonthly magazine *Mouvement*, on contemporary arts) analysed, very interestingly, a particular reaction from one spectator at the end of *Frère&Soeur* by Monnier: 'One particular spectator stands up during the performance and shouts: "it's fucking shit" before leaving. What makes someone feel so important, so sure of themselves, that they can address the whole audience like this?' (Banu and Tackels 2005: 32).[12] A demonstration of strong egos appeared to have taken place among spectators in Avignon that year.

Besides provoking pain, another criticism that these directors faced concerned the absence of texts and therefore clear messages in their productions. 'In the audience, we mainly felt puzzled faced with shows by Jan Fabre, the invited artist, Castellucci, Py, Peyret, Decorte, Abramovic,' wrote journalists Antoine De Baecque and René Solis in *Libération* (2005).[13] Audiences appeared unprepared to watch shows that strongly differed from what they were used to. After attending *Histoire des larmes* by Fabre, one spectator complained thus about 'une absence de théâtre' (Mereuze 2005): 'an absence of theatre'. Drawing on Zola's thoughts on theatre as theatres, one may be tempted to rectify their statement by 'an absence of [their] theatre'. As briefly mentioned previously, the strong reactions triggered by the performances presented in Avignon during 2005 could first be explained by the fact that the artists were deliberately blurring boundaries between different genres. Dance, durational and performing acts were concurrently present in these theatres with the emphasis often put on these things rather than the actors' scripts. While some spectators were happy to see artists expressing themselves through various means and media, others could not understand why scripts were no longer predominant. Close to Antonin Artaud's approach to theatre (which will be explored in more detail later), these productions were inviting the spectators to explore their 'nervous sensibility' (Artaud 1970: 66), while rejecting the 'psychological theatre' (Artaud 1970: 64). Dupont evoked a conflict between 'théâtre de texte' and 'théâtre de corps'; a conflict between intellectual and physical theatres. Yet, this categorization appears a little restrictive since a play is neither only physical nor purely intellectual. In fact, Dupont herself referred to this conflict as 'a debate that need not to take place' (2007: 17).[14]

Many scholars have tried to understand why Avignon, that year, caused such reactions. For Talon-Hugon, the Avignon controversy emphasized a conflict between different art traditions. Most productions, according to her, encouraged the audience to adopt an 'interested attitude', whereas more traditional forms often encourage a 'disinterested attitude' (2006: 13–23). Indeed, in a more traditional view of theatre, spectators perceive the performance in accordance with their aesthetic judgement. The spectators need to feel partly detached from the performance (which, in this case, is perceived as a piece of art) to better judge and therefore enjoy it. This posture enables the spectators to remain masters of their gaze and their critical judgement. For instance, a spectator contemplating a painting that features a naked body will not be offended, as their perception will be aesthetic rather than interested. The performance must then be perceived as an independent object in and of itself in which the spectators 'will get lost in the contemplation of its *qualia*. This means that they will become *indifferent to the represented object*' (2005: 14).[15] Yet in Avignon in 2005, the interested attitude was strongly encouraged. Here she refers specifically to Fabre's play:

Undoubtedly, Fabre floods the stage with real blood in *Je suis Sang*, and actors really do urinate in *Histoire des larmes*. These performances therefore develop strategies of involvement, which run counter to the Kantian imperative for a disinterested attitude to art. [. . .] There is a clear opposition between the two sides: distanciation against involvement, disinterested attitude against emotional participation, aesthetic emotions against real-life emotions. (2005: 19–23)[16]

According to Talon-Hugon, the shows in Avignon that year were of unfamiliar aesthetics, encouraging strong physical and emotional reactions from the audience rather than rational understandings. However, contrary to her assumption, no real blood was used on stage. After speaking with actor Cédric Charron who performed in the play, I was told that real blood was, for Fabre, never an option, due to its impractical coagulative properties. In fact, these shows do not reject narratives and representation as much as the 'stratégie d'intéressement' may suggest. They do aim to reach the spectators' senses; yet arguing that they prevent critical judgement from their spectators is a little strong. I am not sure everyone is capable of suspending their critical judgement for long. One cannot leave such rooted habits behind so easily.

It is interesting to see how French theatre studies often oppose 'la forme' and 'le fond' (which could roughly be translated by 'form' and 'content'). As an ex-French student, I was encouraged to consider a work of art as an articulation between 'form' and 'content'. A performance, or a painting, was a 'message' contained in a shape, a particular form. Never was I encouraged to consider that the form can be meaningful, or that the content could be the form itself. There is little work on the form alone (when not matching a content). In her review of *Histoire des larmes*, Boisseau concluded in *Le Monde*: 'Material beauty does not cover for the absence of meaning' (2005).[17] The content is too often perceived as superior to the form or style. Therefore, if the form is interesting but the content remains obscure, then a show is easily judged as poor. In *Le Monde* again, Darge et Salino referred to shows from Avignon in 2005 as 'artistically weak [. . .] without mediation nor real reflection'

(2005).¹⁸ More recently, in *Télérama* (an influential French cultural magazine), Emmanuelle Bouchez wrote that in *The Sea Within*, directed by Lisbeth Gruwez (former performer for Fabre), 'the formal aesthetic eventually became boring' (2018).¹⁹ The absence of clear meaning is thus perceived as a failure, an unfinished part of a performance. The 'formal aesthetic', which in itself can be very complex and would benefit from the journalist's analysis, is ignored as an object of study. Hans-Thies Lehmann himself argued that when a performance fails to offer signs or references to reality, the spectators' perception is 'thrown back onto the perception of structures', that is, to a formal observation (2006: 98). These approaches reduce the audience's experience to a deciphering activity, which will fail if the unfamiliar cannot be deciphered. Importantly, it excludes understanding created by sensorial and perceptual responses to a play by positioning intellectual response as the only one worth reporting and examining. Avignon 2005 certainly showed the limits of this approach to theatre analysis.

Consequently, some scholars underlined the importance of identifying news ways to analyse and discuss contemporary theatre after the festival that year. During a public meeting at the end of the festival, Bruno Tackels argued that critics and scholars should put more emphasis on the spectators' visual and physical experience of a play:

> If you take that word 'experience', we end up with a polysemic term that enables us to put together things that cannot usually go together. This festival has been extraordinarily intense, we cannot identify a specific art movement, a trend. (Banu and Tackels 2005: 40)²⁰

The diversity in what was on offer that year made performance analysis particularly complex. Yet, if one chose to focus on the audience's experience, one may indeed find a more productive way to approach and understand the mechanisms and strategies used in contemporary productions. After 2005, critics needed new analytical tools, or, as Tackels puts it, 'new mediums', to transmit avant-garde practices to audiences. Importantly, commentators needed to abandon the preconceived idea that theatre must necessarily deliver a narrative and focus rather on what a play can trigger within its spectators. Recently, French scholar Joseph Danan has insisted on this 'false' association between theatre and 'story': 'After all, why would theatre be necessarily based on narration?' (Danan and Naugrette 2018: 25).[21] However, these are not new ideas. Throughout the twentieth century, commentators made a clear distinction between sensitive, emotional experience and rational interpretation.[22] Those debates have had little impact on spectators' expectations, but the rejection of avant-garde theatre in France needs first to be understood as a lack of shared discourse between practitioners and audiences. Many important questions were avoided during a meeting between spectators and artists, at the end of the festival in 2005.[23] The gratuitous violence and the overwhelming dominance of physical theatre were topics raised by many spectators which were avoided by the directors and the organizers of the festival. In fact, spectators and artists never met on the core topics; on the topics that precisely made Avignon this year so sulphurous. There was perhaps a lack of effort, from the festival organizers, to provide the opportunity for both sides to truly communicate. Yet, the 2005 Festival of Avignon nonetheless attracted more visitors than usual. A total of 123,000 spectators attended performances from the 'in' (compared with 108,000 in the previous year). Although various audiences expressed their discontentment, they were still filling theatres and these directors' works were still widely seen. Perhaps this long-lasting miscomprehension of avant-garde theatre by French audiences (the term 'avant-garde', in this sense, has been referred to as redundant) should cease to be discussed in exclusively aesthetical or ideological terms. To overcome this mutual distrust between directors and spectators, and this lack of shared discourse, let us review the issue from a sociological and political perspective instead.

### 1.1.2. Power relationships between spectators and directors

There is a long history of audience-studies work (predominantly in mass-media disciplines like film and TV, as well as in fan studies) on the power relationships between spectators and producers. We now see a surge of 'participatory cultures', where audiences judge and influence productions of artistic works. Series producers are offering alternative endings to satisfy their fans, and some producers directly ask their fan community what they want to see happening in their shows. This is particularly potent in the relationship between fans and musical artists, who are expected to continue to provide the same genres of material but seek personal artistic growth that lead them to territory away from what brought them success. More surprisingly, 'cancel culture' illustrates the rise of a new kind of power given to audiences; the right for the spectators to censor what, and whom, they dislike. Cancel culture has not been much discussed in regard to theatre,[24] but it looks as if some contemporary directors struggle to understand this new generation of spectators. In her article 'Towards a Theory of Producer/Fan Trolling' (2018), Suzanne Scott refers to the term 'fantagonism', first coined by Derek Johnson in 2007 (2007: 287), which describes the 'ongoing competitive struggles between both internal factions and external institutions to discursively codify the fan-text-producer relationship'. Both producers and fans share a deep emotional connection to the object of art (whether it is a series or a film) and struggle to determine who, from the producers or the spectators, have ownership over it. Such a relationship can quickly become toxic, argues Scott, as 'these performances are perceived to be, or received as, just that: calculated efforts to upset and provoke an emotional response from a targeted group' (2018: 145). Some spectators in Avignon in 2005 seemed to have perceived the shows exactly as described by Scott; a manipulation orchestrated by directors to provoke pain and suffering in the audience (*What have we done to you? Why have you made us suffer like this for an hour and a half?*). Scott analyses that 'much of the toxicity within fan/producer relationships is founded on either fans or producers being viewed as attempting to "pass" into the other's role' (2018: 146). Tellingly, some spectators despise the directors for attempting to tell them *what* to feel, and *how* to perceive, while some directors explicitly criticize audiences for not *making the effort* to understand their artistic project. Tensions arise when each side attempts to tell the other one how to perceive/what to create. Spectators claim ownership of the creation; directors claim ownership of the reception.

More than just an ideological battle, Avignon 2005 is a blatant example of how tensions can quickly escalate when producers and audiences are both struggling to assert their role and function in theatre production. The festival that year revealed a great deal about each group's (lack of) esteem towards each other, as well as their respective efforts to affirm their power over each other. Fabre is famously reported to have said, 'People who don't understand think that we are goading them. Nothing has changed in 25 years. It's sad; stupidity can burst forth at any moment' (Talon-Hugon 2006: 53).[25] In the same way, he wants critics to have 'more of a role of mediator between the audience and the work, than one of attacking the work, declaring it a failure' (Talon-Hugon 2006: 23).[26] While he rightly points out the fact that critics sometimes come across as gratuitously judgemental, he also seems to imply that any negative reviews of his shows are void and unwelcome. The rhetoric 'you think my show is bad because you didn't understand it because you are an idiot' would, of course, be insulting to any spectators, whatever they make of the play. The expression 'art without audience, autistic and happy to be so' (2005: 37),[27] is in many respects, appropriate here as Fabre implies that he owns both creation and reception.[28] Theatre critics can also be aggressive and feel entitled to directly attack not only the work of the director but also their personality: Debray describes Fabre as 'his own guide, strolling through his own productions to show his fanatic groupies the exhibition of the abysses of his genius personality; that is to say not much at all' (2005: 45).[29] Similarly, Fabienne Darge et Brigitte Salino considered *L'Empereur de la perte* by Fabre as 'a sham, bloated with his own self-importance' (2005).[30]

Spectators, too, can be aggressive. Those who stand in the middle of a group made of 2,000 spectators must feel like their opinion is important enough to scream how unimpressed they are by a show. Why does a spectator feel the right to interrupt a performance to shout that a show is 'fucking shit', loud enough for everyone in the room to hear them, to stand up, and leave?[31] *Golgotha picnic*, by García, is a good example of a show that gained most of its notoriety because of its spectators' bad reactions. Performed in 2011 in France, the play was judged blasphemous by several Christian groups because it displayed the actors' naked bodies alongside Christian iconography and religious songs. Protests were organized during showings, and many documentaries and interviews broadcasted on public TV illustrated how some spectators felt entitled to 'cancel' the production. In the article 'De l'art et de la religion, ou quand les internautes commentent l'affaire Golgotha picnic' (2020), Geneviève Bernard Barbeau, Marty Laforest and Jessica Rioux-Turcotte gathered all the online comments on the play that they could find (446 comments) and classified them into several categories. Almost 32 per cent of these comments were referring to a disrespect towards religion, 20 per cent were criticizing the large media coverage of the show, and 11 per cent were bemoaning the fact that this production was funded with public money. It is interesting to note that some spectators felt entitled to criticize the extent of media coverage a show *should* receive (especially when they are partly responsible for it: of course, the protests led to more journalists being intrigued and coming to see the play). It is also interesting to see that this entitlement is partly generated by the fact that the show was produced thanks to public funding and therefore taxpayers' money, even though each French taxpayer's contribution was, without a doubt, well under one cent. One of the comments affirmed that art should not be a punishment for the spectator (19), understanding the show as a personal attack on themself. They might well be right; García does like to upset his audience. Some critics have defined García's productions as a series of 'traps' with situations that prevents spectators to fully agree or disagree, thus challenging usual modes of spectating (Lavalette 2020: 16).

In 2013, perhaps to respond to these growing frustrations, French director Jérôme Bel presented *Cour d'honneur* at the Festival of Avignon. As the title indicates, the play was performed in the Cour d'honneur, the largest stage in Avignon. The performance was organized around a series of testimonies shared by spectators on stage. One by one, each spectator was recounting the most powerful theatrical experience they had, there in Avignon. They were fourteen of them, all sat on chairs, waiting their turn to go at the front of the stage and share their moment. They were between eleven and seventy years old and were coming from all over the country. Some scenes were recreated in the background by a group of professional actors. Some of those memories were clearly important and cherished by their owners, others less so; one spectator on stage explained how annoyed he was at another spectator, who, during *Casimir et Caroline*, directed by Johan Simons in 2008, shouted in the middle of the show about how bored he was. Having seen *Cour d'honneur*, I remember how enthusiastic the public was, that night. For once, not only were they given the creation, but the reception was theirs too; they owned both. The show was warmly received by critics, too.

It is tempted to see audience entitlement to disrupt a product of a theatricality that seeks to challenge or upset modes of spectating. One important difficulty in the relationship between directors and spectators is that those directors' works are based on the manipulation of the perception. While directors such as Fabre should probably not tell their audiences *how* to perceive their shows, they do attempt to control some aspects of their spectators' reception. It is part of their aesthetic. But if spectators are willing to let go of their tendency to see in the creation what they want to see, the productions might hit them in unexpected ways. In *Eloge du théâtre*, French philosopher Alain Badiou (who published two essays on theatre)[32] explains how pleasantly surprised he was when he went to see *Tannhäuser* by Wagner, directed by Fabre:

> I arrived at the theatre slightly worried, even convinced that it was going to be a pointless provocation [. . .] It was beautiful. I had to concede defeat: one needs to know when to yield in front of the magnificence of theatre. I came with preconceived ideas, unfounded opinions, that were vanquished and cancelled by the performance. (2013: 27)[33]

Badiou uses some war-related terms, such as 'vanquished', 'provocation', 'yield'. It might be a little too extreme to argue that spectators and contemporary directors are at war. Yet, Badiou's testimony illustrates a relationship based on the dynamics of power between the two sides. The philosopher explains that he came to the theatre with his own intentions, and with contempt. But by abandoning ownership of the creation, he experienced something powerful; *he experienced theatre*. Throughout my education in theatre studies, I have seen how some contemporary directors can trigger hate, adoration or mere perplexity from teachers and students alike. These extreme reactions may be partly explained by the fact that spectators' expectations are often defeated in these theatres. Those productions can rarely be approached with preconceived ideas. While my reactions varied from one play to another, those productions always made me question my perception of reality as a spectator. These experiences cannot take place if spectators do not let directors own the original creation and, in fact, part of the reception. During a meeting with spectators, in Avignon in 2005, journalist Jean-Marc Adolphe criticized the tendency of some French spectators to not be willing to open their perception to innovative forms of theatre:

> When I read that the only valid form of theatre is the Greek theatre, that this has always been the case, a text, some actors, I feel the need to remind ourselves that there's also the commedia dell'arte, the kabuki, many different forms of theatre.... In France, we tend to show intellectual laziness, which I find a bit embarrassing. There is a lack of generosity in how we understand unusual forms of theatre, especially when they do not come with a 'textbook'. (Banu and Tackels 2005: 33)[34]

Similarly, when those productions are not straightforwardly rejected by audiences or critics, they are sometimes approached through critical techniques that have been developed for, what one could name, a semiotic theatre.[35] Some approaches to these theatres, focusing on the spectator's emotional response, do exist of course, but they constitute a minority.[36] Although directors could show more empathy towards their audiences, many spectators appear to miss the opportunity to fully appreciate those shows for what they have to offer. To bridge this gap, I would like to propose a different way to apprehend those shows, based on an exploration of the spectators' own experience, to consider the possibility for spectatorship to be a playful philosophical activity, which is precisely what is encouraged by some directors. Reception can be, first and foremost, creative. But, before I explore this possibility, there are a few other possible reasons why audiences and contemporary directors have such a difficult relationship in France, that need to be discussed.

## 1.2. The French political problem

### 1.2.1. Public funding and elitist theatre

The uneasy communication and miscomprehensions between the two sides must also be understood within the history of French cultural policies. These innovative productions celebrate the end of a tradition that dominated the twentieth century in France: the idea that theatre must have a social impact and be a vector of sanctioned culture. Since the 1930s, ambitious cultural policies have shaped the expectations of French spectators, giving them deeply rooted habits. The fact that these directors benefit from public funds, even though they strongly divide audiences, generates a sense of frustration. Indeed, most of them present their productions in state-funded theatres and, when in Avignon, within the 'in' section as opposed to the 'off', where performances are self-funded or benefit from private patronage. The rejection of their shows appears to be exacerbated by the fact that their work is usually funded by public money. For instance, journalist Armelle Héliot has referred to these practices, in *Le Figaro*, as 'art that aims to trigger a small scandal with significant public funding' (2005).[37] René Gonzales, in *L'Humanité*, labelled them as an 'institutionalised lie' (2005).[38] These reactions are aimed not only at the polemical shows but also towards the directors themselves. Accused of betrayal, they are blamed for not respecting a traditional and implied contract regarding art funding in France. For many spectators, a state-funded play constitutes de facto a public service and needs to engage with contemporary social issues. Régis Debray bemoans, for instance, the absence of social and cultural messages: 'Those abstract brutalities, those LVMH cruelties say at best something about the violence that surrounds drugs and gangs, but nothing about society, about the unemployment rate, the question of national identity, religion, boarders' (2005: 30).[39] Fabre claims, for instance, that his theatre is 'the opposite of social' (Banu and Tackels 2005: 257).[40] Yet, if audiences no longer feel that theatre is an accessible social and cultural practice, how can one justify its public funding? For many spectators, a state-funded show needs to address the audience as a group of citizens, rather than individual characters. This is precisely what these avant-garde practices refuse to do. As Philippe Urfalino asks, in the conclusion of his study on French cultural policies:

> There is one last question. If we no longer consider theatre as a vector for social impact, why should the government continue to guarantee its financial support? Setting aside the economic benefits that arts bring to cities by attracting new businesses, how can one justify public financial aid to the arts? (2011: 401)[41]

The reception of contemporary shows in France is thus compromised by a long-lasting cultural ideology. 'France prided itself on setting up the first real culture ministry in Europe in 1959 and saw cultural policy as a way of uniting the nation after the war,' writes journalist Angelique Chrisafis in *The Guardian* (2011). In fact, as early as the 1930s, during the Front Populaire government, the idea of funding the construction of theatres in the *province* was already being discussed. In 1936, French writer Jules Romains argues:

> The role of the state in the protection of theatre needs to be reformed and amplified. The Comédie-Française should certainly not be abolished. It needs to be divided: on one side, to have a theatre based on the great plays, a theatre-museum, managed with authority by a man thoroughly invested in this task [. . .] on the other side, a national theatre focused on the creation of new plays, of high quality. (Degaine 2000: 369)[42]

According to André Degaine, historian of French theatre, this text is emblematic of the main concerns and aspirations people working in theatre expressed at the end of the thirties. The French state was expected to financially support the creation of 'National Theatres' throughout the country. Indeed, a decentralization policy appeared crucial in a country where theatres were concentrated in Paris. Jean-François Gravier pointed out, among other things, this disparity in his essay *Paris et le désert français* (1947): 'Paris and the French Desert'.

From 1936, two political ambitions were jointly developed: to strengthen the role of the state in supporting theatres and to disseminate French culture across the country. After the Second World War, the first 'Centre Dramatique Nationaux' (CDN) were created, initiated by Jeanne Laurent, assistant director of 'spectacles et musique', a subsection of the Ministry of National Education (one can see the pedagogical mission attached to theatre – the Ministry of Culture only appeared in 1959). The 'CDN de l'Est' arose in Colmar in 1946, while the city of Saint-Etienne was provided with its own CDN, directed by Jean Dasté, in 1947. In 1949, Rennes and Toulouse were the next cities to have their CDNs, followed by Aix-en-provence and Tourcoing, in 1952 and 1960 respectively. Thirty-seven CDNs now spread over France and its main cities. The original purpose of these theatres was not only to provide access to theatre to a larger number of people but also to provide access to the great plays from the 'répertoire'. In fact, theatre was then mainly perceived as a place delivering a pre-existing text. As French historian Pascale Goetschel explains:

> National dramatic centres became the complementary tool to an artistic education for which theatre is first and foremost a book [. . .] Showing audiences well-known plays: that was the ambition of the decentralization. From this point of view, the decentralization of theatre contributed to the shared ownership of the French cultural heritage, in the same way as the education received in secondary schools and sixth form colleges, which developed substantially in those same years. (2004: 146)[43]

Theatres had to serve French cultural heritage, and the term 'patrimoine' was easily associated with the mission of these institutions: 'The state provides the steer: the priority is given to works of national heritage first, then works from abroad. There is not much room for trying something different' (Goetschel 2004: 137).⁴⁴ Since these theatres were largely funded by the state (now, they tend to receive 50 per cent of their financial support from regional and/or local organizations), the directors had to meet certain requirements. This obviously restricted their freedom, especially in the choice of their programme. In 1949, Jeanne Laurent sent several warning letters to André Clavé, director of the CDE ('Centre Dramatique de l'Est') because he was not scheduling enough French plays. In 1951, she asked him to reduce the number of new plays; two new plays out of eight productions were already too many. One year later, she asked him again to offer more classic plays, such as plays by Molière, Racine, Corneille, Marivaux or Beaumarchais. The same year, she wrote down directives imposing strict conditions to Michel Saint-Denis, new director of the CDE: 'a maximum of a quarter of the shows can be based on new contemporary plays and at least one show will be a French classical play. Two thirds of the repertoire will be French plays' (Goetschel 2004: 136).⁴⁵ The importance of the text, and especially French texts, is inscribed in Article 1 of the decree following the creation of the CDO (*Centre dramatique de l'Ouest*): 'Francophone plays need to be presented to the audience, and in particular French classical plays' (Goetschel 2004: 137).⁴⁶ Hubert Gignoux, first director of the CDO, wrote to a young author who wanted his play to be produced that his 'mission does not involve the support of contemporary authors, let alone new plays' (Goetschel 2004: 137).⁴⁷

The Ministry of Culture was established in 1959, with André Malraux as its first minister. Malraux saw in the Ministry of Culture the opportunity to 'tackle cultural inequalities' (Looseley 1995: 40). He opened more CDNs and continued the decentralization policy. He was replaced by Edmond Michelet in 1969. A few ministers followed until Jack Lang (from 1981 to 1986 and again from 1988 to 1993), who is arguably the minister to have been most open to popular culture. One can note, in passing, that movements such as the American 'Happening' or groups such as the 'Living Theater', inheriting from Antonin Artaud's work and based on the spectators' immediate experience, did not manage to establish a permanent imprint in France. Jack Lang launched, for instance, 'Le Festival mondial de théâtre de Nancy' in 1963 where he invited such movements, drawing on Artaud's and Grotowski's theatres. The festival ended in 1983. Throughout the second half of the twentieth century, classic plays[48] would always attract more spectators than contemporary ones. New plays would meet 'local audiences [who] were often ill prepared' (Looseley 1995: 43). To innovate would therefore involve a double risk: to see the Ministry of National Education, unhappy, freezing the funds, and to see the audience deserting the theatre. Thus, directors were first and foremost looking for their audience's sympathy and assent (Goetschel 2004: 148–9). CDNs were among the most important theatres in France, because of their size and their budget. Nowadays they remain the most influential theatres in provincial cities like Bordeaux, Lille, Lyon, Marseille, Nice, Strasbourg, Saint-Etienne and Toulouse. Most French spectators' experience with theatre links back to their experience in CDNs.

According to Philippe Urfalino, such cultural policies gradually disappeared in the 1990s: 'cultural policies have ended, hurray for the public financial support to the arts!' (2011: 406).[49] As said previously, half of the CDNs' budget now depends on regional and local organizations. The requirements that they must meet differ from one city to another, according to local and regional policies. However, this economic shift does not seem to have triggered an important change in programming. First, because they remain a public service, regulated by the dramatic decentralization contract established in 1972 (revised in 1995). Therefore, their mission is still to serve 'the public interest and to encourage the diffusion of high-quality plays [...] to try to gather a large audience and attract more spectators'.[50] CDNs and National Theatres are not the only institutions to receive money from the government and from local, regional organizations. Numerous artistic projects and theatre companies too benefit from public money. While the Culture Minister is funding 7 National Theatres and 39 CDNs, it also funds 69 'scènes nationales', 56 'scènes conventionnées' and 550 production and diffusion structures. In total it financially supports 721 structures and about 1,220 companies. As French historian Gérard Noiriel points out: 'Thanks to this generous funding, public theatre has more or less replaced private theatre, which is mostly concentrated in Paris' (2009: 103).[51] The French budget for culture is one of the most substantial in Europe. Each year, around 3 billion euros is invested in culture, including around 700 million in theatre. Comparatively, in England, the Art Council provides around 350 million pounds per year for arts, including around 180 million for theatre. It seems that there is more flexibility and diversity regarding the performances and associations which obtain funding in France today, and that new works that are not necessarily text-based are more encouraged.[52] Moreover, Angelique Chrisafis states that although 'the private patronage and sponsorship so rife in the UK is almost unheard of in France', 'it is beginning to grow' (2011). It remains to be seen to what extent a greater openness from public funding institutions and a change of sponsorship could change spectators' habits.

In *Politiques du spectateur*, French academic Olivier Neveux analysed the controversy over Avignon 2005 and identified a persistence of the tradition of a text-based theatre:

> Some bemoaned the absence of texts; to which others argued that there were texts. Some said they yearned the golden age of the classics, while others pointed out that such yearning was a symptom of sterile conservatism. *Le Figaro* proclaimed Jean Vilar, founder of the Festival of Avignon in 1947, to be its muse, fifty years after having relentlessly attempted to make him fail. (2013: 18)[53]

Neveux explains that for many spectators, the absence of classic plays was in fact more disturbing than the apparent lack of scripts, or the multidisciplinary nature of the shows. As briefly mentioned in the introduction, Rodrigo García experienced a similar rejection from French audiences when he took charge of the CDN of Montpellier in 2014. When he took office, he wanted to see this theatre 'to grow and modernize' (*Télérama* 2014).[54] He invited many contemporary artists to perform such as Fabre, Philippe Quesne, Lauwers and Tiago Rodrigues.

In 2016, he made the decision to leave his post. According to him, the spectators from Montpellier did not understand him or his art. In fact, as early as 2015, he was already noting: 'In Montpellier, people like to have their little provincial theatre, their classical plays that reassure them, even if they might fall asleep in their seats' (*El País* 2015).[55] In December 2016 he stated, disappointedly: 'I thought the people in this city would be more receptive. I'm offering contemporary shows, but the audience is more used to Molière, to Shakespeare. I think it's a great mission, but I'm not going to continue' (*La Gazette de Montpellier* 2019).[56] He also bemoaned a lack of financial support from the city of Montpellier: 'What happened to the discussions, to the exchanges of ideas, to the collaboration with our partners who support this public space?' (*Scene Web* 2016).[57] Since he took office, the city withdrew 100,000 euros from the initial budget of 450,000 euros per year. During García's direction, the theatre also lost a third of its audience (which represents around 10,000 spectators). A retired spectator explained why he cancelled his membership thus: 'I don't mind the use of different languages, although the openness to Spain and Portugal seems to be a little too restrictive and exclusive, but I do regret the fact that we don't have more plays from the "répertoire", like other national theatres do' (*La Gazette de Montpellier* 2019).[58] Rodrigo García's direction of the CDN of Montpellier is one of the most glaring examples of the persistence of specific spectators' habits and preferences supported by cultural policies. The fact that he resigned demonstrates the victory of the repertoire, praised by the public, over original creations breaking with tradition.

Are French audiences, as García seems to suggest, intellectually lazy? His assumptions need to be nuanced. As stated previously, since the 1990s, the relationship between theatre and the French state has changed. Theatres gained more freedom and programmes have become more varied. Cultural policies (as ministers shaped them after the Second World War) gradually disappeared in the 1990s. Theatres progressively ceased to function as 'cultural schools'. Additionally, in 2008, Jacques Rancière published a highly influential essay *Le spectator émancipé*, promoting spectators' freedom and the end of theatre as a place to *learn*. Not only did spectators start to have access to more international performances, they also became more confident in what they wanted (or did not want) to go and see. Some directors seem to forget this evolution. While most directors claim that audiences can perceive their performances the way they want (Castellucci says that his ideal spectator is a ten-year-old child), they also do seem to put themselves in a position of superiority. Directors say, '*I'll reveal something to you*'; audiences reply, '*We can understand on our own.*' The miscomprehension between French audiences and avant-garde theatre is more complex than ever before. Not only do many spectators not appreciate it, but they are also angry at the directors for not giving them something familiar enough to feel they can process it without explanation. That rhetoric is vicious: the more directors explain their productions, the more spectators will feel infantilized. The less they explain, the more spectators will feel infantilized too. Unsurprisingly, exiting this situation is difficult. But one thing should be made clear: that there are different theatres that invite different levels of perception. A play by Castellucci observed by a political mind will certainly not succeed. Conversely, a spectator coming to see a play by Jean Vilar, expecting to see his perception and emotions challenged, would probably be disappointed. Let us always remember that, as Zola stated, there are theatres. A play comes with a certain practice of theatre, a certain ideology, a certain vision for what role spectators can play. We may forget this too easily, especially during large festivals such as Avignon, where spectators can see up to ten shows in a day. If one wants to have access to a large variety of performances, one will have to be ready to be a different spectator each time. The model of the emancipated spectator has limits: how can one be emancipated if the object they emancipate themselves from constantly changes? Of course, my argument is only valid if one wishes to explore different styles of theatre, from different countries and traditions. But when looking at the number of tickets sold in Avignon, it is safe to say that this is something French spectators are looking for.

## 1.2.2. Contemporary practices in conventional spaces

The performance spaces where many contemporary directors present their productions may also themselves contribute to the spectators' disorientation. Beyond issues of cultural miscomprehension, their physical performances seem to be at odds with the traditional spaces where they take place. What makes their performances particularly distinctive is that while they could be categorized as physical performances, they are often performed in end stage theatres. End stage theatres refer to theatres where the audience are sitting only on one side of the stage, facing it, similarly to cinema layouts. The incomprehension that these theatres create might thus partly be the consequence of a mismatch between the conventional theatres where the shows are performed (which traditionally allow for a peaceful and quiet reception), and the practices and mechanisms of the shows themselves, which actively seek to disrupt the spectators' sense of security and familiarity. For instance, many of Fabre's productions and *Sur le concept du visage du fils de Dieu* by Castellucci (2011) were performed in the Théâtre de la Ville; many of Castellucci's productions and *The Generosity of Dorcas* were by Fabre (2018) were performed at the Odéon and many of García's productions were performed at the Théâtre des 13 Vents (Montpellier). These three theatres are end stage theatres, normally more suited for opera and more traditional forms of theatre. How can one expect spectators to let their perception and emotions be challenged in a space that traditionally let them project their own meanings onto the stage? The modes of theatre being performed do not 'belong' in the spaces where they are performed. It is not a deliberate or knowing act from the directors (they simply produce their plays where they are invited to do so by cultural institutions), but it nonetheless results in a striking mismatch between the theatrical space and the style and intentions of contemporary shows.

This mismatch is only accentuated by the fact that traditional modern theatres such as l'Odéon and the Théâtre de la Ville are places where spectators are in the dark and must stay quiet and watch. As Gay

McAuley notes, the modern spectator's behaviour is often kept under control:

> Spectators' ability to move around in the auditorium and the nature of the social interaction that can take place are to a considerable extent controlled by architectural design, and conventions such as darkening the auditorium ensure that spectators' attention is fixed on the stage. Indeed, some actors get very irritated if there is evidence of anything other than rapt attention on the part of spectators, and the problems incurred by students taking notes for subsequent performance analysis (hardly evidence of lack of attention) indicate that audience behavior is strongly policed even in our ostensibly laissez-faire societies. (McAuley 1999: 57–8)

The imposed darkness and the absence of movement for the spectators are conventions that began in the eighteenth century. They are the first signs of a willingness within Western theatre to progressively tame audiences. Denis Guénoun bemoans this lack of physical freedom:

> It is first and foremost the experience of an immobilization. To sit, in the theatre, means to be in a state where movements are not permitted, for a relatively long time, since once cannot leave one's seat, make any noise, and, especially, because speaking with those around you is forbidden, contrasting with, for example, when you are watching TV. We often said that watching tv is a passive activity, but from a behavioural point of view, this is not true: in front of the TV, one can move and speak. This situation when one is forbidden to move is also at odds with usual spontaneous behaviours of the general public, of teenager, of children: we all suffered from this injunction. (2005: 154–5)[59]

This is, in part, reminiscent of what Michel Foucault argued in his studies on the means of subjugation of the body:

> This subjection [of the body] is not only obtained by the instruments of violence or ideology; it can also be direct, physical, pitting force against force, bearing on material elements, and yet without involving violence; it may be calculated, organized, technically thought out;

it may be subtle, make use neither of weapons nor of terror and yet remain of a physical order [. . .] this knowledge and this mastery constitute what might be called the political technology of the body. (1995: 26)

As in prison, school, the army, the theatre is also a place where bodies are controlled. A few years ago, I saw this invisible authority at play during a performance at the Théâtre National Populaire in Villeurbanne, in France. During the show, one of the spectators fainted. People whispered for a few minutes before deciding to shout and call a member of staff. It seemed to be quite an emergency; yet the decision to speak over the actors' voice was clearly a difficult one. It is a disturbing thought. Because we are due to remain quiet and motionless in a theatre, taking action may be difficult even when a particular situation demands it. Spectators may therefore feel 'trapped', 'victims' of contemporary shows, not primarily because of the performance, but because of the situation they find themselves in. Their frustration with a production might not only originate from what they see on stage, but also from the feeling that these acts are being 'imposed', forced onto them. Rousseau considered that theatre is a prison (Brillaud 2010: 77). Instead of theatre, he preferred 'les fêtes' in which the spectators were free to participate, dance, celebrate. For Denis Guénoun, there is a divorce in today's society, between actors, who are free, and spectators, who remain tamed and docile:

> Actors and artists of all sorts who have taken possession of theatres, but through the stage door, are experiencing a new contemporary form of freedom. They are the actors of today's world. On the other hand, spectators, who obediently queue in front of the box office, are, in my opinion, in a much more critical situation. It seems to me that the aesthetical and political choices that governed contemporary theatres won't always be able to avoid defining themselves through this deep divorce. (2005: 158)[60]

According to Guénoun, while actors would express their freedom on stage, the spectators would remain in a passive position, obeying established rules. For Guénoun, actors and spectators were 'divorced' when the stage and the audience stopped collaborating. The spectators' behaviour is extremely regulated nowadays. Can a physical domestication lead to an intellectual domestication? The spectators who obediently queue in front of the box office are indeed in a critical situation. As Foucault has established, to tame the body also means to tame the mind. Here lies a complex problem: How could innovative productions, which need to be received not only intellectually, but physically too, succeed in spaces that culturally, and historically, do not encourage this?

Moreover, in some contemporary practices, what we may name the 'fourth wall' remains intact. The fourth wall is a dramatic convention theorized by Denis Diderot in the eighteenth century in the *Discours de la poésie dramatique*. It refers to an invisible wall separating the stage or the space of fiction from the audience's real world. This imaginary fourth wall blocks any interaction between the two worlds. This convention to separate the space of fiction from the space of reality is often respected, even in physical forms of theatre. This paradox between physical theatres – borrowing sometimes from endurance arts – and the presence of the fourth wall has not been systematically studied. For French philosopher Jacques Rancière (2011: 13–14), maintaining the fourth wall is a way of guaranteeing the audience's intellectual freedom. According to Rancière, the fourth wall is the necessary condition for the spectator to be emancipated. He believes that it is not a lack of education that paralyzes the spectator's intelligence but, rather, the belief that they need to be guided to *understand* the actions on stage. Trying to eradicate the fourth wall is therefore a paternalistic action; it means disrupting the spectators' own mental space to try to control it. Rancière considers Berthold Brecht and Antonin Artaud as the two emblematic figures who made the mistake of reducing theatre to an educational tool:

> They [Artaud's and Brecht's practices] intend to teach their spectators ways of ceasing to be spectators and becoming agents of a collective

practice. [...] It is the very logic of the pedagogical relationship [...] In pedagogical logic, the ignoramus is not simply one who does not as yet know what the schoolmaster knows. She is the one who does not know what she does not know or how to know it. For his part, the schoolmaster is not only the one who possesses the knowledge unknown by the ignoramus. He is also the one who knows how to make it an object of knowledge, at what point, and in accordance with what protocol. (2014: 7)

Conversely, maintaining the fourth wall gives the spectators the aptitude to believe in their own abilities and to spectate freely. Besides preserving this distance, Castellucci went even further and developed the concept of 'the fifth wall' in *Le théâtre et ses publics: la création partagée*, according to which a performance exists in a meeting point between the stage and the audience: 'On one side, someone is performing, on the other side, someone is watching. From there, a third space appears between the stage and the audience, like a translucent veil, stretched from one side to the other, and that one cannot pierce' (2012).[61] Similarly, one of Fabre's actors explained that the director never considered the possibility of performing anywhere other than in end stage theatres, with a spatial distance between the performers and the spectators.[62] Even though their practices resemble Artaud's theatre of cruelty, the fourth wall remains. That is a contradiction: the fourth wall preserves the spectators' right to be free recipients; to perceive the shows the way they want to, and yet, these directors seek to manipulate their spectators' perception. Consequently, some spectators still complain about the fact that they do not 'understand' such performances, even though the fourth wall is maintained. Perhaps Rancière's theory is missing one important fact: that many spectators have habits of spectating and expect a play to conform to some of their expectations. Rancière wants theatre to encourage a free gaze; but being able to spectate, free from any sort of preconceived ideas on theatre, is far from simple. Contemporary directors who use the fourth wall also aim to trigger a specific perception. They develop strategies to disrupt the audience's expectations and preconceived ideas. In this sense, they do not give complete freedom to their spectators, but it seems that this guidance is necessary for the spectator to, *in fine*, perceive freely, perceive the things as they appear to them. The mismatch between the modes of theatre performed and the spaces where they are performed can thus be confusing for audiences (as seen earlier), but it can also help directors to preserve an ambiguity between different modes of perception, between freedom and manipulation of thought, which in turn serves their own goals.

## *Summary of Chapter 1*

Many factors help understand why debates around contemporary theatre can be so passionate in France, and why, even though France is particularly welcoming of innovative forms of performance, it is also the host of radical rejections and frustrations. Those factors are political, cultural and situational.

The Avignon festival in 2005 crystallized many tensions in 2005 and emphasized a gap between French audiences, whose education shaped some of their expectations, and directors, who, inspired by practitioners such as Bob Wilson, Pina Bausch and Tadeusz Kantor (among others) express themselves through diverse media and aim to question each spectator's perception. Many commentators have pointed out that the gap was an ideological one; some audiences could not understand directors (and vice versa) because they had a different understanding of what theatre should be; its role in society and its ambition as an art. At this point, I would like to remind my reader that not every single French spectator dislike those innovative forms of theatre, far from it! As said previously, even though some audiences were expressing their dissatisfaction, spectators were still filling theatres and, for many, were still applauding those directors' works.

Yet, as often is the case, the unhappy spectators made more noise than the happy ones. The strength of the rejections makes one wonder if, indeed, the reasons are simply ideological. It seems that what is at play is not only theatre itself but also something much more sensitive: the relationship between directors and spectators. Avant-garde theatre has always been sulphurous – nothing is new here. What is quite unique today, though, is how complex and tormented the relationship between artists and spectators is. More than a series of miscomprehensions, this relationship seems tinted with bitterness and resentment. The lack of shared discourse is not just an unfortunate situation, as it is also partly wanted by both parties; no one looks particularly willing to bridge the gap.

What is at stake here is what the spectators' role is in a theatre, what ownership directors have over a production, and how the two sides can, ultimately, share a creation. Some spectators resent directors for attempting to tell them what to feel, and how to perceive, while some directors criticize spectators for not 'making the effort' to understand their work. Tensions were particularly high in Avignon in 2005 because each side attempted to tell the other one how to perceive/what to create. Both the audience and the directors claimed ownership of the reception. Complex power dynamics is one major reason why contemporary theatre can trigger such passionate reactions.

Additionally, a long tradition of French cultural policies has likely empowered French spectators. After the Second World War, France led ambitious policies aiming to promote theatre and the French repertoire across the country. Theatre was then perceived as a vector of sanctioned culture, whose aim was to have a clear and direct impact on society. Being a spectator and a good citizen were jointly encouraged. Those ambitious cultural policies have shaped the expectations of French spectators, giving them deeply rooted habits, but also the confidence to raise their voice when they dislike what they see on stage. Since many contemporary directors benefit from public funds, even though they strongly divide audiences, a sense of frustration has progressively developed among spectators. The rejection of those productions has been exacerbated by the fact that they are partially funded by public money.

Finally, contemporary shows have probably suffered from the fact that they are often performed in traditional theatres, where intellectual experiences are more important than physical ones. The space in which the actions take place does not always seem appropriate for what has sometimes been referred to as physical theatre. The performances and the theatre spaces are contradicting each other regarding the type of experience spectators can hope for. Spectators are invited to experience strong emotional and physical impacts while sitting quietly and obediently in dark theatres. This may well have been fuelling a growing sense of frustration.

It would be presumptuous to assume that such a gap can be bridged, given that so many factors are at play here. Trying to tell audiences how to perceive contemporary theatre is doomed to fail. Spectators should be free to be whatever spectators they want to be in a theatre. Yet, directors should also be able to create what they want without being insulted by spectators who wish to see something else. How could we ease the communication between the two sides while preserving both freedoms to receive and create? Perhaps by clarifying not how those shows need to be perceived, but by emphasizing on how they can be perceived. Those innovative productions do offer the opportunity to explore and question our perception of the world. They can be the opportunity to develop our own 'playground' of the mind, where we make our own personal experiences of our interaction with the world. Before we explore how such experiences can arise, let us try to understand why those experiences can be so challenging and, in some cases, upsetting. We like to recognize our surroundings and, in fact, need to do so to be able to evolve in society and communicate with others.

The aim of the following chapter is to explore how everyday perception can work; how it is based on processes of recognition, how it commonly produces meaning and how directors aim to challenge it. This chapter demonstrates that having these processes of perception frustrated can be shocking. Experiencing the world without recognizing it is indeed far from being obvious.

II

# On stage

## Strategies to challenge perception

### 2.1. Our processes of recognition

#### 2.1.1. Why do we need to recognize our surroundings?

This section aims to consider how our everyday perception is based on processes of recognition, and how uncomfortable having them challenged can be. 'As we negotiate our daily lives, we need to be able to recognize our surroundings, grasp our encounters and communicate with clarity' states Daniel Koczy in his Deleuzian study on Beckett (2018: 21–2). According to Deleuze, the experience of a true encounter with the world is only possible if the subject does not recognize what they are facing; if what they perceive remains 'an unrecognised and unrecognisable *terra incognita*' (Deleuze 2006: 136). Yet, 'recognition' (Deleuze 2006: 140) remains the main mode of our perceptive faculties. For the philosopher, an everyday object (or concept) is assimilated thanks to a pre-existing set of intellectual tools: identity, opposition, analogy and so on. The perception of an object is in fact a more or less complex entanglement of many things already known (memories) articulated by the intellect (concepts). There are thus two different kinds of object which lead to two different perceptions: objects of 'recognition', and objects of '*encounter*' (136). Objects of encounter ('rencontre') force us to think. In fact, for Deleuze, one must be unable to recognize objects in order to produce 'real' thoughts. To not recognize an object or an action is particularly difficult because it coerces the subject to think, that is, to create. In *Les Castellucci. Ecrivains de plateau*, Claudia Castellucci wrote similarly: 'To think, only to think, without using. [. . .] To think is to crave for new things' (Tackels 2005: 25).¹ In contrast, objects of recognition 'do not disturb thought', because they only let the thought refer to itself: 'thought is thereby filled with no more than an image of itself, one in which it recognizes itself the more it recognizes things: this is a finger, this is a table' (Deleuze 2006: 139). To be able to negotiate and navigate through life, one needs to be able to recognize the world as one thinks one knows it. Recognizing the world is not only comforting, but it is vital to maintain healthy relationships with others, to find meaning in what we do, and to define our own identity. 'Representational thinking' (Koczy 2018: 21) is a condition for clear communication and understanding of our surroundings. But as Deleuze underlines, this condition brings along the more problematic assumption that our perception of the world is determined by this strict system of representation, and that experiencing the world outside this system is not possible. Although recognition structures our relationship with the world, it also refrains us from looking for something different. Any thoughts produced outside this system are either 'false, monstruous, or meaningless' (22). Camus's outsider, for instance, is unable to relate to his world, unable to create connections between events, emotions and people: by not being able to recognize his surroundings and by being continuously in the present instead, he is soon perceived as a monster, an outcast at best.

Similarly, Shklovsky has argued that to truly experience an object of art, one must encounter difficulties in recognizing it. If the object remains unrecognized, it can then irradiate its own presence and trigger a different experience of the world. Perception based on recognition cannot lead to such an experience. In our everyday lives, we do not truly see objects, but rather we recognize them. Processes of recognition are essential insofar as they give us indications on how to utilize objects around us. I recognize the pen that I use to write, the bag that carries my materials to work, the clothes that I wear, the pan that I use to cook with and so on. We consider these objects according to us and our desires. To give this another term, we usually 'consume' objects. Consume comes indeed from the Latin *consumo* which means 'I annihilate', 'I destroy', 'I waste', but also means 'I take' (*-sumo*) 'with me', 'for me' (*-con*). Each day, we consume objects; that is, we perceive them in the context of our own needs. To not recognize an object, to not understand its meaning, its usefulness, its role (in the broadest sense of the word), on the other hand, constitutes a real challenge for the perception. Shklovsky considers art as the way to 'restore experience to us – by distorting and slowing down perception, by making the world strange once again' (Gunn 1984: 28). To not recognize our surroundings gives the opportunity to experience the world anew. A child, for instance, who sees snow for the first time, is amazed because they do not recognize the phenomenon. They remain only struck by what they see. Such experiences can be extremely powerful, similar to an epiphany in the sense that meaning – surprisingly – does not seem to come *from* us. Perhaps you did experience the world as an encounter before. Perhaps one day you were sitting in your kitchen, it was the end of the day, the light was particularly beautiful and flooding the room. There was a mug on the table, a mug that you see and use everyday. The light was reflecting on it, highlighting many little imperfections. And suddenly it struck you: this mug exists outside your own world, outside your recognition. This is what many authors have referred to as a phenomenological experience. For Bert States, for instance, phenomenology and semiology both constitute a 'binocular vision' (States 1987: 8). In one day, one may be experiencing the world in a phenomenological as well as in a semiotic way (although the latter overpowers the phenomenal eye). If one loses the 'phenomenal eye', one becomes Don Quixote; 'everything is something else'. On the contrary, if one loses the significative eye, one becomes Sartre's Roquentin, where 'everything is nothing but itself'. He recounts the following experience:

> I am walking to the bus terminal to get my ride home. Suddenly, as I approach, the bus parked in the lot strikes me as being outrageously large and rectangular. It is heavy with material and texture; it is not a bus, it is a queer, unforeseen shape. This may be the result of the sun

coming off it in a certain way, it may be my mood; but I find myself arrested by this *thing*. I see it almost as an artist might: as a study in form. But I must get on the bus if I am to make it home. So I climb aboard, with the help of my significative eye, and I project myself home –is there any mail? Did the plumber come today? What's for dinner? All of these anticipations are softened, however, because on the bus I read a newspaper, which is another way of not being where I am. (1987: 8–9)

Suddenly, the bus appears to him not as a bus, that is, as a means of transport, but as an imposing object in its majestic presence. The experience is surprising as the bus seems to appear to him for the first time. In fact, the bus is no longer a bus, but a 'thing'. There is indeed no word to describe this object (this 'terra incognita'), as a 'bus' refers to a means of transport; that is not what States is seeing at that given moment. That 'thing' is strange, unknown. Experiences of the world through a phenomenological perception can rarely be described with words. Not recognizing what we are facing is difficult, counter-intuitive (or at least it seems to be so at first) and can even be scary since it plunges us into the world as unknown. Yet, are these experiences not our chance to get closer to the world?

## 2.1.2. The difficulty in apprehending shows that challenge processes of recognition

To trigger such encounters in their spectators, directors look at ways to thwart everyday processes of recognition. I call the process that follows these thwarted projections a non-recognition. Directors intentionally make spectators encounter difficulties in projecting meaning onto the stage by ensuring that their performances 'fill the vacuum which has allowed our automatic response to develop' (Gunn 1984: 29). To strike audiences, the meaning of a performance needs to remain unrecognizable. Spectators must be prevented from shaping what they see in their own ways. Instead, spectators are invited to create new ways of thinking in order to apprehend the world on stage. The non-recognition in theatre enables one to encounter the world as it forces one to think (as Deleuze understands it): to create. The duration of an action until it is stripped of any semantic value is one among many strategies that directors use and that we will explore in the next few sections. Many performances involve processes of manipulation of perception and create meaning that is difficult, if not impossible, to translate into words. From that point of view, it is hardly surprising that a certain distrust between directors and the audience has developed. These directors would argue that they seek to intellectually emancipate their spectators by 'teaching' them to free their own perceptual frameworks.

Directors have explained, all in their own terms, how they aim to disturb perception and show audiences how it is quite impossible to fully understand the world as it appears to them (on stage or in the 'real world'). In an interview with Fabienne Pascaud for *Télérama*,[2] Gisèle Vienne argues thus:

> Wilson, Bausch and Kantor enabled a development of our perceptive acuity and have enabled perceptive movements which teach us to hear things that we have unlearned to hear, to see things that we have unlearned to see [...] I try to unfold in space the experience of time. I do not know how to describe this language, but it is a dissection of the perception. To reveal the cultural construction of perception. (2021)[3]

In a more controversial way perhaps, Castellucci has attacked the idea that theatre is a place to recognize; to be reassured in one's representations:

> Theatre is not something to recognize. 'Me-I-go-to-theatre-to-recogni ze-Shakespeare-my-studies-what-I-did': that's not how it works. It is a journey in the unknown, towards the unknown. One cannot calculate conjunctions of elements from the possible. (Castellucci 2001: 118)[4]

Spectators should leave behind their expectations and face performances free from prejudices or ideas they wish to retrieve in them. As said earlier, such a vision of spectating constitutes a challenge for directors as it attracts various criticism. For many people, theatre must precisely facilitate the process of recognition. As Castellucci underlines:

> They [spectators] come to recognize what they already know and to be intellectually comforted. This should stop after school, where one recognizes that which one desires to see. This type of comfort produces inertia, a swamp of dead waters for thought, whereas the theatrical experience needs to be a journey, a path towards the unknown. It is an adventure. (Tackels 2005: 56)[5]

This miscomprehension is also to be found within the approaches by critics. A journalist interviewing Castellucci rightly noted:

> The distinction that you have just made between those two attitudes in a theatre is also to be found in the work of theatre critics. There are those who accept to apply words on the unknown, and those who refuse it lazily, condemning 'falsely avant-garde pretentiousness, really contemptuous and stupid' [. . .] Such simplistic judgements express the fear in front of something one cannot recognize nor identify with – hence the reference (without evidence) to the avant-garde. (Tackels 2005: 57)[6]

The journalist contrasts the readiness of recognition with the difficulty of the encounter for critics and spectators alike. Through such unwillingness to consider something different, some critics seem to assume that recognition is the only valid approach. He also points out the laziness of those who refuse to adventure into the unknown. For Castellucci, this attitude is unacceptable: 'There is an appealing mediocrity in that which just makes people lazy' (Tackels 2005: 57).[7] One could argue that he does not demonstrate much tolerance or empathy towards critics. Calling them mediocre appears relatively unfair. Perhaps he forgets that a long-lasting tradition of theatre, in which the spectators perceive according to recognition processes, is still persistent in Western Europe, and that his vision for theatre remains rather marginal.

In 2005, dance specialist Rosita Boisseau wrote a review in *Le Monde* of *L'Histoire des larmes* by Jan Fabre, presented at Avignon Festival. In the article, she bemoans the fact that 'the material beauty does not cover for the absence of meaning'.[8] She argues:

> *Histoire des larmes* traps itself in a game of props and ends up using them as an alibi. The material beauty is not always sufficient to strengthen the meaning of an image – no matter how vivid it is. [. . .] Even if the celebration of a body in all its truth and rawness is of course crucial in the play, its discourse explodes and lose its perspective. (2005)[9]

These comments are symptomatic of a general stance many critics have adopted towards Fabre's productions. The Flemish director can profoundly displease, if not offend, with shows hosting naked bodies, simulated sexual acts and with animals on stage, while neglecting any clear dramatic construction. Yet, this may be partly explained by the fact that Fabre works according to the devised theatre tradition which involves rehearsals organized and decided collectively with the actors and based on improvisation. Although Fabre remains the director, his shows are thus built depending on various propositions which emanate from various performers. They may therefore appear to lack a common thread, or a clear dramatic intention, which is partly what some critics seem to struggle with. By exclusively favouring a 'travail de plateau' (work on stage) rather than a 'travail de table' (work around a table), Fabre's shows often contain a unique and independent meaning, shaped from accidental actions that have occurred during rehearsals. Still, analyses of his productions that are not focused on a decryption of conventional meaning (mainly produced by semiotic approaches) constitute a relatively rare approach. To study the forms as unrelated to a content – in other words, to study the forms for the sake of it – is rarely considered as an interesting approach. This omission is problematic insofar as Fabre's theatre mainly translates into an extremely rigorous work on physicality: bodies, gestures, voices. Like many other contemporary directors, Fabre's main interest is the physical impact his shows can have on the spectators. He does not seek to send any 'message' to his audience. During a rehearsal for *Parrots and Guinea Pigs*, he is reported to have told his actors: 'Your performance needs to be more playful, like during a quick and light improvisation. Otherwise, people will think that you are trying to send an intellectual message and pass on truths' (Van Den Dries 2005: 159).[10] However, Fabre's productions are not free from references and symbols. Many scenes refer to Flemish paintings for instance, while each animal has a very specific significance for him. Moreover, some shows do seem to convey a strong point of view: *Orgy of Tolerance*, for example, is likely to be a critique of our modern tendency to accept nearly anything; for instance, the play denounces our overly tolerant attitude towards fascist political parties. Yet, this study choses to focus mainly on the forms (or materiality), and what they can trigger within the spectator's perception. This other kind of meaning opens other kinds of perception, as Catherine Bouko states in *Théâtre et reception, le spectateur postdramatique*:

> Spectators' expectations are challenged: used to signs that refer to the 'outside world', they are instead confronted by mysterious forms that only refer to themselves. The codes of drama that they are expert in do not allow them to approach this theatrical language. They are then forced to abandon those codes and open themselves to other modes of perception. (Bouko 2010: 114–15)[11]

Many contemporary productions encourage spectators to produce new ways of approaching theatre, which is precisely the challenge that many critics do not engage with. The experience of an encounter with the world can be triggered by a process of non-recognition, that is, by the disruption of the stage perceived as a space of projection, as an empty stage that can be filled and shaped. In the productions that will be considered in this chapter, it may be that the stage blocks the gaze, making it impossible for one to grasp what is faced. The spectator thus appears unable to recognize, unable to create a second image of what is perceived, challenging the very notion of perception. Actions on stage can therefore strike with their immediacy. As a result, the spectators may have the sensation of losing control over their gaze; to experience an encounter, in this case, also entails a certain submission to the surroundings. Van Den Dries depicts Jan Fabre thus: 'He has a bewitching effect, he absorbs perception and forces us to merge with the image' (2005: 28).[12]

One may consider that while the shows themselves are not meant to scare the audience, the experience of non-recognition can appear scary. To accept that the stage may not always be grasped and assimilated and to lose, at some point, control of one's common sense of reality is disturbing, if not frightening. According to Artaud and his theatre of cruelty, which has very deeply influenced contemporary theatre, theatre should reveal the cruelty of the real. Even though cruelty is not meant to be scary, it involves the rejection of the spectators' reassuring beliefs. To face cruelty means to face a world over which our actions as much as our perception have no control over. Artaud's work is challenging to study because his (adopted) lack of precision leads to multiple interpretations. Scholars have approached his theories from different perspectives: transcendental or primitive forces, ritual theatre and so on. Here I would like to focus on the experience of cruelty as the experience of a loss: the loss of one's position as almighty subject. 'Le théâtre de la cruauté' has indeed the ambition to make the spectators forget themselves as subjects deciphering the world. It seeks to trigger an epiphany inside each of its spectator to lead them to realize that they are driven by forces that they cannot control: 'We are not free and the sky can still fall on our heads. And above all else, theatre is made to teach us this' (Artaud 1970: 60). For Artaud, theatre must remind us that we are only the instruments of a force that goes beyond our mere inner world. Understanding their lack of freedom paradoxically frees spectators; realizing that they are not free to consequently be more free, to some extent. Artaud dreamt of a body predating knowledge and civilizations, a body free from any social and cultural alienations:[13]

> I know a state beyond thought, conscience, being, one which has neither words or letters, but into which you enter through screams and swipes. And it is no longer sound or sense that escapes, nor words, just bodies. (2004: 1351)[14]

This is reminiscent of Jean-Luc Nancy's argument that 'In the absence of an object there is no subject either, no transcendental ground, and that what remains is precisely the body, bodies' (Nancy 1994). To reconnect with this less biased relationship with the world leads to make one's existence more precarious. 'To merge into the image' therefore requires some bravery – or may involve consuming alcohol',[15] as philosopher Georges Bataille (who deeply influenced Vienne) states in *L'Expérience intérieure*. 'This is to play the drunk, staggering man who, in a movement of logic, takes himself for a candle, blows it out, and crying out with fear, in the end, takes himself for night' (1988: 70–1). Yet, performances inspired by the theatre of cruelty, although frightening, can also bring along a sense of generosity and benevolence. I realized this when I attended a training session for actors, directed by Annabelle Chambon and Cédric Charron (two of Jan Fabre's frequent actors) in Lyon in December 2017.[16] The training was physically and emotionally intense for the actors. To a lesser extent, of course, it was also emotionally demanding for me to observe it for ten days straight. Charron and Chambon frequently repeated directions such as: 'Let your instinct take control, don't be in the intention to do, just do', 'don't try to do things right, just do them', 'don't do theatre [. . .] you are athletes of emotions, do it, do not imitate', 'don't think about what you're doing, do'. During a lunch break, Lissandro, one of the actors who had been congratulated for the quality of his work in the morning, told me that for him, only the physical was real. One of the exercises he had just been through was named 'the five emotions'. In this exercise, actors must radically switch from one emotion to another (from joy to disgust, for example) in less than two seconds. Lissandro was particularly good at it because, as he told me, he was acting so fast he could avoid any sort of psychologizing. If he had started thinking about his actions, intellectualizing them, or had tried to 'feel' the emotion, he would not have been able to switch from one emotion to another so rapidly and with so much intensity. Instead, he was finding a physical response to an emotion. When he was performing disgust, for instance, he was contracting his stomach so much that his body would produce acid reflux. I started to understand why it might be hard for a spectator to mentally process the actions on Fabre's stage: intention was lacking. Or, rather, there was a lack of any address to anyone outside the stage (as there was still the intention of acting). In fact, Lissandro did not appear to address the other actors watching him. He appeared to be entirely focused on an energy contained inside himself that he was trying to grow and control. He let the others observe him; but it did not seem that he was doing this for them. As a spectator, I felt like I was invited to witness his actions. I was not a judge, not even a recipient; I was a guest, invited to see, for a few minutes, Lissandro's own private and intimate biological condition. Of course, the conditions in which I witnessed the training were very different from those in which a spectator witnesses a performance. Yet, many exercises that the actors were performing are present in Fabre's shows. I was thus partly able to understand the incomprehension many spectators are facing when coming to see a production by the Flemish director. Although I was a spectator, nothing was ever directly addressed to me. Spectating them without being a recipient was rather disturbing. At the end of a scene, after feeling particularly overwhelmed and somehow grateful, Annabelle Chambon came to me and said, 'They are doing something very generous indeed.' She was probably right. The actors were offering the opportunity to witness a deep and intimate part of themselves, a part that is not controlled by their intellect. They were offering a view of their bodies in their most physical dimension. In some ways, they were demonstrating an act of love to one another by sharing the most private, buried parts of themselves. Unsurprisingly, they all became close outside of the training very rapidly (new friendships and romances began), and they were genuinely kind people. It seems important to insist on this more intimate aspect of the creative process, as it contradicts the first impression one could have before a production by Jan Fabre, as something rather violent and obscene. Fabre states indeed: 'I don't create shows about love. But love is important during the creative process. My best shows have been created by actors who love each other' (Van Den Dries 2005: 131).[17] What may be perceived on stage as merely obscene for some may be seen as sincerely generous for others. By showing 'a state beyond thought, conscience, being, one which has neither words or letters, but into which you enter through screams and swipes', Fabre wants spectators to be able to confront a naked, crude reality. Yet, his shows also demonstrate a certain sense of generosity with actors showing some of their own privacy. Similarly, Lehmann argued that going to see a play by Lauwers was like spending 'an evening at Jan's and his friends (not "with" them)' (2006: 109). If spectators accept to open their perception to this private shared space, then they can experience the stage more openly, where another's intimacy is no longer an object of controversy, but a gift.

## 2.2. Strategies to thwart processes of recognition

### 2.2.1. Duration and exhaustion of the signs

In the next few sections, different strategies used by directors to challenge their spectators' perception will be explored and analysed. The first strategy to be discussed is the repetition of a specific action up to the point that the meaning of the action becomes increasingly confused and eventually fades away. Fabre's shows, for instance, contain many repetitive performance acts. One element that tends to be undervalued when it comes to discussing real acts in these performances (real danger and real physical effort especially) is that these very acts still take place on a theatrical stage, that is, a place traditionally of illusion. In fact, Fabre has always performed in French theatres designed to maintain the fourth wall; the Italian-style theatre Théâtre des Célestins for *C'était du théâtre comme c'était à espérer et à prévoir*, the repurposed opera house Théâtre de la Ville for *L'orgie de la tolerance*, for example. The audience face an action whose danger or physical effort is real and yet which occurs in a space meant to be a space of projection for the spectator. The performance acts in Jan Fabre's theatre thus strongly maintain an ambiguous relationship to representation. It is precisely by playing on this contrast between real actions and theatrical space that Fabre succeeds in making the performance acts striking, especially if they last longer than expected. In fact, the longer it lasts, the more easily the spectator will forget the frame of the stage and will realize that the performing actor is sharing the same space as them. An interesting concept to better understand this process is what Clément Rosset defines as 'la représentation anticipée' (anticipated representation), as discussed before (2004: 162–73). In this theory, the subject perceives the representation before perceiving the thing itself. For instance, a student may perceive Rome first as represented in their history book before going to the Italian capital, and finally find themselves shocked by what stands in front of them. As Rosset points out, the confrontation with the thing itself is usually accompanied by a reaction of surprise, as though the representation did not at all prepare the subject for encountering the real object. Even if we prepare ourselves for an event to occur, we will always be facing it with some surprise. To take a rather radical example, even though we may try to be prepared to lose a family member or a friend who has an incurable illness, there will always be an element of surprise in the news of their death, as one can never be fully prepared for the real event to occur. To a less dramatic extent, even though we might prepare for an exam very studiously, we are surely always surprised to do well (or, indeed, fail). In fact, the 'real thing' is always surprising because it cannot be repeated. This is, to some extent, what Deleuze explains in *Difference and Repetition* (2006). Difference is always to be found in repetition. Deleuze goes even further and explains that it is in repetition itself that difference may be best experienced. Indeed, if something happens repeatedly, the difference may appear clearer. For instance, if one goes to the library every Monday and one day, has their bag stolen, the difference will be better experienced than in the case of someone who has their bag stolen the very first time they go to the library. The second time (the day the bag was stolen) will be compared to the first time and the subject will acknowledge that even though it was the same event occurring (going to the library), there was something radically different about it.

A repetition is never the exact copy of the original: it cannot be. Of course, this example is somewhat simple and trivial; difference may be experienced in more qualified and subtle ways. When Pierre Menard, for instance, decides to (re)write Cervantes's *Don Quixote* in Jorge Luis Borges's novel (1962), using the exact same words, he still produces something new. His novel is unique, even though he uses Cervantes's text, because the context and the impulse of writing are different. To experience repetition is therefore necessarily to experience something new, to experience a *difference*. To assimilate repetition to difference may seem counter-intuitive, but perhaps Deleuze is trying to prove that novelty is indeed everywhere, even in a reproduction, as it seems that humans are normally intellectually not inclined to see it:

> The 'I think' is the most general principle of representation – in other words, the source of these elements and of the unity of all these faculties: I conceive, I judge, I imagine, I remember and I perceive – as though these were the four branches of the Cogito. On precisely these branches, difference is crucified. They form quadripartite fetters under which only that which is identical, similar, analogous or opposed can be considered different: *difference becomes an object of representation always in relation to a conceived identity, a judged analogy, an imagined opposition or a perceived similitude.* (2006: 138)

To conceive, judge, imagine and remember are faculties that enable the subject to 'recognize' things in the world. They recognize them insofar as they are 'identical', 'similar', 'analogous' or 'opposed'. Recognition is our main mode of perception. Yet, for Deleuze, the recognition mode prevents the perception of the difference: 'the world of representation is characterized by its inability to conceive of difference in itself' partly because 'thought is [. . .] filled with no more than an image of itself' (138). On the other hand, the difference 'forces' us to think. This perception is much more difficult; by forcing the subject to think, it forces them to create:

> Something in the world forces us to think. This something is an object not of recognition but of a fundamental encounter. What is encountered

may be Socrates, a temple or a demon. It may be grasped in a range of affective tones: wonder, love, hatred, suffering. In whichever tone, its primary characteristic is that it can only be sensed. In this sense, it is opposed to recognition. [. . .] The object of encounter, on the other hand, really gives rise to sensibility with regard to a given sense. (139)

The real encounter with the world would therefore first translate into a sensory experience. However, this does not mean that this experience does not produce thoughts, on the contrary. This experience of the world brings sensitivity and meaning together. A different, enigmatic meaning emerges: 'that which can only be sensed (the *sentiendum* or the being of the sensible) moves the soul, "perplexes" it – in other words, forces it to pose a problem' (140). Difference enables the subject to encounter the world. This experience only occurs when the subject has difficulty in recognizing something, when they are intellectually struck by what they are facing. Like the 'représentation anticipée', the difference in repetition shows us that the real is unique, 'idiot', and that nothing can prepare us to experience it. It necessarily remains surprising even though it is represented beforehand or repeated.

Many performance artists from the 1960s onwards use repetition as an aesthetic tool designed to challenge usual experiences of the world for their spectators. In Europe, these include (among others) Pina Bausch, Romeo Castellucci and Gisèle Vienne, but also many Flemish directors, such as Jan Fabre, Jan Lauwers, Anna Teresa de Keersmaeker and Wim Wanderkeybus. In the UK, one can also mention Forced Entertainment and Impact Theatre (Peyton Jones 2011). In Fabre's theatre, as mentioned earlier, many scenes feature actions performed repeatedly by actors. The actors often become physically exhausted on stage and are eventually unable to continue performing. Paradoxically, by showing the repetition of an action, Jan Fabre reveals the constant alteration of this very action; its constant *difference*. Actors who repetitively throw themselves on the ground will never do it the same twice, as, for instance, the action will be increasingly difficult and painful. Each beginning of the action might not be particularly surprising as the audience may still be in a process of recognition, figuring out what this action signifies within the play. Yet, by making this action last for several long minutes, the spectator may progressively cease projecting meaning onto it. At some point, they may even stop perceiving meaning in this action and will merely see bodies, throwing themselves on the floor for no apparent reason. Thus, what is perceived at the end of the action is no longer a representation of the action, but the materiality of the action itself. It is precisely this process that Fabre calls 'from act to acting'. Through duration, Fabre can encourage the spectator to finally leave their perception as recognition. As Luk Van Den Dries points out:

> Because the repetition is intensified so excessively and the uniformity is magnified so manically, breaches start to appear out of which the individual can rise up. This is certainly the case with respect to the act of watching. It is precisely in the perfect repetition of the ever identical that the minimal differences between all of these uniform bodies are increasingly enlarged. Amidst what is most uniform, every minimal difference becomes an inevitable rupture in the lake of identity. That millimetre, that second, holds all the time of the individual. (2006: 36)

In *Le pouvoir des folies théâtrales*, performed in Avignon in 2013, the actors tirelessly repeat some basic movements from classical ballet requiring them to keep their balance, until one can see their bodies shaking. Another scene features an actress trying to climb up on stage while prevented from doing so by an actor who repeatedly pushes her back to the audience. This particular action continues for twenty minutes. The actress begins to pant and sweat, and her skin turns red. This may also occur with the repetition of a word, or a sentence. In the same performance, the actors repeat the number 1876, gradually obscuring the meaning of this word, until someone on stage explains that 1876 is the date of the opera *Der ring des nibelungen* by Richard Wagner, being performed for the first time. Similarly, in *Je suis sang*, performed in Avignon in 2001, a scene features knights who kill brides by slashing their veins and waiting for the blood to drain out of their bodies. Once this is done, they carry them in a very gentle way (probably in reference to the Christian Pietà) to the back of the stage and leave them on the floor. The brides slowly wake up and start licking their blood, which had left a stream on the floor right back to their original position. The blood then restores their energy, and the knights must repeat the action. This action is repeated until the actors playing the knights become physically unable to continue. As Luk Van Den Dries states:

> Until the image starts to crack, muscles start to quiver, sweat breaks out and concrete time launches its attack on these exhausted bodies. The loved ones are dragged, rather than carried and finally they get dumped on the floor. (2006: 35)

This scene comes from a training exercise that Fabre gives to his actors to help them understand the difference between act and acting. During the actor training that I attended, Annabelle Chambon and Cédric Charron (who were performing in that scene from *Je suis sang*) gave this task to the actors. I could see how different every action was from the previous one. At first, I perceived the action as filled with references (e.g. I saw a Pietà). Yet, progressively, the action began to lose its signs. After a while, I was finally perceiving it as merely an intense physical effort. As a spectator, it was a powerful experience because my perception was constantly challenged; what I perceived was becoming more and more real, less and less fictitious, as though the image I was facing was gradually more difficult to be grasped, to be recognized. From an image, I was now perceiving an action being performed. Van Den Dries underlines this transformation in the perception in the performance *C'est du théâtre comme c'était à espérer et prévoir*): 'The sound of their bodies that crash into the wood floor is nothing less or more than the sound of any body that crashes into a wood floor' (2006: 19).[18] This statement is close to the experience of the real as developed by Rosset. An idiotic real, that is, without doubles, may be attained if one manages *to see what is being done*.

In 2015, I went to see *Orestie (une comédie organique?)* by Castellucci, performed at the Odéon, in Paris. A particular scene featured the character of the rabbit (clearly inspired by the white rabbit in *Alice's Adventures in Wonderland*), trying to climb on a chair and continuously falling from it. This action was repeated for several long minutes. In the background, there was a short extract of a symphony being played. The extract was repeated each time the action itself was repeated. This scene had a very physical impact on me, and I can still remember the sensation, years later. My body – although I remained motionless – was vibrating and following the rhythms of the scene. It was different from attending a music concert or a dance performance. Music, movements, words, narration, textures and so on. Everything was happening at the same time. There was no space for my own projection, for me to have time to digest and transform what I was spectating. There were no psychological emotions involved (I was not sad because the scene was sad, nor was I scared because the scene was scary). It was rather a diffuse, complete emotion. Something convinced me that what I was spectating was real. I never fully understood what this something was. I simply knew that at a certain point, an intense physical emotion invaded me and united my entire being towards the same, total energy. Intellect, senses, emotions, physical sense of being reached the same tempo. I later came across this quote by Castellucci: 'the entire body needs to feel emotional and convinced by everything that agitates around it' (2001: 17).[19]

*Crowd*, by Gisèle Vienne, is a play that features fifteen young people raving. Hugely successful, the play has toured more than a hundred different locations since its first showing in 2017. At the start of the show, the audience is facing an empty stage covered with soil. Then young people, in casual dressing, come and meet, laugh and touch each other, dance to techno songs. The rave culminates at a certain point, with tensions and pulsion unleashed, then calms down towards the end. Vienne explained she was inspired by raves she has been to herself, when she was living in Grenoble, then in Berlin (2020 in Pascaud 2021). One thing, however, is unrealistic. Each movement of the most trivial actions, such as drinking, smoking, greeting or even dancing, is performed in slow motion. The rave becomes thus a strange ritual, where actions take time to make sense (if they do happen to make sense at all): it takes a few minutes for the spectator to understand that this actor is actually dancing, or this actor is greeting another actor, and not fighting them, for instance. The meaning of the actions gradually disappears because the actions do not happen in a recognizable space-time continuum. The music is loud and high tempo, and yet the bodies are quiet and move very, very slowly. After a while, the audience might then enter a different kind of perception; one that is free from the quest for meaning and allows a 'superficial' observation of uncanny bodies. This temporal distortion is meant to give us a sense of ritual and spirituality that is lacking from our modern Western societies, according to Vienne. She works with her actors on a method she calls 'the sensorial gymnastic' and argues that 'more than slowing down [the show allows one] to be in the real' (2021).[20]

Signs can also gradually disappear when the action is offered to the perception without any given contexts, in medias res. Some of Fabre's performances appear very intrusive for the spectator right from the start. This is, for instance, the case of *L'Histoire des larmes*, performed in Avignon in the Cour d'honneur in 2005. The first sixteen-minute scene (of a total of a one hour-and-forty-one-minute performance) featured several crying women, lying on the floor, seemingly imitating newborns. A harpist, at the centre of the stage, was playing to (perhaps) calm them down. Yet, the screaming soon made the music nearly inaudible. The screaming rapidly invaded the sound space, and the scene became particularly irritating to watch and listen to. *L'Histoire des larmes* offered no possible escape for the spectator (about 2,000 spectators fit in the Cour d'honneur, it is thus rather unlikely to be seated near an exit, etc.). The fact that a harpist was playing very gentle music made the scene even more unbearable as it accentuated the very unpleasant yet dominant screaming. It was surprisingly similar to this situation when spectators are annoyed by some of their neighbours talking in the theatre, making it difficult for them to follow the action on stage and focus their attention. The performance has generally not been well received by the public, and this opening was sometimes met by booing from spectators

(Talon-Hugon 2006). It is difficult, though, to evaluate the percentage of spectators leaving the show during this first scene. It cannot be discerned from recordings, and reviews do not mention it. Yet, it is easy enough to understand why the audience may reject such a start to the performance. But Fabre did make his point. Indeed, the show is about tears and humans' relationship to them. Many characters insist on the fact that tears have been, and still are, wrongly hidden. No positive value is granted to them; on the contrary, they are perceived as indecent. This first scene, in some ways, demonstrates our own intolerance of tears. For Fabre, however, tears are life; the two first things a newborn does are screaming and crying. The scene was disturbing because it could not be grasped, nor could it be stopped. Fabre refused to comfort the audience into their own representations. In many ways, the spectator's experience here may be compared to the character facing a 'panic representation', as described by Rosset. For the French philosopher, 'la représentation panique' occurs when the action and its representation happen at the same time, as described before. In *Duel*, a film by Steven Spielberg, a car driver is pursued by a truck for a whole day. There is no apparent reason. No clues are given to explain the action. The truck, says Rosset, is a signifier without a signify. *It is what it is and that is all.* The action and its representation coexist. A sense of representation is still perceived by both the spectator (and, in a more metatheatrical way, the hero) because the chase remains staged. Through the mise-en-scène, the car driver is recognizing something in this random action, even if he is experiencing it for the very first time. The car driver panics because he does not have time to process what is happening to him. He does not have time to attribute a meaning to it himself.

> Such a coincidence between the real and its representation prevents the subject to find the necessary time to consider what is happening to them: this is why they find themselves in a situation of urgency that refuses delay and forbids deliberation. (Rosset 2004: 166)[21]

*L'Histoire des larmes* plays on the same confusion between action and representation. The spectator is confronted with a scene starting in medias res, with no landmark, yet 'mise en scène'. The action and its meaning overlap each other, chronologically and logically. The meaning of the opening scene is rather to be found in its presence itself; in the simple fact that it occurs on stage. Like the character in *Duel*, the spectator does not understand the situation but may understand its inevitability as this 'idiotic' action is nonetheless staged. Of course, the audience may also feel irritated facing a scene that does not provide any key to decipher it. If they really want to, the spectators will still be able to interpret it retrospectively and connect some random dots together. This is in fact what I did when I interpreted what tears can refer to and symbolize! But at the very instant you are spectating this peculiar action, nothing makes sense. Yet, if we do not reject it straight away, we can enter a different perception where reality strikes and reveals a world unvarnished by interpretations.

The most obvious situation in which spectators will not be able to recognize the actions on stage is when these very actions are missing. Some performances trick the audience and their expectations by blurring any clear opening to the show. The effects on the spectator's perception are particularly interesting. In the introduction to *Theatre and the Body* by Colette Conroy, Marina Abramović evokes a peculiar piano concert by Nam June Paik:

> Years ago at the Documenta exhibition in Kassel, Nam June Paik was supposed to give a piano concert at a Fluxus performance. He took a microphone and said that it was going to be a very boring concert ('please leave the room'). He repeated his appeal for 45 minutes, and finally people started to leave. In the end he was fantastic. It was boring indeed, but it made me realize how afraid we are of doing little or nothing, and yet it is precisely that doing nothing that opens the doors to different perceptions. The performer uses the public like a mirror and vice versa. (Conroy, 2010: viii–ix)

Abramović assumes that the absence of actions on stage ('action' is understood broadly as someone doing something) may lead the spectator to experience 'different perceptions'. While the audience was expecting to attend a piano concert, nothing occurred, and people remained in their seats for forty minutes before finally deciding to leave. Similarly, and more famously, *4'33* is a music score by John Cage featuring a total absence of notes from the beginning to the end. When this piece is performed by an orchestra, musicians simply do not play, for as long as the score lasts. You can easily find online recordings of the piece 'played' (although it is obviously a significantly different experience to watch it on a screen). In *Postdramatic theatre*, Hans-Thies Lehmann quotes Cage about this absence of doing: 'if something is boring after two minutes, one should try it for four hours, if still boring, one should try eight, etc. Eventually one would discover that it is not boring at all' (Lehmann 2006: 90). The idea of writing a silent piece of music came to Cage during a visit to a soundproof room at Harvard University. While he expected to face a perfect silence, he heard two sounds: one very high and the other very low. When he discussed it with the sound engineer, he was told that the high sound was the sound made by his nervous system and the low one was the one made by his blood flowing in his veins. Since then, Cage became obsessed with the perfect silence. In *A Composer's Confessions* (2013), he wrote that his strongest desire was to create an absolute silence. In some ways, his search for silence may be seen as a way to retrieve humans' physical, organic presence. Abramović similarly sought to make the spectators face their own presence with *The Artist Is Present*, at the MOMA in 2010. Sitting on a chair motionless, she was simply maintaining eye contact with each spectator who came to sit in front of her: 'there is no way to go but in yourself. I made a stage for the audience', she explains in the official trailer. Abramović looking back, or the orchestra performing *4'33*, leaves no space for projection for the audience. Viewers are in the spectators' seats but are no longer spectators as either the performance is not given to spectate (*4'33*) or they themselves become an object of contemplation (*The Artist Is Present*). It can be boring (how many people find *4'33* ridiculous?), or it can be, on the contrary, overwhelming. Many people who attended *The Artist Is Present* experienced strong emotional reactions.

Fabre tricks his audience's expectations in a similar way. Some of his performances appear indeed very slow to start. The spectators arrive; they sit down, wait, and soon the scheduled starting time has passed, and nothing is happening. This is, for instance, the case with *Le pouvoir des folies théâtrales*, played in 2013 in the Opéra Théâtre in Avignon. During the first sixteen minutes, the actors stand in line at the back of the stage, with their backs turned away from the audience. As time passes, one can hear in the audience increasing noise coming from the audience: seats cracking, breathing, sneezing, yawning and so on. These various noises gradually build a background sound inside the theatre. Surprisingly, the presence of the spectators becomes significantly more noticeable than the presence of the actors on stage. The stage is not empty, but once the decor, costumes and actors have been analysed, nothing else occurs to keep the spectator's mind occupied. They are left on their own, unable to spectate. Similarly, in *This Is How You Will Disappear* by Vienne, nobody is on stage for the first fifteen minutes of the show. A forest occupies the stage, wrapped up in a cloud of fog, created by Japanese artist Fujiko Nakaya. Vienne explained how surprised most spectators who came to see the show were (2017 in Anna Gallagher-Ross 2017). *We're Pretty Fucking Far from Okay* opens similarly. Presented in 2016 in Avignon, the show was directed by Lisbeth Gruwez, a dancer trained by Fabre and who worked with him for many years. The show *apparently* began once the lights in the theatre were turned off, yet no lights conversely came on stage. It was rather dark; as I attended the performance, I remember being able to see some of the spectators' faces thanks to the exit signs glowing in the dark. I cannot remember exactly how long it lasted, but it felt extremely long. At this point I was gradually becoming more aware of my surroundings; the light of a phone that someone was trying to turn off, the sound of the seats cracking, the whisperings from people wondering whether something was going wrong. We were increasingly reminded of our physical presence. In a way, it showed us that the light switching off in a theatre does not necessarily mean that we, the spectators, must disconnect from our bodies and become solely intellectual entities, as we are still *here* together. After a little while in the darkness, we began to hear the actors breathing on stage, although we still could not see them. The breathing became more and more intense; after a few long minutes, it almost sounded like the actors were having a panic attack. It is only then that the lights illuminated on the stage enabling us to finally see it. The heavy breathing performed by the actors required from them an intense physical effort. As a result, their bodies were nervously shaking and appeared to become increasingly difficult to control. It was rather similar to the five emotions exercise in Fabre's training sessions, as described in the introduction. By forcing themselves to breathe extremely rapidly, their bodies responded to these stimuli and made them end up gasping for air *for real*. My experience as a spectator was, however, very different. The actors' breathing prompted me to acknowledge my own breathing. At a particular point, I felt the spectators' breathing adopting the actors' breathing tempo. For a few minutes, I could hear everyone near me all breathing at the same time. The actors' breathing became too intense for us to follow though. I was feeling slightly frustrated to witness this growing energy on stage without being able to join it. Remaining a motionless, disciplined spectator seemed unfair. Because of this contrasting effect, the spectators were perhaps reminded of their own passivity while the stage grew more and more in physical strength. The fact that we were spectators, and *only* spectators, was thus highlighted. The stage, on the other hand, was manifesting an apparent freedom, and, by doing so, was driving us spectators more and more into our seats. In fact, the system of representation seemed almost reversed. The audience was no longer the first image (reality) and the stage no longer the second image (the representation). Instead, it was rather the stage that was the source, the 'real thing', and the audience the representation. In other words, the stage was the space where a primitive force could take place while we, spectators, were reminded that social and cultural rules control us and force us to remain patiently physically passive. The duration of this repetitive scene challenged our perception and invited us to explore new ways of how being a spectator can feel. The next section explores how the unfamiliar on stage can also prompt audiences to perceive differently.

### 2.2.2. The unfamiliar

The concept of defamiliarization developed by Viktor Shklovsky in *Art, as Device* (2015: 157–74) may help us to understand how unfamiliar bodies or actions on stage can lead to an unbiased encounter with the world. According to Shklovsky (and similarly to Deleuze) to properly experience art, one must encounter difficulties in recognizing the object one is facing. If the object remains unrecognized, it can then irradiate its own materiality. Shklovsky explains: 'things that have been experienced several times begin to be experienced in terms of recognition: a thing is in front of us, we know this, but we do not see it' (2015: 163). The idea that we may know things and yet not see them is significant, as it underlines once more the fact that the encounter with the real is more challenging than the mere everyday perception. The pen we use every day to write, the bag we use to go to work with, the clothes we wear when it rains, the pan we use to cook and so on may be objects that we know but do not see. We recognize all of them, which is precisely why we can have use of them. Therefore, 'to see', for Shklovsky, means to encounter the object (although he does not specifically use the word 'encounter'). We do not see, encounter these everyday objects. Rather, we always tend to consider the objects according to us (the pen *to* write, the pan *to* cook). We may have already paid attention to the colour of our pen, to the material of our clothes, but they may never have particularly stricken us in any way; we may never have faced their presence. For Shklovsky, only art can provide such an experience:

> And so this thing we call art exists in order to restore the sensation of life, in order to make us feel things, in order to make a stone stony. The goal of art is to create the sensation of seeing, and not merely recognizing, things; the device of art is the 'enstrangement' of things and the complication of the form, which increases the duration and

complexity of perception, as the process of perception is, in art, an end in itself and must be prolonged. (162)

Here, the perception of the forms – and only the forms – is precisely the most difficult perception to attain. To experience the way a stone is 'stony' is thus complex and far from plain. To not recognize an object, to not understand its meaning, its usefulness, its role (in the broadest sense of the word) constitutes a real challenge for the perception. For Shklovsky, art helps us reconnect with 'an intensity of perception, forc[ing] us to look again, to see, almost for the first time' (Gunn 1984: 28). To produce an effect of defamiliarization, the artist 'must consciously violate accepted ways of making meanings – whatever they are' (30). It is their responsibility to make sure that the spectators will encounter difficulties in projecting meaning onto the object of art. In order to do so, they must ensure that their object 'fills the vacuum which has allowed our automatic response to develop' (29). In a certain way, to strike its audience, the object of art needs to be full, impenetrable, since it must prevent the spectators from shaping it in their own ways. The border between sensitive and cognitive experience is difficult to establish. It seems rather unlikely that the experience of defamiliarization might only be an experience of the senses insofar as to experience it, one needs also to experience a cognitive failure, that is, a failure in recognition. Here I would like to discuss two strategies to trigger such experiences: showing the obscene, and constructing unprecedented images on stage.

One recurrent criticism of some contemporary productions is that they are 'obscene', due to the presence of blood, urine and nudity or sexual acts. What is seen on stage may be judged as gratuitous and trivial. In many contemporary shows, bodies are indeed no longer beautifully distant and mysterious. On the contrary, they are shown in their raw materiality, their fragility and obscenity. This creates tension and can generate anger for some spectators. The etymology of the word 'obscene' does demonstrate that obscenities should, in theory, not feature on a theatrical stage: the Latin word *ob-scenus* signifies in front of, or outside the stage. The obscene is precisely what should remain hidden, away from our glaze. In fact, showing the obscene on stage constitutes a double transgression. Not only is it shown; but it is shown on stage, the space of observation *par excellence*. Staging the obscene is therefore clearly intentional in theatre. Contemporary directors can shock and disturb their spectators' perceptions by showing what should not be shown. On this matter, Van Den Dries notes:

> Consciousness tends to envisage the body as necessarily an obscene residue, *ob-scaena*, meaning outside the stage as a place of observation. Perhaps the body, in everyday life, needs to stay away from the consciousness' space. Theatre is here to make this regularity an exception, to succeed in making it problematic. (2005: 6)[22]

By staging the obscene, directors attempt to impose uncomfortable realities upon their spectators. The stage becomes a space that deconstructs representations and projections and instead, that makes the real strike. It no longer represents reality; it unveils it. The discomfort that some in the audience may experience can be explained by two reasons. First, the vulnerable (often naked) body reminds us of our physiologic and animalistic dimension. Our own image as civilized human beings is being challenged. Second, the naked body on stage can be way more disturbing than any naked bodies seen within our private sphere because it is seen in groups. The experience is intimate but also shared, collective, therefore social. The gaze is not only *my* gaze, but *our* gaze. The private body is public. The transgression is not only social and cultural but also political. The social rules that ease and enable our living together are transgressed; the private and the public are reunited. By showing obscene bodies or acts, the director takes the risk to betray the trust between them and the audience. To illustrate this breach in the tacit contract between directors and spectators, let me give you an example. In November 2015, I went to see *4* by Rodrigo García at the théâtre des Amandiers (Paris). During one scene, the actors were joyfully dancing and singing on the stage. At some point, one of the actors asked a young woman in the audience to join them on the stage and dance and sing with them. The lights went on in the audience, and the actors encouraged us from the stage to clap with them. This moment was particularly enjoyable, a nice alchemy between the stage and the audience was forming, and we, spectators, felt like we had become active participants in the show. One of the actors then asked the young woman to get into a sleeping bag that was on stage. We laughed at her clumsiness, and she also looked to be enjoying herself. They then made her sit on a chair and asked her if she knew the meaning of the English expression 'doggy style' (the play was in French). She said no. At that point, only a few were still laughing in the audience. The music was turned louder and louder and an actor zipped up the sleeping bag entirely, trapping her inside. They carried her on the floor and acted as if they were, indeed, doggy-styling her. Of course, no one in the audience was laughing at that point. Instead, I felt incredibly uncomfortable, and stupid, for not foreseeing the obscene – and extremely intrusive – action this spectator was enduring. After what felt an eternity, the actors finally released her and asked her to go back to her seat. After leaving the show that night, I wondered if she were part of the cast. I only saw the performance once, so I would never be able to know for sure. But that probably doesn't matter; the scene was shocking, disturbing, and years later I still very much remember how it made me feel. I remember feeling like García, and his actors betrayed my trust. I also remember thinking that I should not have to pay for feeling uncomfortable! And, yet, I've rarely seen a scene that questions our role and position as spectators so brilliantly – and brutally. I was told later that one of the spectators went on stage to try to rescue the young woman during one performance. García, who was then backstage, apparently went straight on stage to shout at that poor spectator trying to help and ask him to leave immediately. Showing the obscene is not chaos; it is a subtle art with specific codes that need to be rigorously followed.

The obscene shocks, challenges our perception and complexifies our relationship to the stage. To better understand the implications of showing obscene acts or bodies on stage, it might be useful to discuss the concept of Genius, as developed by Italian philosopher Giorgio Agamben in *Profanations* (2007). Genius refers to the 'impersonal element' (11) every human lives with; Genius makes us eat, sleep and urinate for instance. It is a vital force that surpasses our will and upon which we have no control. According to the theory developed by Agamben, humans are split between Genius and their 'I'. The latter refers to the individual's ego, their personal part, that is, what makes them who they are (tastes, desires, feelings, opinions, etc.). We can control 'I' as we are its source, its creator, on purpose or not. While 'I' is specific to each of us, Genius is universal and was seen by the Romans as the divine part of humans: 'Genius was, in a certain way, the divinization of the person, the principle that governed and expressed his entire existence' (10). Existing, in this way, means living together with 'an impersonal, preindividual element' (11). Genius is timeless; we breathe and shudder in the same way at eighty years old as at any age.

> Everything in us that is impersonal is genial. The force that pushes the blood through our veins or that plunges us into sleep, the unknown power in our body that gently regulates and distributes its warmth or that relaxes or contracts the fibers of our muscles – that too is genial. It is Genius that we obscurely sense in the intimacy of our psychological life, in which what is most one's own is also strange and impersonal, and in which what is nearest somehow remains distant and escapes mastery. If we did not abandon ourselves to Genius, if we were only ego and consciousness, we would not even be able to urinate. Living with Genius means, in this sense, living in the intimacy of a strange being, remaining constantly in relation to a zone of nonconsciousness. (12)

Consequently, this unknown and mysterious constituent leads humans to practice various spiritual activities, in an attempt to understand it. Since Genius is free from the individual's 'I', experiencing only Genius – in the hypothesis that it might be possible – may be related to an ecstatic state. This is precisely this state that some actors are trying to reach. In Fabre's theatre, the 'warriors of beauty' (the way he calls some of his best actors) attempt to reconnect with their physiological existence; with life as it does not belong to them: 'Genius is our life insofar as it does not belong to us' (13). For Fabre, everything that relates to the body in its organic dimension is beautiful. Van Den Dries insists on the fact that he is working with his actors 'like a biologist'. Actress Annabelle Chambon told me once that she and other actors have been treated like laboratory rats by him, as he made them pass several tests to examine their heart rates, their blood flows and the way their brains were reacting while facing different sorts of danger. Fabre is always seeking to reveal the animalistic energy inside each of his actors. Fascinated by the function of the human body and the way the organs are related to each other, his directing is in fact close to a dissection. He seeks to demonstrate to his audience how bodily joints are activated, how pain affects the control of the body, and so on. This approach to theatre is shown concretely in *Requiem for a metamorphosis*. In a particular scene, a doctor explains how dead insects are preserved, and how the operation involves the use of many chemical operations. She uses a human body to illustrate her talk, describing all of the organs and their functions. This scene looks similar to the painting *A le De anatomische les van Dr Nicolaes Tulp*, by Rembrandt, painted in 1632 (translated as *The Anatomy Lesson of Dr. Tulp*). A similar scene occurs in *Je suis sang*. Several characters are cutting other characters' bodies laid on what seem to be old school surgery tables. The actors scream very loudly and eventually pretend to be dead. Once all their organs have been taken out, the characters wake up with a large hole in their stomachs and start eating their own organs, in order to regain them. In *Je suis sang*, bodies are similarly externalized as much as possible. Fabre's theatre may be experienced as a ritual insofar as it tends to make the actors' 'I' disappear in order to present them as mere bodies crossed by a vital force. The actors appear thus as trying to reconnect with Genius.

But how can the actors experiencing their physiological dimension, their 'Genius', transmit their experience to the spectator? When discussing *Mount Olympus*, a twenty-four-hour performance by Fabre, one actor explained in an interview:

> We tend to feel as we do not belong to society anymore [...] but I think it is just part of us and it is good to reembrace it. That is actually how you achieve the catharsis.²³

He seemed to assume that the actors' 'catharsis' necessarily transmits to the spectators. He argued that the audience will eventually forget that they are in a theatre and will instead feel this vital energy. In the same video, the actor Cédric Charron claimed:

> During the 24 hours, something is growing, and we are putting layers on layers on layers until the very big fireworks at the end. And the audience is feeling as [if they were] living this physical experience with us. And so, the catharsis; [...] of course, it is on stage, we are [in] a state, we are becoming something else. But the audience as well. And at the end of the 24 hours, that you will see [...] People are transformed. There is a before *Mount Olympus* and an after *Mount Olympus*.

This assumption of a necessary transfer of energy from the stage to the audience remains extremely obscure. The actors and Fabre himself are never clear on how this life energy might be circulating from the actors to the spectators. Moreover, the word 'catharsis' is often mentioned, yet there are different and competing definitions. Fabre seems to assume that the Aristotelian catharsis is similar to Dionysian rituals, which is very debatable. In fact, the actors' and the spectators' experiences are always confounded in Fabre's comments. The actor training that I attended was all about the actors, their relationship with their bodies, with their own energies. I sometimes felt like the catharsis was first and foremost for them, and mainly in a therapeutic way. When I asked Annabelle and Cédric about the experience of the spectators, they remained very vague. Cédric argued that it was through the actors' catharsis that the spectators could experience their own, which remains a rather unclear answer. They seemingly do not really know in what way the spectators could feel that which they feel as actors. This probably would not be an issue in more traditional forms of theatre, but it appears problematic when it comes to engaging with the spectators in a theatre boasting to be a ritual.

While naked bodies and obscene acts on stage can be seen as part of a strategy to make bodies and behaviours look strange and make them difficult to process for the audience, there are other strategies to challenge spectators' familiar representations. One of them is to associate various elements that emanate from significantly different registers. Doing so contributes to defeat the spectator's recognition as it usually creates a sense of the uncanny. Before mentioning examples from various shows, I would like to briefly refer to a specific exercise often given to Fabre's actors during training sessions called the five idols. While attending one of those sessions, I witnessed five actors being asked to perform one idol each. The first three idols were a saint, a prostitute and a clown; the remaining two were to be chosen by the two remaining actors. They were not asked to reproduce stereotypes but rather to find a certain physicality in every character (the exercise appeared similar to the commedia dell'arte in this sense). In a line at the back of the stage, they were waiting to receive the signal to start performing. There were always at least three actors performing at the same time, embodying different idols, creating quite a festive energy. Yet, because they were all acting alongside each other, interpreting characters from completely different worlds, a sense of the strangeness emerged. The characters, as archetypes, were very familiar but their gathering was odd. To spectate a nun and a rapper having a lively discussion, for instance, was bizarre yet cheerful because it contained something somehow transgressive. In a way, it felt like what philosopher Giorgio Agamben calls a profanation. Agamben explains in his essay *Profanations* that to profane something means to 'return to use what the sacred had separated and petrified' (2007: 74). He argues that capitalism (as a new form of religion) has taken humans away from the profanation: every object now has a very specific function and serves a specific purpose. To consume an object means to destroy it as purely an object, since the purpose of the object and the object itself are confounded. For instance, a child – who is not yet a consumer – will turn the family sofa into a playground and will ignore the fact that this is not its purpose; which, for Agamben, is the attitude towards objects one needs to reconnect with. Indeed, the child knows how to *use* the sofa while their parents may only know how to *consume* it:

> If, today, consumers in mass society are unhappy, it is not only because they consume objects that have incorporated within themselves their own inability to be used. It is also, and above all, because they believe they are exercising their right to property on these objects, because they have become incapable of profaning them. (83)

To profane an object leads thus to experience it as an infinite number of possibilities. In extension, it means to combine different objects to see blossom new ways of using them. For Agamben, museums are the ultimate symbols of our capitalist cult of the 'unprofanable' (92). Art, religion and philosophy are now classified into different sections and left as dead and immutable representations. By associating different images that appear to have nothing in common, directors fight against good taste and try to create unprecedented images. The spectators can recognize different elements on stage but simply cannot recognize – or *consume* – their assembly. They are constantly failing to grasp the representation, even though it is composed of familiar elements.

In Fabre's theatre, sinister surgeons are playing electric guitars in *Requiem for a Metamorphosis*, and the character of the bee who embodies a sort of fool imitates God and his mighty power by waving two table tennis rackets. In *My Movements are Alone like Streetdogs*, the actress sings 'La mauvaise réputation' by Georges Brassens while pretending to vomit, in a gloomy and worrying atmosphere. She then puts two party hats on two dogs' corpses (although this image might be more complex than a mere strange combination, as a play between life and death is engaged). In *Another Sleepy Dusty Delta Day* (2008), the actress repeats, 'Oh oh, je crois que j'ai vu un gros minet!' (famous quote from the French version of the animated movie Tweety: 'I tawt I taw a puddy tat!') to a canary in a cage, in a mine decor. She then pretends to give some beer to the bird. In *Je suis sang*, which features a medieval setting, one of the actresses, Lisbeth Gruwez, starts to sing 'Son of a preacher man' by Dusty Springfield while playing with a sword and wearing a nappy. The song 'Le tango des joyeux bouchers' by Boris Vian is then played in a particularly bloody scene. In *Orgy of Tolerance*, Jesus has a makeover done by a professional stylist. His cross becomes a guitar. The images we are facing as spectators appear unprecedented and therefore unrecognizable. While it is still an association of common representations (the more common the representations are, the more bizarre the final scene will in fact appear), the new image that emerges from this is not a recognizable representation. It is rather an uncanny object that leaves the spectators unable to consume it and invites us instead to perceive more freely. The examples seen usually create a disturbing or worrying atmosphere, except the scene featuring Jesus and the bee, which is deliberately comical. The combination of registers can indeed also lead to some very funny, grotesque scenes. In *Requiem for a Metamorphosis*, the actress playing the character of the bee brings a dissonance to the rest of the play; a play that raises existential issues and whose tone is generally serious.

In García's productions, worrying atmospheres are often created by playing a popular, familiar song during a distressful situation. *ACCIDENS (mata para comer)* is a twenty-five-minute-long performance which features a single action and was first performed in 2006. At the very start of the show, a man comes on stage holding a live lobster. The man hangs the animal on a hook and places a microphone next to it so that the audience can hear its heartbeat. The man goes to sit down on a chair, looking at the lobster and at the audience in turn. He goes to water the lobster with a bottle, then goes back to his seat. One can hear the lobster's heartbeat fainting. After many long minutes, the man unhooks the lobster, puts it on a cutting board, lights a barbecue, chops off the lobster's claws, cuts the abdomen in half, puts some salt on the flesh, places the lobster on the grill. He then eats it with a glass of wine. Shocked and disturbed by what they were witnessing, some spectators got up and left during the show (Reynolds 2017: 144). While the actor was eating his meal, Louis Armstrong's 'What a Wonderful World' was played in the background. The association between the horror of seeing an animal put to death on stage and a song about happiness and peace might have been the final trigger for some spectators leaving. By doing this, García creates not only a sense of uncanniness but also mixes up happy memories with the obscene (the showing of death is, in Western countries, normally kept out of the public space). The scene is therefore a double transgression, with the action of killing being clearly shown and acted alongside a song about pretty rainbows and red roses. Gabriele Sofia has tellingly called this mechanism in García's shows the 'images' betrayal' (2018: 355).[24]

With puppets on stage, Vienne goes even further in challenging the spectators' sense of familiarity. 'Experiencing something that is familiar through strange is a recurring experience in my work,' she states in an interview with Anna Gallagher-Ross (2017). In *Une belle enfant blonde* (2005), adolescent dolls appear next to human actors. As Julia Dobson argues, Vienne plays on the 'hierarchical binary between reality and the constructed image' (2013: 21). The way we construct our own reality is challenged: although the puppet looks real (i.e. alive), unlike the actress, it is not. The way we identify the 'living', what is flesh and blood, is actually not that obvious. This puppet reminds us that our perception is partially constructed through a series of preconceived ideas. There is a strange temptation for our gaze to recognize the puppet as alive simply because it *looks like* a living body. So much simplicity is troubling. We seem to think it is alive but know it is not. The puppet triggers a constant oscillation between what is perceived and what we make of this perception. But it also questions our understanding of being. What does it mean to be? The puppet certainly seems to exist in its own right. It has presence, much more than, let's say, our kettle has. And yet, we know it is just an object, just as lifeless as a kettle. Many have discussed the strangeness of the puppet on stage (Craig, for instance, famously discussed the concept of the 'super-puppet' in *On the Art of Theatre*, in 1911). In *The Theatre and Its Double*, Artaud talks about it as 'a fabricated being [. . .] made of wood and cloth, completely invented, resembling nothing, yet disturbing in nature, able to reintroduce on stage the slightest intimation of the great metaphysical fear underlying all ancient theatre' (Artaud 1970:

32). Puppets' presence is mysterious – they can be as fascinating as they can be frightening (one can think of Kantor's *Dead Class*). In the play, one of the dolls, laying down at the front of the stage, contains a mechanism that makes her chest rise at regular intervals, giving the impression that it is breathing. So much likeliness is troubling. The 'uncanny valley' is a term coined by Japanese robotics engineer Masahiro Mori in the 1970s. It designates the strangest experiences one can have when facing something that is non-human and yet resembles us. The hypothesis made by Mori is that the more realistic a non-human object is, the more our emotional response become positive and empathic, until it reaches a certain point where reactions become negative – emotions such as fear and revulsion can then develop. If the object is almost identical to a human being (with more than 90 per cent resemblance) then reactions become positive again. The gap in between is what he calls the uncanny valley, where objects are different enough from us to understand that they are not 'real' human beings, but ressemblant enough for us to struggle to process them as mere objects. Vienne knows how to find this specific spot, and can make her puppets both ressemblant and odd enough to really challenge her spectators' perception. She also plays with her real actors, asking them to perform jerky actions using slow motions; and the more mechanical the actors appear, the more 'real' the puppets seem to be, confusing even further the audience's sense of reality.

### 2.2.3. Children and animals

The term 'animal' in this section refers to a non-human animal. Having animals and children on stage is, of course, ethically questionable. Many performances have been heavily criticized for this, in France, and elsewhere. García's use of animals in his shows, for instance, has generated more than one controversy. In *Accidens*, a lobster was killed, cooked and eaten on stage each night. On the 7 April 2015, a few protesters were gathering in front of Montpellier public theatre singing, 'torture is not our culture' (*La torture ce n'est pas notre culture*).

They tried to get the show cancelled and collected 29,000 signatures to support their cause. They were unsuccessful, but García did write a letter to explain himself, published in *Le Monde*. Showing clear signs of annoyance, he called the protesters complete idiots and argued that thousands of lobsters die every day in restaurants. The lobsters that are killed on stage are, in fact, the only ones to die for a poetical cause (2015). The same year, hamsters were thrown in a fish tank in *Et balancez mes cendres sur Mickey* (and eventually saved by actors before they drown). Although those animals are undoubtedly suffering on García's stage, the dramatic reactions from some spectators can seem surprising. Aren't most of us eating meat and passively endorsing all the animal suffering generated by the current food industry? A very interesting anecdote on this matter can be cited here. In *Theatre and Animals*, Lourdes Orozco reviews the controversy about *After Sun*, another play by García where two rabbits are used in the first scene. They are grabbed by the neck by an actor who then pretends to perform sexual acts on them. This profoundly shocked the audience. Later on in that very show, the same actor appears as a McDonald's manager, training a young employee how to cook a hamburger. The meat cooked on stage is real meat. Lourdes Orozco recounts:

> The audience watched without complaint. No one expressed disgust at animal meat being cooked onstage. The spectators could not relate to the body of an animal that was no longer visible. The animal had become food, and that, somehow, seemed more acceptable than the mistreatment of the love rabbits. (2013: 2)

This perhaps must be related to our unwillingness to face up to the way humans treat animals. As soon as the animals are present, alive, they are 'able' to look back at us and remind us of our own violence. On the other hand, to watch real meat being cooked did not shock the audiences because they could forget that this meat used to be an animal. The two rabbits were indeed abused, and this submission only echoed the much larger exploitation that animals experience every day; yet, to look at this directly on a stage proved unbearable for many.

Although I am very aware of the ethical issues raised by the presence of animals and children on stage, this section will not be argued on ethical grounds. Here, I will rather focus on ways our perception is challenged while witnessing the presence of an animal, or a child on stage, and Castellucci's philosophy, in particular, will be discussed. In Castellucci's theatre, the use of animals is significant. Unlike in shows by other directors, animals are not treated as secondary characters, and certainly not considered as mere tools. For the Italian director, humans only constitute a small part of the living world. In this sense, animals and humans are being put on the same level. Animals have thus the power to reveal humans (actors) as animals among others. Tackels recalls here a quote from French playwright Valère Novarina that echoes Castellucci's vision:

> Men today need to be expelled from theatres: their unbearable and perpetual penchant for self-portrait. In theatres, we have to be animals. Question not our humanity – but our 'pantinitude'. To see words coming out from wooden mouths and be surprised by it. Be surprised by this material ribbon that we blow. (2005: 34)[25]

Castellucci's theatre does not contain any anthropomorphist views. It is rather the opposite; he does not search for human features in animals but looks instead for animalistic features in humans. This goes against a long tradition of domination over animals. There is no need to explain that animals were and are exploited by humans. The word 'animal' expresses this domination by distinguishing non-human animals from human animals. In Castellucci's theatre, animals are usually motionless, or doing very little on stage. They are trained, of course, to be able to stay on the stage, and standing still is already a result of domestication. Yet they are not performing tricks that would give them human features. Animals are not considered as props, and their presence is just as important (if not more so) as the actors'. Castellucci explains:

> I am a true animalist because I do not confuse animals with humans. I do not give them feelings that are mine nor do I give them an expressive face like mine. I do not give them names. I do not believe in

Dumbo's human tears [. . .]. To have an animal on stage is like taking revenge because the animal comes back alive, silent, without any human features; it is there, splendid, occupying the front of the stage; but an animal on stage is also a form of speechless prayer, a form of forgiveness. (2005: 34)[26]

One cannot claim that Castellucci does not control and restrain animals on stage. However, the way he includes animals in his productions is very different from other artists such as Rodrigo García (and to some extent Jan Fabre), who merely use them to serve a dramatic purpose or to create a certain effect on the spectators. For Castellucci, the presence of the animal in itself is to be valued. Although a largely questionable notion, Castellucci claims that he does not tame the animals but instead prefers to let them express themselves through their presence. Yet, the presence of animals on stage, even in his shows, is always controversial. In *Moses Und Aron*, presented at the Opera Bastille in 2015, the presence of a bull on stage irritated many charities. But if we chose to only consider the presence of animals on stage from the perspective of the spectators' perception of the world, then animals' presence is extremely valuable and certainly constitutes one of the many ways Castellucci and other directors disturb the spectators' sense of reality.

The presence of animals on stage can challenge the spectators' perception, especially when their presence is not motivated by a clear purpose. An almost motionless animal whose presence does not directly serve the dramatic action can be uncanny to observe. In her article 'There and Not There: Looking at Animals in Contemporary Theatre', Orozco explains how unusual this particular use of animals still is:

> When the animals that appear on stage are perceived to be not-acting (and am not referring here to accidental appearances like that of the mouse, but rehearsed ones), when the animal performance is not based on 'visible' tricks that the animals has learned to perform for the pleasure of the audience (like those in the circus or the aqua parks), the animal is perceived to be just an animal, rather than a performing animal. This way of participating in the theatre is what audiences are still struggling to comprehend. (2015: 193)

One could argue that to watch an animal on stage is similar to watching one in a zoo. Yet, it seems that animals on stage, when they are only trained to remain almost motionless, have a strange presence, that animals in zoos do not necessarily have. In zoos, the presence of animals constitutes a show; people come to see what they look like and to observe their behaviours. They live in artificial environments that reproduce their natural environments; they are fed at certain times, sometimes in front of an audience. Their presence is justified by people's curiosity. In fact, it is quite rare to see an animal whose life is not, at least partially, controlled by humans. Pets are usually trained and may also live in – what might be for them – unnatural environments. Even animals in the wild can now constitute a show through safaris. The circus is probably the place where animals are the most tamed. Zoos, certain homes, circuses and safaris are all spaces designed or designated by humans to domesticate animals. Theatres are simply not animal-friendly places. Therefore, and quite surprisingly, theatre might be the place where animals' presence is finally no longer a show. As a result, their presence can make the audience feel uncomfortable because they appear to be in the wrong place. In *Stage Fright, Animals and Other Theatrical Problems*, Nicholas Ridout underlines this uncanniness:

> The impropriety of the animal on the theatre stage is experienced very precisely as a sense of the animal being in the wrong place. In the circus there are still a few tawdry reminders of nature. [. . .] The theatre, by contrast, rigorously excludes nature. It stays where it is, in the city. No natural light comes in. [. . .] Bringing an animal in here is courting disaster. We'll have them in our homes, so long as they have been properly trained, but in the super-artifice of the theatre, we fear that even the best-trained creatures could run amok at any moment. (2006: 98)

Theatre is the artificial place par excellence, possibly the furthest one from nature. It is thus the most inappropriate place to have animals. Moreover, putting animals on stage is always a risk, as they are more unpredictable than actors, no matter how well trained they are. In this sense, animals on stage can strongly contrast the rest of the performance as they disrupt any form of theatrical illusion. Let us recall Shklovsky's concept of defamiliarization. To see, for Shklovsky, means to encounter; and we actually very rarely *see* objects. It seems that humans are doing this even with animals: such as the animal to eat, the animal to stroke, the animal to observe. Humans tend to consume animals in the sense that they always domesticate them in one way or another. Coexist, on the other hand, means to exist together, simultaneously. Therefore, putting an animal on stage, away from any familiar background, away from a context in which they become useful makes them look particularly unfamiliar; and so, according to Shklovsky's theory, they appear more present than ever. In a similar way, Ridout recalls Michael Peterson's reflections on animals in theatre in his book 'Stubborn as a Mule':

> Peterson is quite right to affirm that 'the presence of live animals introduces a non or anti-intentional force', an observation related to animals who are supposed (intended by others) to appear, but which must clearly also apply to those whose appearance is uncalled-for. This 'force', Peterson suggests, 'lends itself to the perception of difference and to an encounter with the uncanny'. The lack of intention presumably highlights the intention applied in performance by humans, and herein lies the accentuation of difference, while the uncanny presumably arises from the illusion of intention generated by animal activity matrixed in performance in such a way as to fabricate intention. (2006: 101–2)

The strong presence animals can have on stage may then be explained by a contrasting effect between illusion, artificiality, and the living world. In Castellucci's theatre, their presence is accentuated by the fact that no intention can be projected onto them. For once, they do not serve humans. Of course, one could argue that as soon as they are participating in a theatrical production, they are necessarily exploited. However, on Castellucci's stage, they are no longer exploited in the way they are perceived; for once, they do not seem to be there for us. According to Romeo and Claudia Castellucci, what gives the presence of an animal on stage so much strength is their apparent indifference: 'it's the cold indifference that is beautiful' (2001: 105).[27] Actors always try to improve their work, to be better from one performance to another, to become 'lords of the stage' (106).[28] Conversely, animals are never trying to 'shine' and the stage, for them, does not contain any particular significance. This apparent detachment gives them a strange charisma: 'The animal is more impressive because it does not try anything, because it respects fully and unintentionally the stage's alienation' (106).[29] The decalage between the live animals and the theatre as a codified place may lead the spectators to finally rid themselves of any utilitarian projections. In fact, animals on stage prompt us to enter a different perception. As Castellucci explains: 'The animal comes on stage to bring a little bit of itself: a bit of this world, of this reality, of this time' (2015).[30] The animal on stage can encourage us to perceive the real as the living world, as not necessarily processed through human eyes. Castellucci adds: 'The animal teaches me that technique is not necessary, as I cannot be wrong. And I cannot be wrong simply because I do not know exactly what it is I am doing' (2000: 26–7).

While animals on stage can challenge the perception of the spectators, causing them difficulties in processing and recognizing what they are facing, they can also make them experience shame in Castellucci's theatre. French philosopher Jacques Derrida describes thus this peculiar feeling that one can experience while facing the animal's gaze, referring to his own experience:

> I often ask myself, just to see, *who I am* – and who I am (following) at the moment when, caught naked, in silence, by the gaze of an animal, for example, the eyes of a cat, I have trouble, yes, a bad time overcoming my embarrassment. (2008: 3–4)

Derrida explains later that he felt uncomfortable in this situation because while he is naked, his cat, that looks at him, is not. Animals cannot be naked because they are not familiar with the concept of nudity. But humans do have this modesty, and so Derrida feels ashamed of his nudity in front of the cat that does not know a single thing about nudity. This consideration leads him to realize that he, as human, is only following animals (*L'animal que donc je suis* – the original title of his book – means both the animal that I am and the animal that I follow). Indeed, humanity appeared rather late in the living world: animals were here much earlier than we were. And yet, humanity took control over animals; named them and dominated them in various ways. The cat looking back at Derrida reveals to him all the violence his self as dominant species has engaged against animals. This triggers his shame. The sense of shame is particularly strong in this case as it is not the look from a stranger, but from a familiar cat, the one that Derrida raised and lives with. An animal looking back can thus be quite a strange and uncomfortable experience as they seem to remind us the violent history we, humans and animals, share.

The animals on Castellucci's stage do look back. The bull in *Moses Und Aron* is facing and looking at the audience for a very long time. Of course, it is not accusing anyone in particular (that would be quite the anthropomorphist view!), but it is in the spectators' gaze that this realization along with a sense of shame can occur. The bull that is looking back engages in a form of communication, showing the spectator that it is capable to do so and that the violence animals suffer from humans is real. By looking back, it simply reminds the spectators that it is alive, just like they are. Ridout states:

> The animal, restored to the stage, does what anyone on stage always has the uncanny capacity to do: it looks back at those who look. Animals are only a safe (and exceptional) presence on the stage for as long as they are denied this capacity for looking back. The moment they do look back they disturb us by being just like us. [. . .] The strangeness of the animal on stage comes not from the fact that it ought not to be there, has no business being there, but rather in the fact that there is suddenly nothing strange about it being there, the fact that it has as much business being there, being exploited there, as any human performer. (2006: 127)

By looking at the animal that is looking back, the spectators might feel like they are participating in this domination, or at least that they are an accomplice to the animal's submission, which is being forced to be on stage. Suddenly, the animal on stage flushes the spectator out by revealing them in their act of domination. The spectators may then become ashamed of the fact that they have not realized this sooner; they are ashamed that they did not see their own violence before. Ridout explains that bringing the animal on stage is to bring this history of violence 'back into view' in Castellucci's theatre:

> Castellucci seems to be suggesting that the division of labour, the death of God, the establishment of human dominion over the animals and the birth of tragedy may all be seen as simultaneous, as moments of the same historical moment, and that the historical moment in question is, in effect, the moment at which history begins (made through labour and available through writing). Western theatre has kept the animal offstage in order to hide its origins in these moments of inaugural violence and the institution of labour. (114)

Animals on stage challenge the perception of reality by challenging our gaze but also bring back into light a history of violence that Western theatre has tried to hide. In *Accidens* by García, a lobster is being killed and eaten by an actor on stage. The action is violent, brutal, and aims to demonstrate how suffering has necessarily been experienced before any meal containing meat has been prepared. Regardless of where the meat is coming from (a slaughterhouse, a restaurant, a farm, a theatre), it originates from the killing of an animal that rarely takes place without pain and distress. By confronting spectators to the transformation of a living animal into a ready-to-eat product, García reminds us of a hidden history of violence that is still very much happening.

Let us discuss the rarer (perhaps because legal permissions are so difficult to obtain) presence of children in theatre. Children are, again, often present on Castellucci's stage. In *Genesi – from the Museum of Sleep*, Castellucci's and Chiara Guidi's six children appear on stage in a scene featuring Auschwitz. Many people protested, considering that the children were used to recall a violent history that they should not yet have to face. Similarly, in *BR.#04*, Castellucci puts a baby in the middle of the stage, at the start of each performance. The mother of the child must arrive at least thirty minutes before the start of the show and, when it is time, leave the baby on his own on the stage. It is important that she makes sure that the baby does not get upset so he does not start crying right away. The baby is the only person on stage and stays there for a maximum of ten minutes. There is no music, no particular light; only him on the stage, looking around. If he begins to cry, Romeo Castellucci asks the technicians to draw the curtain and the mother can take her child back offstage (Ridout 2006: 90–2). Perhaps the presence of a baby triggered a sense of shame in the spectators, just like the presence of animal does; a shame to find oneself in front of a young person being manipulated, exploited. But more generally, a shame triggered by the realization that there are some things in the world that cannot be turned into a meaningful double; such as a birth or a baby. On the strangeness of the baby's presence on stage, Ridout explains:

> That is because there on the stage she does not occupy her infancy as a story but as a slice of sheer enduring. From the point of view of an adult spectator, enduring is the infant's action, and it is by way of her action that she keeps time open for us. We are incapable of not watching. (96)

Watching a young child on stage can be captivating as the spectator can then experience time differently: enduring it, and leave their everyday perception of time, usually imbricated with their perception of space. They can see the real just as the babies may do: with a constant surprise, and perhaps, with the feeling that they are not *outside* but *inside* the world, that is, not facing the world, but inhabiting it. Ridout has this great turn of phrase: '[the baby] seems to disrupt a sense of spatial propriety' (108). In this sense, the baby maintains a 'sheer unrelation to [the] place' (107). Like the animal, the baby does the exact opposite of owning the space.

It should be underlined that babies and small children are not masters of language yet. In this way, they have a particularly strong presence for

Castellucci. In *Inferno*, a scene features a large see-through cube in which several young children are playing together. They are still too young to articulate proper sentences. The cube is covered by a black veil. Once lifted, the spectators are able to see and hear the children playing (which is undoubtedly what they were doing before the lifting of the veil). The scene lasts a couple of minutes before the cube is covered again. The children clearly did not notice the fact that they were being observed by an audience, which is precisely what confers upon this scene a sense of strangeness. The way that they communicate is also striking. As they are still young, they produce approximate sounds rather than words. As Castellucci states: '*Enfance* [childhood], in the sense of "en-fance", meaning the condition of whom is outside the language' (2001: 112).[31] Young children are arguably still in this phase where their 'I' is not split yet; when they still do not have to communicate in the way that adults do through a compromised common ground. In this sense, children, before language, still live in the world as its objects and not as almighty subjects. Children, just like animals, remind us, spectators, that there is a world outside our perception. We are masters of nothing. They invite us to let go of our perception of the world as our property.

## *Summary of Chapter 2*

Some directors use various strategies to challenge their spectators' perception and tendency to recognize their surroundings. Such experiences are particularly disturbing because they often come with a sense of loss; the loss of one's position as almighty subject. Being aware of these strategies helps us understand why mistrust has developed between certain directors and the audience. Challenging perception often involves manipulating it.

I started this chapter by exploring how our everyday perception is based on processes of recognition and emphasized how uncomfortable and uneasy having them challenged can be. Yet if we do let go of our tendency to attribute meaning onto the stage (or, indeed, onto the world), we can experience, as Deleuze, Shklovsky and States argue in their own ways, an encounter with the world.

I then discussed what I coined as the 'non-recognition' and explored how the spectators' thwarted projections can create confusion. Yet they can create anger from the audience, who may think that they are being deceived. The meaning created from these experiences is also difficult, if not impossible, to describe; to translate into words. Therefore, communicating and transmitting these productions is difficult and might partly explain why they are often misapprehended or can trigger frustration. Directors try to intellectually emancipate their spectators by 'teaching' them to let go of their familiar perceptual patterns. Freeing by teaching works only when the subject is happy to be taught, which, as we have seen in Chapter 1, is not always the case.

Some strategies were analysed along with examples from the shows; duration of one action until exhaustion of its signs is one of the most famous (and intentional) strategies. Although repetition as an aesthetic tool has been used since the 1960s in Western 'avant-garde' theatre, it is still widely practiced by contemporary directors to challenge the audiences' experience of the world. To be able to fully appreciate how such a strategy can open our field of perception as spectators, it is important not to be looking for a linear narrative or for meanings based on semiotics. In other words, to be able to take full advantage of duration and repetition on stage, one must know what the intention is or, at least, understand the potential that its contemplation can have on perception.

I then turned to strategies that trigger a process of defamiliarization. The concept of defamiliarization as developed by Shklovsky helped us understand how unfamiliar actions and bodies on stage can trigger a non-recognition of the world, thus narrowing the barrier between the world and ourselves. To experience art, one must experience difficulties in recognizing what one is facing. Obscene actions and bodies on stage; use of hyper-realistic puppets; mixing of representations from radically different registers are all strategies used by directors to instil a sense of the uncanny in the spectators' mind.

Finally, I discussed the presence of children and animals on stage. I was particularly interested in analysing how children and animals, in a theatre, can force us to face our own violence and history of domination, as human beings. A feeling of shame can develop for us spectators. Moreover, children and animals have the power to make us feel pretty stupid for trying to decipher everything that stands in front of us. This shame is also triggered by the revelation that some things cannot be grasped and shaped by our understanding. A bull looking at us disturbs our system based on representations and recognition. A baby playing on their own on stage tells us that some things in this world cannot be comprehended. Children and animals help directors to reinstate a mystery of the world.

This chapter has tried to offer different notions with which to approach some contemporary theatre makers, based on a more spectator-focused approached. Through these different strategies, I have demonstrated how crucial the experience of the spectator is in this practice of theatre. Paradoxically, it is in theatre, a place of illusion that directors seem to have found the perfect medium to reveal the real.

In the next and final chapter, these shows will be explored as tragic performances. I make the hypothesis that spectators, here, are invited to become tragic men. Spectatorship becomes thus a philosophical practice. This chapter will mainly focus on the theatre of Romeo Castellucci and Jan Fabre (especially when exploring examples) as they are the two directors who have most clearly articulated the analogy between their theatre and the tragic. Nonetheless, I hope that the following considerations will encourage spectators of shows by Vienne, García, Lauwers, and by many other contemporary directors, to appreciate how their role as spectators is fluid and how theatre is at its best when it becomes a playground for the mind.

# III

# Spectatorship as a philosophical practice

## 3.1. Do we really want to encounter the real?

### 3.1.1. A cruel world

Lehmann explained that in some contemporary plays 'the gaze finds no occasion to detect a depth of symbolic significance beyond the given, but instead [. . .] remains stuck within the activity of seeing the surface itself' (2006: 99). One can ask if this experience, after all, is to be searched for. Perceiving the world without attempting to understand is scary. Interpretations and projections help us to produce meaning. Meaning reassures us by giving us the impression that we are in control of our surroundings. I mentioned Artaud previously. He is undoubtedly one author who still inspires contemporary artists.[1] The most famous concept he is remembered for is his concept of cruelty, as developed in *The Theatre and Its Double*. This concept has been interpreted in various ways. The most convincing interpretation (and possibly the most common one) is to assimilate cruelty to the tragic. Artaud explains:

> I suggest a Theatre of Cruelty. With this mania we all have today for belittling everything, as soon as I said 'cruelty' everyone took it to mean 'blood'. But a *'theatre of cruelty'* means theatre that is difficult and cruel for myself first of all. And on a performing level, it has nothing to do with the cruelty we practice on one another, hacking at each other's bodies, carving up our individual anatomies, or like, ancient Assyrian Emperors, posting sackfuls of human ears, noses, or neatly dissected nostrils, but the far more terrible, essential cruelty objects can practice on us. We are not free and the sky can still fall on our heads. And above all else, theatre is made to teach us this. (1970: 60)

The theatre of cruelty is not necessarily a physically violent theatre. Artaud wrote in many letters that cruelty must be differentiated from mere bloody violence. Instead, cruelty designates the unpredictability of the world, the world insofar as it cannot be controlled. For Artaud, theatre should remind its spectators that the sky can still fall on their head at any moment; nothing and no one is safe. To perceive the cruelty of the world means to perceive the world while it is acting: 'Everything that acts is a cruelty' (65). Cruelty is 'strictness, diligence, unrelenting decisiveness, irreversible and absolute determination' (79). Artaud insists on the fact that the perception of cruelty does not only translate into sensations; cruelty may in fact be intellectually processed:

> Above all, cruelty is very lucid, a kind of strict control and submission to necessity. There is no cruelty without consciousness, without the application of consciousness, for the latter gives practicing any act in life a blood red tinge, its cruel overtones, since it is understood that being alive always means the death of someone else. (80)

The world is tragic, cruel. It occurs without us, does not 'care' for us. No matter what we do, our actions will necessarily remain meaningless. Through the different strategies discussed in the previous chapter, some directors offer this raw vision of the world. For example, the repetition of an action unveils the cruelty of the real, as Van Den Dries argues:

> The body is no longer a flesh inhabited by the mind, but a mere skeleton. [. . .] the mechanical movements, repeated in series, showing nothing more than a skeleton. No individuality is expressed in these movements. [. . .] No 'I' inhabits this body, only the experience of the skeleton's emptiness remains. (2005: 30–1)[2]

Strategies of repetition enable some directors to display a cruelty on stage; a world of mere mechanics, empty of any signs of empathy or, in fact, of humanity. In *Crowd* by Vienne, each actor performs an action (dancing, smoking, drinking, etc.) in slow motion, which seems to isolate them from one another. They are all focused on their own movements, their own self. Even though they are partying all together, their loneliness is emphasized. Social relationships appear superficial and only remain a cruel reality: that we are alone and will eventually die alone. The jerky movements prevent the audience from understanding the overall actions. As spectators, we are forever confronted with unfinished and mechanical movements that look more and more like disarticulated and dehumanized actions. Audiences cannot recognize neither feelings nor emotions in these bodies. We are reminded of our own death; of our body as mere corporality. Additionally, the repetition of an action on stage brings a new apprehension of temporality. To perceive the world as cruel, one has to adopt a different perception of time, not as a chronological succession of instants but rather, as Rosset explains, 'a fixed mechanism', 'a motionless time' (2014: 8).[3] The tragic prevents one from perceiving time *spatially*. In *Penser la mort*, Vladimir Jankélévitch argues:

> We consider the human life as a long line between two extremities. One is on the left, the other on the right. It is a myth of symmetry, a spatial myth, just as the clock is between the two candelabras on a chimney breast. But life is time. Time cannot be deployed in space. [. . .] The past is not an upside-down future and the future a right side up past. The past and the future are not each on one side of the present. I live in a perpetual present. Beware of myths of symmetry! (1994: 17–19)[4]

Similarly, for Rosset, humans tend to spatialize their perceptions of time. He refers to the example of a passer-by who witnessed a builder falling off of a scaffold (2014). After the accident, the passer-by perceives the temporality of the accident spatially, confusing time with space: he reconsiders the 'itinerary' of the event, and believes that he witnessed: 'the passage between the state of life and the state of death' (9).[5] Yet, if we consider along with Rosset that the real is 'insignificant' (2004), then time does not follow any paths. In this sense, time should not be considered as a line in space, connecting instants between them; this perception of time is indeed only an illusion, prompted by the myths of symmetry. The repetition of an action on stage invites the spectator to perceive time without projecting spatial interpretations onto it. It defeats the spectators' potential attempts to link instances between them. Time does not seem to *go* anywhere. Repetition is a tragic trap for our perception.

For Rosset, cruelty is to be found in the irremediability of the real; it prevents humans from distancing themselves from the real by means of intellectual patterns. Rosset reminds its reader of the etymology of the word; cruelty comes from the Latin terms *crudelis* and *crudus*, meaning 'raw, not digested, indigestible' (1988: 18).[6] Cruelty hurts because it has not been yet shaped, digested by the perception. To open our perception to cruelty leads us therefore to a rather inhospitable world. The notion of cruelty appears rather similar to the concept of 'insignificance' as defined by Rosset (2004). The insignificance of the world is experienced 'when reality shows itself in a visibly incoherent and disorganized manner, in a state of pure and arbitrary contiguity' (27).[7] For Rosset, the whole Western philosophy has not adequately explored the notions of chance, disorder and chaos, as if human intelligence managed to get rid of those realities just by intellectually organizing the world. According to him, only tragic philosophies have aimed to explore these more obscure paths. He writes:

> Tragic philosophers, whose goal was to dissolve the apparent order to refind the chaos buried by Anaxagore [. . .] Philosophy thus becomes a destructive and catastrophic act: thoughts are produced to deconstruct, to destroy, to dissolve – generally, to deprive humans from everything that they intellectually have created in the event of their own misfortune. Just like Artaud, at the start of *The Theatre and Its Double*, uses the vessel to symbolize theatre, tragic philosophy brings to men not a cure, but the plague. (2013: 10)[8]

By wishing to return to the study of the world as an uncontrollable force, and by destroying every intellectual construction that perhaps aims to reassure us, tragic philosophies may not seem very attractive. There is no message, no signs – who would want to explore this vision of the world? Yet, they may still appear rather intriguing as they attempt to reconnect with a fundamental mystery; the tragic is the world as necessarily surprising and mysterious. Rosset goes further and states:

> no, human love does not exist, human greatness does not exist [. . .] The tragic man finds himself without love, without greatness, and without life: that is the situation to which he will never be able to give interpretations, in front of which he will always have the perpetual astonishment, the surprise of a child whose toy was confiscated for the first time. If his stupefaction ends, he is no longer tragic. (2014: 21)[9]

The tragic revelation goes cruelly along with the destruction of any human values. This revelation is not so much about destroying these values; it is simply about realizing that they do not exist outside one's own interpretations. As depressing as it may seem, Rosset considers love as merely a human interpretation; the tragic man therefore realizes that there is no such thing as human love. Facing the cruel world means perceiving without any of these reassuring references. Yet for Rosset it also means getting closer to the world, narrowing the barrier between oneself and the real. In a different way, French philosopher Georges Didi-Huberman distinguishes the man of tautology from the man of belief (1992). While the man of tautology sees things as they simply appear to him, the man of belief cannot help himself from seeing beyond the things:

> The man of belief prefers to remove shapeless rotting flesh from the tombs, to fill them instead with sublime, purified corporeal images made to comfort and inform – i.e. to *fix* – our emotions, our fears and our desires. (25)[10]

The man of belief has a common Western perception of the world while the man of tautology appears like the tragic man, able to perceive the world free from any intellectual or emotional interference.

The tragic as a philosophical concept has been first developed by Friedrich Wilhelm Joseph Schelling. Peter Szondi begins his essay on the tragic by stating: 'Since Aristotle, there has been a poetics of tragedy. Only since Schelling has there been a philosophy of the tragic'

(2002: 1). Instead of approaching the genre of tragedy, as defined by Aristotle, through dramatic analyses, Schelling develops a philosophical approach to the tragic. Referring to the tragic hero, he states: 'It was a *great* thought: to willingly endure punishment even for an *unavoidable* crime, so as to prove one's freedom precisely through the loss of this freedom and perish with a declaration of free will' (quoted by Szondi 2002: 7). The tragic hero demonstrates their freedom by fighting for their freedom *while* acknowledging their absence of freedom. The notion of indifference in the conflict between the tragic hero and the 'objective necessity' (seen as a superior force) is essential. Schelling explains:

> The essence of *tragedy* is [...] a real conflict between freedom in the subject and objective necessity. This conflict does not end with the defeat of one or the other, but rather with both of them simultaneously appearing as conquerors and conquered in perfect indifference. (Quoted by Szondi 2002: 9)

The tragic hero's freedom and the objective necessity complement each other; the hero can only manifest their freedom within the objective necessity, and the objective necessity is the only reason for them to be willing to manifest their freedom. This conflict leads to a scission between the hero and the world insofar as the world has revealed itself as objective necessity. It appears now indifferent to the hero. Consequently, the hero must remain indifferent to the world in order to demonstrate their freedom. As Szondi puts it: 'Schelling's entire system, whose essence is the identity of freedom and necessity, culminates in his definition of the tragic process as the restoration of this indifference in conflict' (10). In *Propos sur la tragédie*, Miquel develops interesting thoughts on what occurs when a character enters the tragic world (i.e. when they become a tragic hero):

> Tragedy often comes with a transgression, which is a way to cut ties; but also a way to demonstrate a detachment – in its full sense – from the world. The world no longer matters [...]. It is no longer despicable; it becomes indifferent. (1997: 21)[11]

The detachment is characterized by an 'indifferent' relationship to the world. This appears rather paradoxical; as though, to reach the tragic, the hero would have to distance themselves from the world. Yet, by refusing to 'recognize' the world – that is, by refusing to perceive the world according to their own desires – they may indeed face the frightening revelation that the world exists de facto without them. They are bound to remain in their own loneliness. As a result, communication is impossible in the tragic world. In Greek tragedies, heroes becoming tragic heroes communicated by singing (rather than speaking), demonstrating thus a different attitude towards the world.

Schopenhauer is the first philosopher to adopt an ontological approach to the tragic. The situation of the tragic hero is thus viewed as the condition of any human being. In *The World as Will and Representation*, he argues that the tragic is inherent to the word's 'will' (a concept close to the objective necessity by Schelling). Anyone can experience the tragic as anyone can experience the world's will, through, for instance, incontrollable desires. Yet, for Schopenhauer, the tragic as world's will is perceived negatively. Only art can appease humans and show them the world as 'representation'. He writes:

> To this extent the effect of tragedy is analogous to the effect of the dynamic sublime, since like this, it elevates us above the will and its interests and then brings us around to the point where we take pleasure in the sight of something precisely repugnant to our will. What gives everything tragic, in whatever form it might appear, the characteristic impetus to sublimity, is the dawning of the recognition that the world, that life cannot afford us true satisfaction, and is therefore not worth attachment to it: this is the spirit of tragedy: and this is why it leads to resignation. (2018, Volume 2: 450)

In Schopenhauer's philosophy, humans can only *submit* themselves to the tragic. On the contrary, Nietzsche sees the philosophy of the tragic as optimistic. According to him, tragic men fully adhere to the tragic world, thus proving their freedom.[12] The Dionysian refers to the primitive instinct, the human's life insofar as it belongs to the living world, made of desire, violence and – adds Nietzsche – of joy. The tragic man, in his philosophy, is emancipated because he discovered that the things in the world are beyond his control:

> In this sense Dionysiac man might be said to resemble Hamlet: both have looked deeply into the true nature of things, they have *understood* and are now loath to act. They realize that no action of theirs can work any change in the eternal condition of things, and they regard the imputation as ludicrous or debasing that they should set right the time which is out of joint. (1956: 51)

The tragic man is free because he knows. However, to perceive the tragic is not, for Nietzsche, a comfortable experience: it requires some bravery. As Nietzsche put it, to perceive the tragic leads to accept the world's 'dissonance' (1956), to accept that the real is not harmonious and that harmony is only to be found in the filter of human perception. In the same way, Max Scheller insists that the tragic is an interpretation-free perception:

> The tragic is not the result of an interpretation of the world and the important events of the world. [. . .] it is a sort of sudden bewilderment in the face of the defects of the world against which one knows of no help, or – what is the simple consequence of this as stated by Maeterlinck – no helper is at hand, no helper to put the matter in order. (1965: 5)

Scheller concludes: 'Every interpretation fails before the inflexibility of reality which reduces it to silence' (5). The tragic goes against our natural tendency to put the real in order to reconcile our expectations with our relationship to the world.

In the previous chapter, I have explored how directors develop strategies to prompt us to abandon our interpretative gaze. In the following sections, I will go further and explore to what extent some performances can be defined as tragic, and how, as spectators, we can embrace the tragic hero's view of the world. By better understanding the implications on an interpretation-free perception, we, as spectators, can oscillate between quest for meaning and tragic worldview, maximizing each production's potential. We can turn spectatorship into a philosophical practice. Of course, to perceive the tragic as an indifferent world is far more complex on a theatre stage, which contains dramatic intentions. Yet actions on contemporary stages often appear indifferent towards the audience. Castellucci does indeed use the word 'indifference' many times when referring to his productions. In this way, he claims that the stage must remain indifferent and never aim to communicate, regardless of the audience's expectations. Having animals on stage is, for instance, a way to give the impression of an indifferent stage. He explains:

> The animal on stage is fully at ease because it is not perfectible. What it knows for sure, is its own body; it does not know, though, about the whole strangeness of the atmosphere around it. [. . .] The indifference, yes. It is this cold indifference that is magnificent. (2001: 105)[13]

According to him, animals on stage emit a certain majestic aura insofar as they do not seem to realize that they are being observed. Unlike the actors who endeavour to become the 'lords of the stage' (106), Castellucci claims that animals do not attempt to possess the stage; they simply appear as being part of it. Replacing actors by animals is therefore a means to communicate as little as possible with the audience and to show an indifferent world on stage. The sensation of facing an indifferent stage may also be conveyed by a close observation of matter. By exploring only matter, communication can be avoided, as Castellucci states in *Les Pèlerins de la matière*:

> The problem is to be a pilgrim in the matter. Matter is the ultimate reality. [. . .] It is, therefore, a theatre of elements. Elements are what is most purely communicable, like the lowest level of communication possible. That's what interest me: communicate as little as possible. And the smallest degree of communication is to be found on the surface of matter. In this sense, and paradoxically, it is a superficial theatre, made of surfaces, because it is a theatre that searches for emotions. (2001: 111)[14]

In a letter to Frie Leysen, Castellucci adds:

I am definitely outside ethics; I am in a no man's land, in the false, wandering condition of someone who looks for a thing that, in reality, he does not know anything about: not the name nor the entity [. . .] A form is a form only if it is with indifference that it crosses our humanity. A form is a form only if its inhumanity moves our humanity. (2001: 183)[15]

By going back to the organicity of matter, he may indeed succeed in showing the tragic; a world, *in fine*, made of chaos and unpredictability, a world indifferent to interpretations. Communication through language removes the possibility for the tragic to appear; in order to communicate and be intelligible, one has to organize one's perception of the world. It is therefore in the mere observation of matter that the spectator may best see the infinite potentiality (and the scary unpredictability) of the real. Matter is the only reality, Castellucci claims, as only matter we know to exist (or at least seem to exist) outside our perception. Moreover, the observation of matter can trigger, in an unexpected way, deep emotions for the spectator. When its indifference (in the sense that it remains unshaped, unconcerned with our perception) meets our humanity, waves of emotions may cross the audience as a result; just like observing someone without them knowing can sometimes be a moving experience. By exploring materiality, a new meaning can emerge. In *Giulio Cesare*, directed by Castellucci in 1997, Antoine is played by an actor who happened to have had surgery on his vocal cords. Therefore, every time he inhales air, he makes a strange, unusual noise. Similarly, Brutus's voice is altered by the helium he inhales before speaking. The first scene of the performance shows a video of a human larynx projected on a screen, thanks to a camera inserted inside an actor's throat. Castellucci seems to want to show the *physical* process of speech and language. Here the physical pain and the violence involved throughout the play are emphasized by the image of the actor's internal flesh. But the observation of matter does not necessarily serve a specific sign (the inside of a throat, for instance, might not necessarily refer to the capacity to speak). Often, it merely refers to itself. Castellucci plays extensively with colours, shapes, material and bodies. Through matter, he creates a world on stage by contrasting different shapes to different materials, by combining different bodies with different colours and so on. The visual impact is essential and participates in the creation of new thoughts (like the iconic Deleuzian thought, generated from scratch and leading to a real encounter with the world), while generating strong emotions for the spectators. *L'Orestie, une comédie organique?* was a particularly visual production performed in 2015 (originally performed for the first time in 1996). The confrontation between solid and liquid substances, between warm and cold colours, fat and thin bodies, round and square shapes, light and obscurity is designed to strongly impact on the spectator. As discussed before, I attended this performance and I remember how powerful the created effect was on me. Strangely, despite there being no physical interaction with the audience, the show was received in a very physical way. Yet, I was not considering myself merely as a body, as I was still producing thoughts, which would have been more difficult without some distance from the stage. I was somehow understanding something with my body. Some people complain about the fact that Castellucci often employs actors with unusual bodies (e.g. anorexic or obese people, bald women), comparing his productions to 'freakshows' (Ridout 2006: 99). However, there are no judgements made on these bodies in these shows, and, although those concerns are legitimate, adopting such a cultural point of view does not suit Castellucci's conception of theatre.

Going further, the sensation of an indifferent stage can quickly turn into the uncanny impression that the stage is looking back at us, spectators. Castellucci comments:

> When you are before a piece of art, you have the sensation to be looked at by the piece, and not the opposite. Your gaze does not lay on an object, you become instead the object of the piece. You have the sensation to be naked, discovered, like a thief, you feel unprotected, deeply touched in your intimacy. You are suddenly in the piece, and not before. I felt this before the Tate's Rothko, before *Mulholland Drive* by David Lynch; to be stripped, skinned. You find yourself in the condition of the animal that has been flushed out of its hole. (Banu 2005: 55)[16]

The impression that the relationship between oneself and the thing one observes is reversed when something in the perception changes. When the thing perceived ceases to be recognized, the spectators enter a new dimension where their positions as subjects vanish. Because they can no longer possess what they perceive, they strangely begin to feel as if it were them, who were possessed by the object of contemplation. Discussing Castellucci's theatre, Daniel Sack writes:

> Utterly alone in perception, where the question of possession falls away, I can no longer determine whether an event belongs to my experience or I belong to its enactment. The limits of my body are no longer determinate and I cannot discern a possible end to my actions or the event's motions. (143–4)

The experience of non-recognition can move the spectators to a reality where boundaries between themselves and the world become less obvious, which is perhaps why they can have the sensation of being observed. This experience goes along a different apprehension of time. Time is still experienced but no longer as a linear path, rather as a condensation of layers of moments. While there is a physical distance between the stage and the audience, this is how directors such as Castellucci invite the spectators onto the stage and 'plunge' them into the representation:

> There is an economy of the gaze, a circulation, a flow of the gaze, which is capable, I think, to carry the spectator onto the stage. [...] We are really – literally – carried within the representation: we are here. (Cassiers 2012 : 46)[17]

Strangely, this perception, that could almost be judged as hallucinatory, prompts some lucky spectators to feel closer to the real. As mentioned earlier, the sensation of the stage looking back might be a result of the spectators realizing that they are failing to recognize what they see, and therefore suddenly see themselves trying to recognize. In other words, by failing to recognize, they become aware of their attempts to recognize: 'I have caught myself in the act of looking' (Sack 2015: 133).

This is particularly striking in Castellucci's *Purgatorio*. The first half of the play features the inside of a bourgeois house in a very realistic decorum. Everything is in proportion and the time of the representation matches the time of the fiction; the spectator's perception of time is thus the same as the characters'. We see a mum and her son in their everyday life. The boy is playing with his toys; the mum is preparing food. There is no play of light; the staging is minimal. But, as Castelluci warns, this play is designed to be a trap for the spectator. It starts off too simple, too plain but also too recognizable. In the middle of the play, the dad comes back home. He tells his wife about his day while she prepares dinner. He then asks where his son is, goes in his bedroom and rapes him. Although nothing is directly shown as it happens in the boy's room which is offstage, the spectators can hear for several long minutes both the boy (played by a very young actor) screaming and the dad groaning. The scene is incredibly violent, especially because the rape takes place out of the blue, in a world that was previously recognizable and seemed relatively safe. Moreover, it may give the spectator the impression that their perception is being attacked. The real hits them, as for Castellucci the real can only manifest itself through violence, following Artaud's thoughts on cruelty (although violence does not necessarily mean physical violence for Artaud). Along with this cruel perception of the stage comes a sense of shame for the spectator. 'In witnessing the performance we become coproducers of the shameful act [. . .] we, too, are responsible for making this happen and envisioning what might happen next' (Sack 2015: 173). Shame precisely intervenes when one feels looked upon. There is no fundamental shame in the recognition (in the Deleuzian sense, as opposed to the encounter), because the recognition mode only let the thoughts refer to themselves. It is only in the non-recognition that a real sense of shame can occur because it is only in the encounter that oneself can visualize oneself spectating.[18]

There was, in *Purgatorio*, a progressive unveiling of the tragic in the sense that the spectator may have understood that something was not quite right, at the beginning of the play. For instance, the child and the mother were speaking with the same seemingly foreign accent (why would not they speak their first language when together?). French did not appear to be the first language of the actors, and the dialogues between the two characters remained extremely basic. They pronounced each word carefully and slowly, articulating a lot so as to make sure to be intelligible, which seemed to put even more distance between them. Communication was difficult, and both characters appeared rather lonely. There were some long sequences where the two characters remained silent and motionless. The child was also taking pills because he saw 'everything in purple'. During the first half of the play, one would be tempted to see the aesthetic of the Brechtian distancing effect. Indeed, the bourgeois and realistic décor seemed at first quite common, recognisable. Yet, it then became increasingly strange and distant. It is this uncanny feeling (strangeness into a familiar background) that creates the distancing effect. What was first perfectly recognisable became more and more difficult to grasp, to understand. There were also 'clues' that a terrible event was about to happen. Once home, the dad started to act strangely, and the mum began to cry and implored her husband not to 'do it'. He asked the mum to call for the child and to leave. He opened his suitcase and took out what seemed to be a dildo. At this stage many spectators may have already guessed that a sexual assault was going to occur; if not then it is probably at this very instant that everyone in the audience may have understood what is going to happen. Although I did not spectate this show live, watching on a screen was in itself a violent experience. As a spectator, I did feel like a witness to a horrible act. Since most of the spectators were probably guessing what was going to happen next, the play was particularly tragic; the spectators knew the outcome before the terrible act occurred. Yet there certainly was no tragic pleasure because it just felt 'too real'. The actor playing the child really was a child, and the fiction's temporality matched the performance's (and so the spectators') temporality. The rape scene occurred without any apparent reason: in a gratuitous way, some would say. The world on stage (or, in this case, offstage) may have suddenly appeared extremely crude. It may have left its spectator in an emotional shock. Yet, more interestingly, the rape scene may also have left them in an 'intellectual shock' (Rosset 2014: 8). There was a thin veil, between the stage and the audience, that short descriptions of the actions on stage were projected onto. Every action was narrated except the rape scene. When the violent scene occurred, the description ceased to be accurate, and the veil narrated something different from what was happening. It ended up showing the word '*Maintenant*' (now) for the rest of the scene. The rape was too violent to be narrated, to be translated into words. Yet, by not acknowledging the tragic act, by refusing to narrate it, the descriptive veil made the rape scene even more striking. The rape was outside the representation, outside the narrative, which made it appear more real than the rest of the performance. This aesthetic distance between the spectators and the violent act established by the explanatory veil was a trap; it tricked the spectators by omitting to relate the horrible act and by leaving them as lonely witnesses, voyeurs, of the shameful act. This is perhaps what Artaud has sometimes omitted; by wanting to destroy any form of distance between the real and the stage, he may have forgotten that theatre will necessarily remain a representation, and that one can in fact play on that distance to better reveal the cruel world. The tragic may therefore be better revealed if the spectators are initially distant enough from the cruel action: the distance comforts, reassures them. When it disappears, it leaves audiences shocked and lost for words.

To continue exploring how *Purgatorio* reveals the tragic on stage, the concept of 'dissonance', as developed by Nietzsche in *The Birth of Tragedy*, and then borrowed by Rosset (2014), is quite useful. The tragic pleasure and the pleasure taken in listening to a dissonance in music are described as similar: 'The delight created by tragic myth has the same origin as the delight dissonance in music creates' (Nietzsche 1956: 143). The idea of the tragic pleasure will not be mentioned in the case of *Purgatorio*, as it is difficult to imagine that there might be any. Although the extremely violent scene of rape might question the possibility for a perverse pleasure, this is a ground that I do not wish to explore. However, the concept of a tragic dissonance understood as an interruption of harmony is particularly interesting. Nietzsche makes an analogy between harmonious music and the world insofar as it is commonly perceived. Music is generally an organized harmony; conversely, the world is generally perceived in order and making some sense. To understand this analogy, the concept of duration ('durée') in Bergson's philosophy may help: our representation of the world is similar to the way duration is experienced (2003). Our consciousness is constantly moving towards the next instant, while keeping the previous instants in the memory in order to have 'instant T' making sense (T refers to the present instant, $T_1$ to the instant following the present instant and so on). Hence, we can say that T is followed by $T_1$ which is itself followed by $T_{1+1}$ and so on. Each instant is connected to the previous and the next ones, exactly like in a harmonious piece of music: for harmony to exist, a specific succession of notes must occur. Instants, like notes, fuse together. In Bergson's philosophy, this fusion is triggered by intuition. The world seen as harmonious is then a world in which meaning has been created, in which chaos has been turned into harmonious order. Everything is connected; therefore, everything seems to make sense. The tragic, on the contrary, features a fundamental dissonance. The tragic instant does not make sense because it cannot be connected to a past or future that would confer it some meaning. The rape scene was, in this way, a dissonance. It occurred in a world that looked at first reasonably harmonious; recognizable. As soon as the spectator may have realized that something terrible was going to happen in this comfortable bourgeois setting, this dissonance may have been experienced. The rape scene was the B-flat intervening in a reassuring harmony. Yet, it is precisely because this dissonance happens *in the harmony* that the tragic emerges. Hence, Rosset states that:

Harmony + Dissonance = tragic chord (2014: 70)[19]

A dissonance without harmony cannot exist; B-flat on its own cannot constitute a dissonance. It becomes one once confronted to a harmony, as it is only then that it can express its difference. Therefore, to have dissonance, one need to have primarily harmony. Similarly, to be able to no longer recognize, one must be familiar with processes of recognition.

In this very dissonance, the tragic may suddenly be perceived. The organized and harmonious world falls apart and reveals a fundamental instability. In *Purgatorio*, the world on stage appears very common, yet contained some anomalies: disharmonious language, a very monotonous routine and so on. But the rape scene screamed the most violent dissonance, and with it came the revelation of the cruelty of the world.

### 3.1.2. *Terra incognita*

Have you ever imagined a world where nobody understands anybody, a world in which everyone has their own unique language, making communication impossible? In this section, I am focusing on the absence of verbal communication in theatre. If we consider that language is a complex system of representations, as Derrida has, for instance, demonstrated in *Writing and Difference*, communication will then only exist if one found a common ground with others. However, finding common ground leads to the creation of 'fictitious significances' (Rosset 2004: 7). Communication necessarily distorts one's perception of the real. Therefore, some directors want to find a connection with each of their spectators that is not based on a verbal communication.

Castellucci has claimed that theatre should reconnect with a 'pre-alphabetic language' (Banu and Tackels 2005: 256),[20] while Fabre claims for his part that his theatre is 'the opposite of the social' (Banu and Tackels 2005: 256).[21] For Lauwers, 'Art stands alone. Art doesn't need to communicate' (Lauwers 2010: 452). They are positioning theatre outside the social sphere. They even claim that their theatre may take the spectators back to a non-verbal state, a state where words are yet to emerge. In this sense, they explain that they are not addressing the audience as a whole but are instead addressing the spectator as an individual. In 2005, Christian Longchamp points out this apparent paradox regarding Castellucci's and Fabre's theatres:

> I would like to react to a comment made by George Banu about how these plays show us our own loneliness. These last few days I often

thought about paintings by Rothko, by Fautrier, by Bacon, about this primordial loneliness. Therefore, it would put into question the conventional idea that theatre should create a community. (Lauwers 2010: 452)[22]

Indeed, while theatre is usually considered as an art to share in a community, these directors approach it as a medium that first and foremost reaches the individual. Interestingly, Lauwers notes that applause in a theatre 'puts too much emphasis on the entertainment value' and, in fact, is the reaction of a group, not an individual. Applause marks the presence of a community. Therefore, for Lauwers, applause is 'the tragedy of theatre' (Lauwers 2010: 450). According to Fabre, his and Castellucci's relationship to art is in fact 'different' (Lauwers 2010: 450) because their stages aim to establish a connection that is not based on social grounds. They argue instead for a stage that would instil a secret and strong relationship with each of its spectator. This connection, they say, cannot happen in a social atmosphere. They are therefore seeking to communicate in a very different way:

> We, artists, are not against something (the group. . .) but respond to an internal need to directly address the individual. This asks for a different dramaturgy, different images, different states or sensations, and that is why the current reactions demonstrate an incomprehension of it. (Lauwers 2010: 258)[23]

A different communication leads to a different work on stage. Fabre, Castellucci and García, in particular, are often accused of being pretentious artists, to consider themselves as geniuses and to display on stage their own obscure and incomprehensible inner world. Carole Talon-Hugon argues that such personalities may be understood through the theory of the 'metaphysic of the artist' (2006): according to her, these directors have established themselves in the long tradition of artists seen as Nietzschean 'genius': these artists claim to be 'inspired' by a transcendental force, hence offering an art that cannot be judged upon its quality, but can instead only be admired for its originality and the beauty of the artist's inner world: 'The whole value of the artwork comes from this occult, transcendent and mysterious force' (2006: 38).²⁴ This would partly explain why the stage cannot address the audience as a community. Indeed, the inner world of the artist may echo differently depending on the spectator's sensitivity. Yet Fabre's and Castellucci's theatres are very structured, observing precise and strict rules. Their shows conform to a form of science established by the directors in an attempt to create a certain effect on the spectator and answer a large range of inherent rules. To better understand how they address the spectator rather than the audience, let us try to understand how this non-verbal language is developed on stage. Here, I will be exclusively focusing on Castellucci's and Fabre's philosophies and productions, as they have been the two directors who most profusely talked about the possibility of a non-verbal communication between the stage and the audience. By understanding their thinking, one can start to see how one can spectate shows differently.

A non-verbal language, for Fabre and Castellucci, does not refer to a subjective reading of the world but rather to a vision of the world free from verbal language, that is, free from the most invasive form of representation. In order to have a glance at this obscure and primitive language that does not use words, the spectators are encouraged to abandon the human tendency to name, and therefore give meaning, to the objects of the world. It is precisely this experience that cannot be shared. For Fabre and Castellucci, it is the most intimate relationship with the world that someone can experience in a theatre. This statement needs, however, to be qualified: their shows partly rely on predetermined scripts. A verbal language is indeed present. Their performances do contain words, dialogues, quotes, poems. Fabre and Castellucci argue that they are searching for a non-verbal language, but they do not use such a language continuously throughout the performance. If these theatres were only addressing the individual, I would not even be able to share my reflections. Language and its representations cross each of the performances, which is why the criticism made by Florence Dupont, in her essay *Aristote ou le vampire du théâtre occidental* (2007), does seem relatively irrelevant. She argues that even though Jan Fabre wants to associate his theatre to a non-mimetic art, there are still some symbolic elements, some representations, some traces of what she names, rightly, the Aristotelian tradition. Yet, as it has been shown in Chapter 2, representations may be found outside the concept of *mimesis* and may paradoxically participate into the exposition of a world without doubles. Moreover, the presence of some symbols, some doubles, does not fully alter the tendency of a performance to remain outside the sphere of representations. In Fabre's theatre, the search for a non-verbal communication passes through an exploration of organisms. His stage is a place where bodies are dissected and biological mechanisms studied; he wants to show the human body before its cultural transformation. Annabelle Chambon and Cédric Charon explained that Fabre is fond of some of Michel Foucault's theories, such as the analysis of human's body as turned by societies into a regulated and docile machine, developed in *Discipline and Punish*.[25] In *Corpus Jan Fabre*, Luk Van Den Dries compares Fabre to a biologist:

> Fabre observes his actors and works with them like a biologist. He is fascinated by the body's structure, the limbs' implantation, the organ's functioning. His work technique is similar to a dissection: he examines articulations, analyses each movement in great detail. But he is also the biologist who wants to know how living beings develop, breed and die. This cyclic evolution intrigues him and is a source of infinite inspiration. (2005: 133)[26]

Beauty, for Fabre, is then not to be found in sophisticated bodies but, rather, in primitive, physiological bodies. His theatre appears to want to un-domesticate, rewild the body. This is one way to reconnect to a non-verbal state. According to the Flemish director, theatre should make the actors and, consequently, the spectators (although the transmission from actors to spectators is not always clear, as seen in Chapter 2) rediscover their physical instincts. Instincts would be 'hidden' behind a 'thick cultural layer' (2005: 352).[27] He is interested in a body full of impulsions, reflexes and 'insignificances'; beauty would lay in this relatively uncontrollable physical force. Jan Fabre is very close to the German philosopher Peter Sloterdijk's concept of 'domestication' of humans.[28] According to Sloterdijk, the domestication of the human body is one of the least studied and thought through truths. Sloterdijk and Fabre both consider that animalistic instincts have been dissimulated behind what we may name a cultural training. Sloterdijk aims to rediscover this very force present in all humans whereas Fabre wants to manifest it on stage. In other words, they are both interested in the ob-scene, that is, what must remain offstage as it cannot be represented; only shown. By reconnecting to this primitive state, a new kind of knowledge may emerge. Spectators are invited to unlearn and lose themselves in a new, raw reality. This return to an animalistic state (if we consider it were ever there) would bring along a new form of language; not a language made from words, but a more essential one. This is what Hugo de Greef and Jan Hoet state in *Jan Fabre, le guerrier de la beauté*:

> The comprehension of a forgotten language. This language that we all carry in us, but which we suppress because it contains nature's anarchy. This language is based on a different logic to that of our civilized society. This language is closer to the essence of things and expresses empathy towards life. [. . .] It is a language of intensity, instinct, intuition. (1994: 25–6)[29]

This language is chaotic insofar as nature is seen as chaotic; it does not attempt to put order in disorder. This language refers to things as they are first perceived, and not as they are culturally assimilated. It deconstructs our 'I' as civilized and social beings. This is a significant theme in Artaud's reflections. In *The Theatre and its Double*, he makes a famous comparison between theatre and the plague. Five pages are dedicated to the description of the effects and damages the plague has on the human body. He depicts, in a rather meticulous and detailed way, the internal destruction of every organ. He concludes by stating that just like the plague, theatre is a delirium. Theatre results in an organic disaster, aiming to empty the spectators' abscesses. Fabre's theatre is significantly influenced by Artaud's writing. Characters on stage often describe their bodies bursting (see for instance *Je suis sang*), similar to the bursting of the body that the plague can provoke, as described by Artaud. However, in Fabre's work, the theme of a bursting body is first related to the cycle of life and death as a transformation of state. Indeed, according to him, theatre should reveal to the spectators their bodies as temporary forms destined to disintegrate. Having the impression that their bodies could 'burst' during of one his shows constitutes a first step: 'All my work is a preparation to die in a sense. We're born with death inside, with a dead skeleton inside us.'[30] Luk Van Den Dries mentions, for his part, this experience in the following terms:

> It is a moment of transgression. The body wants, for a minute, to extract itself from its exclusion. It wants to be part of the big stream, it wants to drown in a form of continuity in which it feels connected to the energy of life. It wants to break barriers. The experience is incredibly violent. We lost all control. (2005: 32)[31]

It seems that the spectators who would be willing to give up their identities as subjects (their 'I') would be going through one of the most powerful experiences one can have in a theatre. This would be achieved through a form of communication that is no longer verbal and based on pre-established meanings, but through the transmission of primitive forces. The present study does not suggest that this is what any spectator going to see a performance by Fabre will experience, nor does it argue that this is the ultimate goal to reach as a spectator. Fabre is only claiming to be able to provoke it within some of his spectators. Some people do experience it (as is the case for Luk Van Den Dries); some simply do not. Some people appear indeed capable of letting the borders between their self and their consciousness blur in an attempt to let themselves merge into the 'energetic mass' (2005: 29). Yet, Fabre's performances may still be appreciated (or not) without what he and his actors loosely name a catharsis.

Fabre calls his actors 'warriors of beauty' and often talks about their 'aura'. The aura is a fascinating concept to explore in theatre, and may help us, here, to grasp how a communication without words or pre-established meanings can be established between the stage and the audience. In *Presence in Play*, Cormac Power defines aura through what he names 'the auratic presence':

> An actor can convey a powerful sense of charisma, or a famous play or theatre company can project a sense of prestige and authority to a knowing audience. The term I am using for this mode of presence is 'auratic presence', derived from the term aura. What makes 'auratic presence' so difficult a term to pin down is that it doesn't immediately refer to the presence *of* anything in particular. [. . .] Aura is a term with mysterious connotations, referring to a presence which is above the ordinary, an abstract quality that can be attached to people, names, objects or places which have more significance than appearance might suggest. The auratic mode of presence is thus very different from the fictional mode; while the latter is concerned with the *making-present* or fictional phenomena, auratic presence refers to the *having* of presence. (2008: 47)

Aura is thus a term difficult 'to pin down', whose presence remains 'above the ordinary'; it refers indeed to a more complex presence than the mere *hic et nunc*. Yet, aura is 'easily recognise[d] and experience[d]' (47). As Power points out, even though everyone may have experienced an auratic presence, it usually remains obscure, unexplained. No one (or nothing) 'possesses' aura. It appears to be a mysterious force that simply lies onto certain objects, certain people. Therefore, it is not the object or the person themselves that strike but, rather, something about them. Facing an auratic presence leads paradoxically to the experience of a strong presence, yet one which appears distant, unattainable. On stage, it appears extremely difficult to understand why some actors might have more of an aura than others. Denis Guénoun argues that theatrical presence is not an address ('une adresse') but is instead 'a very singular and enigmatic presence' that only shows itself as a pure phenomenon (2014: 94). Aura is thus problematic to apprehend as it is located somewhere between here and elsewhere. Fabre's warriors of beauty seem to be trained to achieve this auratic presence. Fabre names warriors of beauty actors who have worked for him more than five years and are very much used to his exercises. They are trained to be able to enter a 'physiological state'. Thus, they do not tend to 'address' the audience; they rather focus on what is happening inside themselves. During the actor training that I attended in 2017, Cédric Charron insisted on the fact that actors must not 'monkey something, it [is] about [them], about [themselves]'. Fabre seeks actors who can reach a state close to ecstasy and can become not someone else but something else. With reference to Els Deceukelier, one of his favourite actresses, he explains:

> You can see her change. Her eyes, her face, her body, her hair, you can see it change. It is a form of ecstasy. The dividing line is very thin, and one needs to be careful. Good actors, who learnt how to develop their personal cruelty, also know how to retrieve their balance at a certain moment, before they completely lose it. Of course it is a difficult journey, both mentally and physically. (Luk Van Den Dries 2005: 363)[32]

When Luk Van Den Dries asked Els Deceukelier to explain this state, she said: 'It is difficult to describe [. . .] For me, it is a sensation of complete abandon, a state of authenticity that one cannot explain' (382-3).[33] Her aura seems to originate from some primitive energy that she is able to convey, which is why she does not possess aura, but something about her is auratic. Since the warriors of beauty are capable of entering a state bordering trance, spectating them appears to go along with perceiving the unpredictable quality of the real. The spectators' perception of the stage as representation is defeated because the actors are changing into an unrecognized something, emphasizing their own presence. As an example, see Cédric Charron's performance in *Attends, attends, attends* by Jan Fabre, available on YouTube. This new reality is unfamiliar, unstable and difficult to apprehend. What is perceived seems thus here and now as well as distant and enigmatic. These bodies on stage are in perpetual mutation. They are constantly changing, continuously moving from one form to another. The theme of transformation is in fact central in Fabre's theatre. During the actor training I witnessed, the actors were routinely asked to go through a series of metamorphoses at the start of each day. They were, for instance, tasked to act like a cat, to then mutate into a tiger, then a lizard, to finally changed into an insect. Every time they were acting like the cat, Cédric and Annabelle insisted on the importance of the physical embodiment: 'try to activate each body part. A cat has a tail, whiskers, how do you integrate this information? [. . .] Connect your imagination to your stomach'. When they were asked to switch to the tiger, Cédric and Annabelle insisted on the time of the transformation itself: 'Taste this transformation, taste the in-between [. . .] You are becoming much stronger, your muscular structure is changing.' When it was time to act like a lizard, the fact that it involved a physiological mutation from a hot-blooded creature to a cold one was always highlighted. This exercise's aim was to teach them how to apply a particular animal's anatomy to their own human one and 'taste' the moment of the transformation. The transformations were rapid, and actors were encouraged to explore the limits of their physical conditions. I witnessed some actors crying or shaking after such exercises or looking disorientated. One actress even broke her nose during training yet did not realize it straight away. It seemed that Fabre made up these exercises, with very precise rules, to make the actors reach a state without control, of pure disorder (and only then teach them how to remain physically safe). The actors were experiencing a chaotic relationship with their surroundings (this is how one of them put it) while I, as spectator, was watching this very chaotic world being suddenly revealed to me. They were possessed by forces much bigger than themselves; in that sense their presence was auratic, and they were communicating with me in mysterious and archaic ways.

Fabrian bodies never stagnate or take a break on stage. They use the space to transform themselves into animals, to switch between different ages (from the child to the elder for instance) or to constantly switch between sexes (male to female to male to female and so on). Their bodies are, in this way, unlimited. In *Preparatio mortis* (2012), for instance, Annabelle Chambon, who is the only performer on stage, spends an hour being alternatively 'possessed' by Eros and Thanatos. In Greek mythology, Eros symbolizes life instinct, pleasure and acceptance while Thanatos symbolizes death drive, destruction and pain. She was thus switching between two radically different states at an extremely rapid rate. Again, this was also a recurrent exercise during the training. The actors were told to avoid any dance movements to rather be in a fight with forces penetrating their bodies, whether they were positive (Eros) or negative (Thanatos): 'Think of your body as a shell. Forces are penetrating you and are pushing. Play with the extremes. Is it good, is it painful. Give textures.' This example demonstrates how the constant mutation of the body may disorientate the spectator's recognition. Indeed, after repeating Eros and Thanatos a great number of times, they both start to look the same. As Annabelle pointed out, extreme pain and extreme ecstasy can end up resembling one another. This is, for instance, what is seemingly shown by the famous sculpture of Saint Teresa by Gian Lorenzo Bernini, in the Santa Maria della Vittoria church, in Rome. Saint Teresa is being pierced by an arrow launched by an angel. The violent sensation, sent by God, appears to put her into an orgasmic pain. In fact, these sequences of different physical and emotional states blur the spectators' understanding because not only can they not recognize any definitive shapes but these shapes seem to be related in a mysterious way. Bodies on stage are cats, tigers, lizards, babies, elders, driven by life preservation or self-destruction. Yet in their hybridity they are all the same: bodies which are simply free from any determined shape. They are elusive as they avoid any form of exterior control to remain fluid and autonomous.

These training methods ask the actors to reconnect with a tragic perception of the world. Fabre claims:

> In my shows, this return to the origins turns the actors and dancers almost into Greek gods. Indeed, my shows are built so as to become structures against which they have to fight, to lose or to win. In this aspect, the shows are very close to the idea of a Greek tragedy. (Banu and Tackels 2005: 246)[34]

Yet, there is a fundamental difference between his actors and actors in Greek tragedies: on Fabre's stage, actors are fighting for real, in the sense that their bodies are physically being challenged. Their bodies fight, whereas the Greek tragedians do not fight; only their characters do. Similarly, he argues in *Corpus*:

> The warrior of beauty has perhaps enough freedom to understand that they are not free, but thanks to this freedom, they oppose their finitude. They aspire to be a god. The warrior is a mortal, such is their fate. But they are also pretending not to be, and there lays their sin. It is the essence of my tragedy. (2005: 344)[35]

Fabre has his own definition of tragedy, differing from the Aristotelian genre. There are some similarities, yet also many crucial differences between the Aristotelian tragedy and what he names 'my' tragedy. His vision of the tragic hero is indeed quite traditional: a man or a woman fighting against dominating forces, knowing that they will eventually lose, yet manifesting their freedom in engaging in this very battle. However, tragic heroes, for Fabre, directly refer to the actors as individuals, rather than the fictitious characters. Fabre's actors are indeed performers who put their bodies into real pain or at least in a real conflict. In *Je suis sang* (2001), for instance, the opening scene features actors wearing a heavy suit of armour and dancing until physical exhaustion (other examples can be found in Chapter 2). Yet, the most obvious example is probably *Mount Olympus* (2017), a twenty-four-hour performance where the actors, eventually exhausted, perform continually for an entire day and night. These warriors of beauty fight against their biological condition, which is precisely what makes them tragic heroes; not as characters but as human beings. Fabre takes the tragic heroes out of their tragedies and rather trains actors to become tragic heroes (hence the expression 'from act to acting'). The way Fabre understands the Aristotelian tragedy is loose, yet it enables him to free himself from the rigidity of the genre and to offer an experience *in* the real, rather than *of* the real (I will come back on this later). Fabre calls this state the 'post-mortem' state. This experience is difficult to describe with words because it is difficult to explain it rationally, which is perhaps why Luk Van Den Dries refers to it in *Corpus* in quite poetic terms. As

Artaud demonstrates in *The Theatre and Its Double*, it appears that the ineffable can only be approached through a poetic expression, as though unfamiliar ideas (especially when referring to sensations) would need a looser use of language to be linguistically communicated. The ecstasy of the actor (or the post-mortem state, the catharsis; Fabre remains rather approximate in his choice of words) would thus qualify a moment, in the acting, when actors reach a certain state. From what I understand, this point is often reached through either emotional or physical exhaustion – usually both. During the training that I witnessed, actors were, at the end of each day, exhausted because of the physicality of the training, but also mentioned an emotional fatigue, since they were sharing their nudity and uncontrollable reflexes with a large group. The showing of an extremely private dimension of themselves was making them vulnerable. It appears that this state of fragility is necessary for them to reach an ecstatic state. Luk Van Den Dries mentions, for instance, in *Corpus Jan Fabre* some actresses who, during a rehearsal, contracted their muscles so much that they ended up peeing on stage. Besides the physical fatigue, the fact that these actresses involuntary displayed such an intimate act in front of everyone added to their own vulnerability; social rules were left behind, and as a result, they were no longer able to distance (and protect) themselves from others. Yet, it is precisely through this very fragile state that actors may experience a form of trance, for they may finally have overcome others' gaze. We are in *terra incognita*.

Romeo Castellucci's quest for a non-verbal language is quite different and in a way more complex because his thoughts on the matter have been developed further in his writings. He affirms that his performances do not communicate with the spectators. Instead, they would allow them to enter a space that prevents all forms of messages. His theatre resists the 'society of the spectacle', as described by Guy Debord in 1967. Castellucci refuses to consider theatre as a modern medium through which the artists deliver a message. For the Italian artist, art should, on the contrary, interrupt communication, and should offer the audience a moment of rest in a society overwhelmed by images and messages. One might struggle to understand what the artist wishes to deliver to his audience, if it is not a communication. In fact, a communication does occur but one of a rather different kind. In *Les Pèlerins de la matière*, he explains:

> There is a completely forgotten, erased, outdated tradition of Western theatre which is that of the pre-tragic theatre. It is outdated because it is a theatre linked to matter and the terror of matter. It is, without doubts, linked to a female presence or power. [. . .] Art, in pre-tragic theatre, had this privileged connection with the mother in relation to the conceived body and to the recomposed body for the tomb. We are leaving the linguistic sphere. (2001: 112–13)[36]

His definition of a 'pre-tragic' theatre has many similarities with the tragic as it has been defined in this chapter. The 'pre-tragic', as understood by Castellucci, could thus be the tragic as described by Clément Rosset: a crude vision of the world as concentration of matter, unconcerned with human interpretation. The mysterious feminine force that he mentioned refers, perhaps, to the mystery of life itself. As women give birth, they are the ones to release deaths yet to come. Moreover, childbirth also questions the formation of matter into life. Castellucci regularly claims that his theatre raises questions, yet never provides answers for them: it is, in this sense, a theatre of enigmas. The stage questions matter, and through questioning matter, it may question the spectators' relationship to their lives and deaths. For Castellucci, linguistic language took humans away from this initial '*terror* of matter' (note that the original French word 'effroi' is particularly tricky to translate). 'A pre-tragic theatre is, to extend the image, a theatre of infancy. Infancy understood as in-fans: the condition of those who are outside language' (2001: 112).[37] Tragedies, as first codified by Aristotle in *Poetics*, are thus, for Castellucci, an attempt to control the world; to remove the enigmas and to attribute artificial meaning to it. By becoming a 'pilgrim of matter', Castellucci wants, on the contrary, to show that the real is enigmatic, difficult to reach, and that matter is too complex to be described by words. His theatre is thus much closer to the tragic as a philosophical concept than the genre of tragedy, based on Aristotelian *mimesis* (as an aesthetic reconstruction of reality). According to him, it is in this archaic vision of the tragedy that an experience of catharsis can truly be experienced. He points out:

> Against Aristotle, [Walter] Benjamin thought that the tragedy was missing catharsis. The comedy allows for this immense burst of laughter that will resolve the nervous and hysteric tension, biological and social, that accumulates in the tragedy. This laugh enables the catharsis of the tragedy, and not in the tragedy. It is a liberation 'from' the tragedy itself, and not 'in' the tragedy. This vision is completely anti-Aristotelian. (Tackels 2005: 54)[38]

The distinction between a liberation *from* the tragedy rather than a liberation *in* tragedy is particularly interesting. While catharsis, in Aristotelian tragedy, would begin and end within the tragedy (the tragedy being the trigger of this very catharsis, leading eventually to the purgation of the spectators' emotions), catharsis as understood by Castellucci does not belong to the tragedy as a genre. Instead, the catharsis that the director seeks to trigger in each of his spectators would allow these very spectators to overcome their fears, tensions, concerning their own world, the tragic world. The stage would reveal the tragic, frighten the spectators to then, through the catharsis, liberate them from this very fear. In this sense, tragedy is for Castellucci 'a tension permanently open; opened towards the unknown, opened towards the openness. It is openness itself' (in Banu and Tackels 2005: 242).[39] Those forms of tragedies reveal the world as chaotic and open to an infinite range of potentialities. They display the world's openness by inscribing in the real the field of possibilities that have not happened but simply might. In this sense, they remind their spectators that the world is nothing but uncertainty. Catharsis would hence intervene to crystallize this anxiety, push it to an unbearable level and eventually purge it and make the spectator overcome it. This view of catharsis is in fact also close to the image of the theatre of plague as developed by Antonin Artaud. Let us now see how these projects are materialized on Castellucci's stage through one example.

I'll go back to one show that I have already mentioned in this book: *Le Metope del Partenone*. I saw the production in November 2015, performed in the Grande Halle de la Villette in Paris (the description of the performance can be found in Chapter 2). I have witnessed some accidents before, with injured people requiring medical assistance; and although the fictitious accidents, in the Grande Halle de la Villette, were obviously less traumatic and alarming, they looked extremely real. In some ways, they were even more striking. In everyday life, if passers-by observe an accident in the street, they will perceive it as an ongoing action, whose ending (the death or the survival of the injured person) would still be uncertain. But in the play, after two or three accidents, the spectators may rapidly understand that more representations of accidents are to come; and that they will all lead to the death of the characters. Every time we saw a new character coming with their own medical condition, we already knew how it was going to end; they will not be saved and will die. The long repetition of the action revealed the absence of dramatic or symbolic meaning; the show rather invited us to 'only' witness characters dying. The play was thus tragic for this first reason: the spectator ended up knowing the end of the actions before they occurred. As soon as a new character entered the dramatic space, the audience had guessed that the character was going to die. The play, in this sense, may have felt like pure determinism, a tragedy. Yet, it was the way death was shown that made this performance an exposition of the tragic. To help understand this, I would like to review the example of the builder falling off of a scaffold developed by Rosset in *La philosophie tragique*:

> Let us examine, for instance, the case of an accidental death: I am walking in the street, at the bottom of a building under construction; a builder trips on his scaffold, falls for 20 meters and lands at my feet, dead. Nausea comes to my throat, but while they take the body away on a stretcher and I contemplate the pool of blood on which they spread sand, I realize that I dove into an intellectual horror and not under the knock of a physiological shock. (2014: 8–9)[40]

The passer-by dives into an intellectual horror because they appear unable to process the temporal chain of actions that they just have witnessed. The builder was working, he fell and now his corpse is lying on the ground. One may consider that the passer-by may simply be in a state of shock. Yet Rosset does not consider this reaction to be a shock. This intellectual horror is instead the result of an intellectual failure in processing the event: the passer-by experiences first an intellectual crisis and then a nervous breakdown. His immediate experience of the accident is irreconcilable with his everyday perception:

> We find ourselves, for the first time, absolutely unable to find a solution, to vanquish the obstacle that stands in front of us. For the first time, we are stopped, we cannot continue on the path we have taken [. . .] We are truly trapped: it is impossible to move back and turn right or left, we are condemned to remain motionless. (2014: 25)[41]

The passer-by suddenly knows no longer how to perceive as they do no longer recognize the real. To see the builder dying is to see the transformation from a living person to a corpse. Rosset continues:

> It is no longer just the worker who is dead, but it is all of the other humans, but it is ourselves [. . .] Suddenly, it is no longer a life, it is life that dies! We discover that the insurmountable death of a human being condemns life in an irremediable way. (2014: 28)[42]

One may easily contemplate death as a concept, but to spectate death is obviously different. Rosset thus draws a distinction between 'the idea of death [. . .] which appears around the age of four' and 'the intuitive discovery of death, the tragic discovery' (2014: 27).[43] Death as a concept constitutes the intellectual approach whereas death as witnessed leads to the tragic revelation. The passer-by did not see a dead person, he saw life ending. In *Penser la mort?* Vladimir Jankélévitch argues: 'I know I will die, but I do not believe it' (1994: 29).[44] He quotes Jacques Madaule in *Considérations de la mort*: 'I know it, but I am not intimately convinced. If I was convinced, absolutely certain, I could no longer live' (1994: 29).[45] Everyone knows that they will eventually die, but cannot truly believe it. We know that we will necessarily die, yet we usually also know that we will not necessarily die tomorrow, or the day after, or next week, and so on. In this sense, we never have to believe in our future death. As Jankélévitch puts it, dying is never a necessity (1994: 30). The tragic reminds its observer of the inexorability of death. In some ways, the spectators were confronted to a similar experience in *Le Metope del Partenone*. The performance was emphasizing the transformation from a person to a corpse, from life to death and the mystery in this very change. The spectator was invited to witness this process, even though it was only represented. As a spectator, it was indeed difficult to understand how the bloody corpses laying on the ground were 'the same' as the characters who were standing up, a few seconds ago: 'The tragic is not this corpse that we take away, it is the idea that this bloody pile of flesh is the same as the one who fell an instant ago' (Rosset 2014: 9).[46] A strange process had been witnessed. At the end of her review, Fabienne Darge, in *Le Monde* (2015b), states: 'At the end, two sweepers come to clean all this blood, all these human flesh remains. Life goes on. What did we see ?'[47]

This sense of revelation could be associated to what some called the 'iconic thought'. The term 'iconoclast' commonly describes someone who destroys religious and/or sacred objects and images. From the Greek *eikonoklastês*, it etymologically means 'breaker of images'. The iconoclasts refuse representations as they consider that representations would necessarily weaken the religious or spiritual entities. In the New Testament, the transfiguration of Jesus designates the moment when, while he is praying on a mountain, his body begins to shine, with rays of light emanating from it. A voice coming from the sky then calls him son. For Castellucci, iconoclasm and transfiguration are similar concepts: they both refer to the resurrection of a greater force by deconstructing its representation. There is an initial obstacle with regard to such a statement: how can one create something greater than the mere visible reality with a material that is reality itself? How can one show something on a stage, while destroying representations? These questions are raised by the artist in *Les Pèlerins de la matière* (30–2). Castellucci wants to go beyond the concept of theatre as merely Aristotelian *mimesis,* that is, an organized representation of the real, establishing an aesthetic distance with the real. He rather wishes to reach something more obscure, less intelligible: essences. And to be able to show essences, he must destroy images, doubles of the real. In this regard, he agrees with Plato to consider that ideas (understood as essences) are more real than visible reality, which can be misinterpreted. Yet he goes further by trying to find and give materiality to these very ideas in order to be able to show them on stage. Iconoclasm is not a mere destruction. On the contrary, it is the promise of an unprecedented image that refers to nothing but itself. The concept of profanation developed by Giorgio Agamben is quite similar and can help us to better understand this process (the concept has partially been explored in Chapter 2). According to Agamben, the consumer society marked the start of a tendency towards the 'possession' of objects. Yet, by always wanting to possess more and more, people have forgotten how to profane objects. In other words, they have forgotten that they can use objects in a different way to the falsely exclusive use that they have been designed for. A common example is the cat playing with a woollen ball: the primary use of the woollen ball is to knit warm clothes. Yet, the cat does not know this function and prefers to play with it. It is also true with young children taking various objects for toys: they are 'profaning' them in Agamben's vocabulary. The cat and children are iconoclasts as they destroy sacred objects, that is, objects reserved for one very specific use (he thus opposes the 'sacred' to the 'profane'). They release the object from its representation by breaking this very representation. Suddenly, the object does not serve a single purpose and does not belong to anyone; it is free and inalienable to any system of thought. The cat, the child (or some spectators attending a performance by Castellucci) have thus a closer access to the 'essences' of objects. As mentioned earlier, the main purpose of iconoclasm on stage is to lead to the possibility of an 'iconic thought' for the spectators. The notion of 'iconic thought' is difficult to grasp and complex to define but very powerful when experienced. Here is one definition, provided by Catherine Bouko:

The iconic process calls for a pause during which the perception remains at a primitive level [*niveau de la priméité*] and is released from all searches for meaning. The iconic thought is fragile and fleeting; it can only be reached during short instances and demands an open attitude from the spectator: the latter must accept to abandon its (dramatic) landmarks to apprehend this scenic language. If they oppose the floating perception, they cannot reach this type of reception. (Bouko 2010: 143)[48]

One can see partly why the experience is complex to define; it requires a 'floating' perception, a term which is just as vague as it is intangible. Besides, as soon as the spectator returns to a more focused perception, this brief moment vanishes: 'as soon as it is intellectualized, the iconic thought disappears and is replaced by the dramatization process' (Bouko 2010: 143).[49] However, iconic thought does not refer at all to a state of trance as the spectator remains fully aware of their surroundings. The ability to reach such a level of perception strongly depends on the spectator's capacity of 'letting it go'. It varies from one individual to another and is relatively impossible to translate into exact words. But we can say at least that iconoclasm and its attempt to deconstruct representations on stage invite spectators to open their fields of perception. A new meaning without intellectual significance can emerge from reality and the mere presence of the object on stage can appear rather mysterious and full of possibilities.

To conclude, and as Artaud said in *The Theatre and Its Double*: 'words mean little to the mind' (1970: 66). According to him, language condemns humans to communicate, that is, to find a superficial common ground. This is a compromise that erases the individual. As Daniel Sack explains:

> Artaud wrote with terror about the everyday act of speech not only because sound cannot stand still or it would cease to be, not only because it must always leave us, but also because in order to appear in speech, one's peculiar singularity must disappear behind the uniform word I. (2015: 180)

For Artaud, birth inexorably leads to a person's duplication, as it causes the birth of their double: they become divided into their real being and their representation. The simple act of talking (and more broadly of expressing) recalls this division. In this sense, Derrida's thoughts on language appear to be quite similar (as Sack points out); language does not belong to the speaker but to a much larger and general system of representations, a necessary condition for anyone wishing to be understood by others. Thus, language and its complex entanglement of meanings cannot appear except on a common ground; their existence is due to a series of compromises that individuals make. This reality is terrifying for Artaud as it means that there is a fundamental split in every human being. On a purely ideological level, the only solution to escape this scission, and regain our being as a whole, is to commit suicide, since it is only in death that one can retrieve their pre-language state and kill their double. Daniel Sack quotes Derrida's *Writing and Difference* and summarizes thus:

> To be born is to be born for something: the most definite end, death, but also any number of subsidiary ends along the way. In Derrida's understanding of Artaud, this scission marks the 'judgment of God' and the making of the human in distinction from the divine: '[God] is the difference which insinuates itself between myself and myself as my death. That is why – such is the concept of true suicide according to Artaud – I must die away from my death in order to be reborn "immortal" at the eve of my birth'. (2015: 154)

Although Castellucci is not religious (although his productions contain many religious references), he considers that theatre is born with the death of God. For both Artaud and Castellucci, God is to be considered as a force that imposes representations on any human being; a certain sense of identity, defined by comparison to the divine. Theatre, according to them, overcomes this split between being and representation that God created. The cruelty of theatre refers thus to its capacity to express the world without words, without having to find a common ground, without doubles. For Derrida, Artaud's concept of cruelty is 'the access to a life before birth and after death' (quoted by Sack 2015: 166). Cruelty is a rather similar concept to what Deleuze calls 'difference' in *Difference and Repetition*. As we have seen previously, difference designates something not that distinguishes itself from something else but, on the contrary, can only distinguish itself from itself. In other words, the object of 'difference' contains its own reference, its own representation. Difference is creative and cannot be found in representation. To perceive the world prior to the acquisition of language therefore leads to the perception of a difference, a cruelty. It also means, in some ways, to perceive the 'determination' of the real. In *Le Réel, traité de l'idiotie*, Rosset explains that the real is necessarily 'somehow anyhow' (14). The real is cruel because it occurs independently from us, in a way that does not answer logic and is irrevocable. Language, in this sense, constitutes an illusion: it brings logic in a world that is nothing but chaos. 'The sky can still fall on our heads,' states Artaud, as for him, the ultimate purpose of theatre is to remind us of this frightening truth. Theatre, for Artaud and Castellucci, should thus allow the spectators to leave the 'everyday world of productive objects and produced subjects' (Sack 2015: 143) in order to enter the real as cruelty; this 'moment of conception, when and where stuff is forming, becoming, but taking action becomes impossible' (Sack 2015: 143). Entering a pre-language world can be terrifying because it means leaving a safe, reduced and partitioned environment to let an endless potentiality invade our field of perception. On this account, Castellucci considers that Genesis is scarier than the Apocalypse because it offers a 'terror of endless possibility, the open sea of potential' (quoted by Sack 2015: 133), for the same reasons that life, with its infinite number of representations, is scarier than death for Artaud. But is this the only way to access the real? Jean-Luc Nancy considers that presence is 'the coming that effaces itself and brings itself back [. . .] To be, is not yet to have been, and already to have been' (1994: 5). Presence (which we can directly relate to the real here) is vertiginous and chaotic because nothing settles in it; it is a permanent non-recognizable instant. Like Nancy, Deleuze and Guatarri qualified chaos 'not so much by its disorder as by the infinite speed with which every form taking shape in it vanishes. [. . .] Chaos is an infinite speed of birth and disappearance' (quoted by Sack 2015: 144). By witnessing a stage that communicates through chaos leads the spectator to experience something that they cannot grasp. Apocalypse comes in fact from a Greek word meaning 'unveiling' (Sack 2015: 146). The Apocalypse, in this sense, is not the end of the world; it is its revelation.

## 3.2. Becoming masters of our gaze

### 3.2.1. Accepting simplicity

To call a spade a spade: sometimes we need to go back to basics. This simplicity is far from being obvious: to let go of our interpretations and quest for meaning is uneasy, and can, as seen in the previous section, be scary. It involves getting lost in a world that does not exist for us. If we accept this simplicity, then, hopefully, we can regain control over our gaze. Our perception won't be influenced by external factors, and our gaze, for once, will truly be ours. It is easily said! Perhaps such a level of perception can be reached only by some, and only in very brief moments. Yet if we are aware of the possibility for our perception to lose itself and wander on the simple surface of things, then we can spectate productions more freely and be more open to new, sometimes disturbing, emotional and physical experiences. The contemporary stage gives objects and actions their freedom back. It is precisely because they are on stage that they can be perceived as being free from any system of representation; that they can be profaned. In other words, the objects and actions owe their existence to only one thing: the stage, and the only purpose of the stage is to be observed. The stage is the only reason for them to exist, so what occurs on stage will always have the possibility to occur only for the sake of it: a spade will always be able to shine as a spade and nothing more. In this sense, nothing is more real and simple than the objects and actions on stage, because they can contain their own reference. Presence comes from the Latin *prae esse*, which means 'be in front'. The stage shows presence better than anything else. As said previously, an actor walking on stage might be perceived as more real than a pedestrian crossing a road, because his action only answers the necessity to walk on the stage while the pedestrian crossing the road is doing so for a particular purpose, in order to go somewhere. On stage, the action can match the intention. On this matter, Artaud defined theatre as 'that momentary pointlessness which drives [people] to useless acts without immediate profit' (Artaud 1970: 15). The real in theatre can be more powerful than the everyday reality; '*It is the real* against reality,' claims Castellucci (in Banu and Tackels 2005: 256). Theatre, for the Italian director, offers a perception close to what the 'phenomenal eye' sees, as described by Bert States (as seen in Chapter 2). States contrasts phenomenology with semiology. According to him, the 'phenomenal eye' and the 'significative eye' are both necessary for an everyday experience of the world (although the latter remains, by far, the most significant); they constitute a sort of 'binocular vision'. When mentioning his phenomenological experience of watching a bus, he describes it as though he were seeing the bus for the first time. The bus appears to him not as a bus, that is, a means of transport, taking people from one place to another, but as an imposing object in its majestic presence. Perceiving the world through the phenomenal eye leads in fact to perceiving things as unnamed. There is no word to describe it because there is no longer any specific meaning attached to it. Bert perceives this 'thing' free from language, letting it remain in its full potentiality. The only thing that he is able to describe with words is its matter. This bus appears more real than a bus that would be perceived through the 'significative eye', because, within a short instant, it seems to only exist in its material reality. In theatre, Romeo and Claudia Castellucci explain that the use of parables in their work can also be used to defeat the quest for deeper meaning that the spectators seek. Without going as far as promoting a phenomenological perception, they ask their audience to accept simplicity:

> This new pragma-theatre uses parables for its communication. [...] what is said is too intimate to be told with a journalistic and popularising tone. The parable has an extremely simplified aspect, which is why a good number of people – outraged by such decadent symbolism, leave, disgusted by so much simplicity. Good on them for despising us, as they are expecting a language full of poetical double meanings, of which they want to decipher the 'complexity', thanks to their humanist culture. Well, here, the cultivated man and the one who is not have exactly the same possibilities [...] because this theatre completely transcends culture. (2001: 16–17)[50]

Several interesting statements are made here. The first one claims that the company does communicate; only the nature of it is too intimate to be delivered in a common way, that is, in a descriptive way, even though a broad range of theatrical practices do communicate in this 'journalistic' manner. Consequently, these types of theatre can appear too simple to some because they refuse to overfill their stage with doubles, with complex entanglements of meaning, and therefore refuse to turn their theatre into an intellectual practice to which only a few have access. But as previously said, as soon as theatre takes some distance from cultural environments, it becomes paradoxically simple and yet demanding, as it asks the spectators to leave some entrenched habits to enter a world that is perhaps more straightforward but nonetheless unfamiliar.

> Theatre that tries to produce a resolution is unacceptable. It makes me feel like I'm still in school. It is even worse, because this type of theatre wants to make us believe that it is speaking the truth. Even Brecht fell into that trap and this pedagogical pretention. It is much better if theatre lets a feeling of anxiety pass. (Tackels 2005: 56)[51]

Castellucci is against the reassuring intellectual resolutions of problems, against the production of doubles that hide or falsely organizes chaos (similarly, Lauwers affirms that questions are more important than their answers). He rather prefers to show the existence of a disturbing disorder. He wants to allow the spectators to experience it, to no longer ignore it. As a result, his performances can be anxiety-provoking. Some people find the productions very difficult to watch as they display the infinite possibilities that chaos exposes, its absent solutions, its missing responses. This approach to theatre is similar to Jan Fabre's, for whom theatre should not 'hit people with some truths' (Van Den Dries 2005: 159)[52] and to Gisèle Vienne, who believes that answers and firm interpretations are irrelevant in her approach to theatre: 'It is important to get it wrong and be wary of ready-made solutions. As a director, I do not pretend to be God, and I do not want spectators to imagine that I am' (Turk 2011b: 161).[53] Many contemporary artists believe that theatre should not try to solve riddles, to provide answers, but, on the contrary, should provide unanswered questions.

For Clément Rosset, simplicity means idiocy (2004) yet with no pejorative connotations. Idiocy defines that which is without doubles, reflections, that which is unique. For instance, an idiot is someone who cannot see beyond mere reality. According to Rosset, we should try to recapture this 'idiotic' perception insofar as it leads to a closer relationship with the real. In many ways, projecting our own meanings onto the real appears to be much easier that trying to perceive reality without this tendency. Some contemporary productions can be judged as too simplistic because no complex intellectual meaning is to be found. Some spectators may be offended perhaps because they believe that simplicity of perception means stupidity. They are offended by the fact that they are not being given 'intellectual food', offended that artists dare present something so simple. But again, simplicity, or idiocy, is uneasy. Taking the example of the theatre of Societas Rafaello Sanzio, Nicholas Ridout explains that one can feel lost or abandoned, while attending one of their performances, because one believes that one does not possess the keys to decipher the show. The author describes how many spectators – including himself – want to have access to the (non-existent) master code; the master code that would clarify everything seen on stage and make 'enigmatic actions [. . .] understood to be standing for other actions' (2007: 104). Because they believe that what they see on stage stands for some doubles only discoverable through the mastery of codes, many spectators fail to grasp the entire project of the theatre company. Ridout adds, referring specifically to the show *Brussels BR.#04*:

> Then, everything became very clear. The veils had been lifted, and we looked straight into the wide open space of a marble box in which every action seemed to have its own proper name and to need no explanation. In English, there is a phrase with which one can signal one's approval of this kind of straight-talking: calling a spade a spade. Suddenly, this theatre seemed to be presenting spades as spades. [. . .] With no gauze interposed between the gaze of the spectators and the action itself, everything that appeared, appeared to do so intensely as itself: lucid, in focus, most definitely here and now. (2007: 104)

Ridout then describes one of the scenes where a policeman is beaten with a truncheon by two colleagues. The scene is very long; repetition is a crucial aspect of the aesthetics. Ridout concludes and states the (apparent) obviousness: there is nothing else to see than a policeman being beaten by two other policemen. The only thing we can account is therefore only facts: 'If a spade is a spade then there is nothing to be written about spades' (2007: 104). However, there is another much more complex aspect worth explaining: the spectator's perception. He concludes that

> Nothing strange about that, even though the theatrical effect of the action's duration (it felt like fifteen minutes) makes it unusually intense and difficult to endure. Indeed, the simplicity not just of this scene but also of others around it suggests that a certain experience of enduring is being engaged, as though allotted hours are being passed on stage, the fact of their passage perhaps as important as the matter treated. As though the act of our witnessing these actions, or these images of actions, were the point of the exercise. (2007: 104–5)

For Ridout, there is not much to say about simplicity itself. However, there is a lot to question in terms of what simplicity can provoke for those whom are willing to see it, especially on a theatrical stage. By accepting a simple, unique world, the spectator can attain a perception of the real that is full of promise. But much remains to be said about simplicity in terms of the mere physicality of things. As Rosset states, there is no mystery *in* the things but a mystery *of* things (2004: 47). The mystery lies upon their surface rather than in some deep invisible layers of meaning.

Castellucci persistently claims that his theatre is a theatre of matter. However, as we have just seen, this apparent simplicity can lead to complex reactions from spectators. Moreover, his work on matter appears to trigger the creation of 'a transcending matter'. This may appear as rather paradoxical, yet transcendence must be differentiated from metaphysics. Metaphysical primarily defines anything that exists beyond the physical world. For Rosset, metaphysics is precisely a path to avoid as it encourages affinities with fictitious meanings (2004: 7). Thus, metaphysics and matter appear to be two incompatible notions. This apparent paradox can already be found in Artaud's reflections upon the theatre of cruelty: 'In our present degenerative state, metaphysics must be made to enter the mind through the body' (1970: 77). Monique Borie understands Artaud's fascination for Balinese theatre as a fascination for this unexpected reunion, where bodies, robes, costumes, colours but also movements and sounds meet to manifest the invisible (1997: 11). Castellucci does not use the term 'metaphysics' in his philosophical work. He does not mention a search for a metaphysical matter but, rather, for a transcending matter. Transcendence refers to anything that 'goes beyond normal limits or boundaries, because it is more significant than them' (Collins English Dictionary). He aims to unite the perception of materiality with an experience that goes beyond the mere observation of this very materiality: 'paradoxically, it is a theatre made of surfaces, searching for emotion,' he says, adding: 'matter is the ultimate reality' (in *The Animal Being on Stage*, 23). Since matter is the ultimate reality, they consider their work as a pilgrimage into this very matter. Through the exploration of matter, they aim to reach some senses of reality that are perhaps too obvious to be seen in the first place. The highly religious term 'pilgrimage' refers thus to this spiritual quest. Rosset similarly wrote in *Le Réel, traité de l'idiotie*:

> There is no mystery in things, but there is a mystery of things. No need to dig into them to tear away a secret that does not exist: it is on their surface, at the edge of their existence, that they are incomprehensible. (2004: 47)[54]

The company claimed to explore the mystery laying on the surfaces of things – the matter – which is why, for them, matter does contain something invisible and inexpressible (whereas Rosset does not question that very mystery and certainly does not try to explore it). Castellucci does not hesitate to use almost magical terms when he mentions this quest. In a letter addressed to Festival director Frie Leysen, he explains:

> I am in a no man's land, in the wandering, erroneous condition of someone who is looking for a thing, about which, in reality, he does not know anything: nor the name nor the entity, but only (if one is very lucky), the enchanting glimmer of its shape. (2001: 183)[55]

In many ways, Castellucci explores a field that Rosset has refused to venture into; and by doing so, the director reconciles real and transcendence. The 'emotional waves' (in Banu and Tackels 2005: 256) he aims to provoke inside the spectators' bodies are thus the physical reactions triggered by a certain perception of matter:

> I am a shape hunter. [. . .] The sensation, in front of each discovery of a new form, is a wave, a tremor [. . .]. A shape is a shape only if it crosses our humanity with indifference. A shape is a shape only if its inhumanity moves our humanity. (Banu and Tackels 2005: 256)[56]

The mystery of matter can be approached when matter is perceived free from any interpretations, but more strikingly, when it is perceived without carrying any humanity. Therefore, emotion can be felt when the inhumanity of the object meets the humanity of human perception; when the 'insignificance of the real' (Rosset 2004: 14) strikes our humanity with full force, opening our perception to a new emotional meaning. For Chiara Castellucci, revealing matter is precisely the strength of theatre:

The concentration on a gesture was of the utmost importance, and here it was on this gesture. Here it's as if, by means of naturalness, the apparent insignificance of a gesture, although prolonged, this gesture could give access to a metaphysics, to another world – as if producing a moment of pure and complete suspension [. . .] for you see nothing other than this hand which completes a gesture and the repetitiousness of this hand that follows it. You enter, or rather you find yourself in, a state, a metaphysical state. For me, this is also the power of theatre. It is to return to this power. (in Ridout 2007: 224–5)

Repetition is a means to achieve this revelation of the real because it has the power to exhaust signs and interpretations the spectators might have projected onto the stage at first. 'You see nothing other than this hand,' Castellucci said; and this, apparently, has the power to plunge the spectators into the observation of a mystery. Thus, by observing closely the physical world, one might eventually be spectating this very world under a completely new light.

### 3.2.2. Peace of mind

The real, in some contemporary productions, has been depicted as paradoxically simple and mysterious. It appears before the spectators in its obvious and indubitable presence while remaining at the same time unknown and enigmatic. To better understand this phenomenon, I made a connection between the perception of the real and the perception of the tragic. Following Rosset's philosophy, I argued that these two kinds of perception are indeed significantly alike insofar as they both aim to get rid of human interpretations projected onto the world. The tragic washes away our reassuring projections, interpretations, optimistic beliefs, to reveal a world ready to crush us at any time: 'no, human love does not exist, human greatness does not exist, life – meaning life as we picture it when we are happy, life as always existing and young – life *does not exist*' (2014: 21).[57] However, the tragic vision is not always considered as a particularly negative view of the world; this perspective can in fact be valued.

In his article *Tragedy and the Common Man*, Arthur Miller points out:

> There is a misconception of tragedy, with which I have been struck in review after review, and in many conversations with writers and readers alike. It is the idea that tragedy is of necessity allied to pessimism. Even the dictionary says nothing more about the word than that it means a story with a sad or unhappy ending. This impression is so firmly fixed that I almost hesitate to claim that in truth tragedy implies more optimism in its author than does comedy, and that its final result ought to be the reinforcement of the onlooker's brightest opinions of the human animal. (in Robert W. Corrigan 1965: 150)

Although Miller is referring to the tragedy as a genre, this reflection appears relevant to the tragic as I have defined it. The tragic is not necessarily sad. To perceive the tragic implies to perceive the brightest side of humans. Paradoxically, the tragic emphasizes human freedom. Similarly, Karl Jaspers argues:

> The tragic looms before us as an event that shows the terrifying aspects of existence, but an existence that is still human. It reveals its entanglement with the uncharted background of man's humanity. Paradoxically, however, when a man faces the tragic, he liberates himself from it. (Corrigan 1965: 43)

To be able to perceive the tragic, one must be aware of it; and that already constitutes a liberation. Facing the tragic consequently leads to free oneself from any doubles, that is, any misleading filters. Moreover, in the tragic world, nothing is permanent, nothing is settled, and therefore, everything remains possible. This is precisely why the vision of the tragic cannot be but optimistic: 'for a moment everything is in suspension, nothing is accepted' (Robert W. Corrigan 1965: 150). Miller mentions, in this regard, the existence of a 'tragic right': the right to 'flower' and 'realize' oneself. By opening infinite possibilities, by showing a total indetermination and chaos, the tragic also offers an incredible liberty; inherent rules or norms are indeed non-existent. 'Everything may occur' means thus 'everything is possible.' In this way, the access to tragic is a 'path' for Jean-Pierre Miquel, powered by our own will (1997: 7). The tragic goes along with a certain state of mind which might not be comfortable at first. But once adopted, the tragic gives some distance with the everyday problems and allows one to acknowledge one's ontological freedom.

The idea that the tragic may instil joy in its observers is particularly present in Nietzsche's and Rosset's philosophies. For Rosset, being able to accept without anxiety all versions of reality, no matter how desirable they are, brings a sense of tragic joy. Nietzsche, in *Ecce Homo*, claimed to be the first tragic philosopher, that is, the exact opposite of a pessimistic philosopher. Following Nietzsche's approach to the tragic, Rosset states:

> the tragic is first and foremost what enables us to live, what is most rooted in man's body, it is life instinct *par excellence*, insofar as without the tragic, we could not live: we would not consider that life is worth it, if the tragic path was obstructed. (2014: 51)[58]

The tragic joy ('la joie tragique') is the only true form of joy for Rosset. The world is tragic, and that is precisely why life instinct exists; and this very instinct brings joy into life, makes it valuable and tells us to enjoy it while it lasts. Furthermore, according to Nietzsche, to perceive the tragic is to adopt an optimistic attitude towards life, while refusing the tragic means to negate life. In the tragic, life appears appealing, exciting; in the *dissonance*, men can reveal a better version of themselves. In *The Twilight of the Idols*, he states:

> [The tragic is] not in order to escape from terror and pity, not to purify one's self of a dangerous passion by discharging it with vehemence – this is how Aristotle understood it – but to be far beyond terror and pity and to be the eternal lust of Becoming itself – that lust which also involves the *lust of destruction*. (1911: 120)

For Nietzsche, the tragic joy partly comes from the fact that the tragic men know that they do not owe anything to anyone. They face the chaos with joy while looking forward to seeing where the total indeterminism of the world will lead them. They see it as an emancipation. Destruction is therefore not perceived as a negative phenomenon insofar as they know that destruction also means rebirth. The tragic man (or 'the dionysian' in Nietzsche's vocabulary) 'has unlearned how to walk and speak and is on the verge of taking off into the air, dancing' (Rosset 2014: 53).[59] This incessant movement between chaos and renaissance brings joy and energy to the tragic man.

Moreover, the tragic may also provide some appeasement to its observers. This appeasement can be particularly well experienced at the end of the tragic. Once a particularly tragic moment has ended, the subjects, through a form of catharsis perhaps, may be left relieved and purged. In *On the Tragic*, Max Scheler argues:

> This kind of grief is free from all indignation, anger, reproach, and that accompanying the desire 'if it had only been otherwise'. It is a calm, quiet fullness; a special kind of peace and composure is characteristic of it. The atmosphere of tragic grief will be absent if we are aroused to do something about it. (1965: 9)

There is something surprisingly calming in the tragic; funerals, for instance, may have a peaceful atmosphere, even though their circumstances are particularly sad. Someone died of old age: there is indeed nothing else to do but to honour their memory. Scheler adds rightly that 'a feeling of contentment' is joined with what we may name 'the tragic appeasement'. In many ways, this appeasement appears to be due to a form of fatalism: 'This resignation banishes the weakness and pain that would come from contemplating a better-made world' (1965: 9). By acknowledging the determined indetermination, one cannot but go with the flow and find peace in this way of living: 'a certain reconciliation takes place' (1965: 9). In fact, this tragic appeasement usually follows the realization that the world cannot be changed; it is what it is. Some people may find it appeasing to see that things are simply what they are, and to know that it is not in their power to attempt to change them. A burden is thus lifted. If the real is necessarily occurring by chance, as Rosset claims, then nothing can *change* it. Nothing can modify chance. Human actions are bound to remain, in this sense, meaningless. One may find this statement controversial, if not dangerous, as it seems to indicate that good actions (preserving peace, fighting poverty, etc.) are pointless and have therefore no reason to be. Of course, social standards should always be improved. However, this criticism misses the point because it wrongly implies that one should never settle for what one has at the present time; that one cannot feel contented before various major improvements. A world that would perfectly match our expectations will never exist. To address this criticism leads to delay one's adhesion to the world. The tragic does not challenge the idea of social improvements, it rather 'authorizes' us to enjoy the present; it demonstrates that the world is the best possible world simply because it is the only world that exists (rather than the best of all possible world as claimed by Leibniz who argued that God *chose* the best possible version of the world).

The American film *Being There*, directed by Hal Ashby in 1979 and based on a 1970 satirical novel by Jerzy Kosinski, conveys this view of the world. The film focuses on a character named Chance (played by Peter Sellers), a gardener who worked his entire life for the same man. When the man dies, Chance must leave a house that he has seemingly never left before (all his needs were looked after by the housekeeper). Chance is apparently very simple; he is an idiot as understood by Rosset. He cannot see beyond things, does not understand irony and only perceives what he perceives. After a string of misunderstandings, Chance ends up under the protection of a wealthy freemason family whose motto is 'life is a state of mind'. Everything that Chance says (with great simplicity) is wrongly interpreted into deeper reflections. People will understand his gardening tips as political metaphors, his empty look as profound depth, his uninspired meeting with the American president as strength of character. They will even change his name: from 'Chance the gardener', he will become 'Chauncey Gardiner'. As the title of the movie implies, Chance is the only one to 'be there'. His presence among the members of the freemason family will appease them. The head of the house, an influential industrial CEO whose multiple responsibilities are constantly underlined, is sick and kept alive thanks to a range of medical assistance; Chance's company will provide him peace. He will finally confess to his doctor, talking about Chance: 'since he's around, the thought of dying has been much easier for me.' Chance simplifies people's relationship to the word and to their death. He peacefully slides on the surface of things; he is the one who is light enough to walk on the water, as the last scene of the film shows. Chance the gardener does not know anything about frustration and unmet expectations. Happy, he takes life as it comes, just like the tragic man does.

The same tragic joyfulness can also be expressed on stage. For instance, Fabre's productions attempt to show the tragic on stage while remaining extremely joyful. A sense of the 'fête' crosses many of his performances. *Requiem for a Metamorphosis* is probably the most obvious example. Dance, music and laughs are omnipresent. Although the themes on stage are sometimes rather dark, they are treated with fun and enjoyment. Death itself is celebrated, as Fabre points out:

> As a human being I am already dead, I've been socially dead for years. It's my artwork's breath that makes me live. I see my artistic work as a preparation to die. I see death as a field of positive energy. By accepting death and by giving it a central place, you can see life differently. (Van Den Dries and Beauviche 2013: 119)[60]

Death is seen as a positive energy. *Preparatio Mortis*, for instance, features an intense one-hour dance performed by Annabelle Chambon, who is the only actor on stage. She is surrounded by flowers, and one can see at the back of the stage a coffin with her date of birth engraved (the date of death still yet to come). As the title implies, this performance is a preparation for death. Fabre created it especially for her. This preparation to die appeared, in this case, to go with a state of trance. Annabelle explained to me that during the show she had to feel alternately 'possessed' by Eros (god of desire) and Thanatos (god of destruction, death). It was in this very trance that she experienced a power, an energy that was helping her overcome her own fear of death. The show, in some ways, was leading her to accept her death to come, to accept her own finitude. This force has thus to be found by the actor through an inner journey: 'it is a grace of the instant, that is not divine in its origins, nor in its objective. It is an exhilaration [ivresse],' states Miquel, referring to the tragic revelation (1997: 21).⁶¹ It appears that in many ways, the tragic revelation, in Fabre's theatre, is first and foremost an experience for the actors. However, the simple observation of trances may provide the audience with a similar energy. In *La philosophie tragique*, Clément Rosset mentions the experience of one spectating dancers (it must be noted that Fabre's actors are usually former dancers):

> We admire these dancers and we feel proud to exist, because we know, through their tragic grace, that they know that grace is not for men [...] we love them because they have, while they dance, the acute revelation, very much more acute than in other moments of their existence, that they are ephemeral and mortal, that their fathers are dead, that they themselves are going to grow old, and perhaps that the friend with whom they dance in this moment will die tomorrow in a car accident. Our *fête* is the sudden revelation of the tragic: it is happiness' veil that tears ... and that is why we are so joyful! (2014: 65)⁶²

Through dance, dancers appear to celebrate everyone's fragility and mortality as human beings; and not only theirs. 'Life is a spark between two identical voids,' wrote the American writer Irvin D. Yalom (2016). Hence, life must be a celebration. In *Le Cas Avignon*, Fabre, close to Rosset's views on the tragic, argues:

> I mainly defend the body's vulnerability. Simply, I remind us that we constantly live in a post-mortem state, or to say it differently, that in order to stay alive, one has to be aware that one constantly comes back to life. The smallest of movements is a joy. This joy is a rejoicing. (2005: 254)⁶³

The post-mortem state, according to Fabre, aims to remind his actors (and seemingly his spectators) that life is never to be taken for granted. To live, for him, is to be constantly brought back to life. Similarly, and as stated before, Jean-Luc Nancy wrote in *The Birth of Presence* that presence is 'the coming that effaces itself and brings itself back' (1994: 5). To reuse Irvin D. Yalom's metaphor, one may consider that each instant of human life is comparable to a burning candle, ready to go out, but in a flickering, continues to burn for a little longer. Interestingly enough, many of Fabre's performances contrast the bright actors' bodies with a dark background as to accentuate the fugacity of life, its precarity, similar to a burning candle in the darkness; seemingly demonstrating that life must be celebrated.

Some of Fabre's performances take place late in the night or are even sometimes produced throughout an entire night and day, as is the case for *Mount Olympus* which lasted twenty-four hours. Luk Van Den Dries reported in *Corpus Jan Fabre* his own experience as a spectator when he went to see *Prometheus Landschaft*, first performed in 1988. The play was starting at four in the morning. He describes the tiredness of the spectators, waiting for the show to begin. Fabre wanted his spectators to be tired, as a tired spectator necessarily spectates differently. On this matter, Simone de Beauvoir rightly wrote in *Les Mandarins* that the idea of death is always less scary when one is tired (1954). On a more prosaic note, it is true that tiredness makes us put aside our everyday problems. Yet, it may also make us more aware of our surroundings. Van Den Dries explains:

> We were for some time tangibly immerged in this nocturnal blue, a 'total' experience. It felt like my body, the movement and things around me were intensely connected. And Merleau-Ponty, who used to say that we do not just look at things, but that things also look at us, came back to my memory. Until the point when everything disintegrated with the light becoming too bright. (2005: 26)[64]

It appears that Van Den Dries felt like he was no longer a subject facing the world as object but, rather, was part of a larger whole, as though he were finally belonging to the world. For Fabre, this experience can only occur at night and, more specifically, at the 'blue hour'. The blue hour qualifies this period of time, around four in the morning, when the night ends and the day begins, when they are both, for a short moment, in symbiosis: when death and rebirth occur jointly. The importance of a nightly perception is also very present in Rosset's philosophy. In *La philosophie tragique*, he states:

> There is no *fête* in the morning. Mornings are only good for masses, or at best, for scientific conferences, for political meetings: for the 'small' *fêtes*. It is not for them that we dress with our best clothes, our true 'evening clothes', us, tragic men. We reserve them for our own *fêtes*, those that celebrate the cult of mystery of men and life, and which occur invariably in the evening, when all the men's lights have turned off. (2014: 55)[65]

It is indeed usually only at night that normal social life is put aside, and that we freely celebrate one's life as mere existence.

'Genesis scares me more than the apocalypse: the terror of endless possibility, the open sea of potential,' confesses Castellucci in the programme notes to *Genesi: From the Museum of Sleep* (1999). The tragic as perceived on Castellucci's stage can indeed be terrifying; especially in *Purgatorio* and *Le Metope del Partenone*, as seen previously. Yet, I would like to review these two performances to demonstrate that a certain tenderness actually prevails. We have seen that the tragic can be followed by a phase of decompression, of relief. This occurs in *Purgatorio* after the rape scene. It has also been seen that appeasement may be found *in* the tragic: by accepting the indeterminism of the real, one can be relieved. This can be experienced in *Le Metope del Partenone*.

In *Purgatorio*, after the rape scene, the stage gradually darkens, while a bright and full circle emerges in the centre; the son appears inside it. Progressively, many enormous flowers (which seem to be made of paper) appear and disappear, crossing the circle. From an extremely violent episode, the spectator is now invited to spectate a very poetic one. Yet, the same poetic world gradually becomes more threatening. Large clouds darken the sky, and flashes of lightning begin to manifest. The flowers now take monstrous shapes. Screams are heard. The dad appears in the circle, seemingly trying to reach for his son; but the son manages to escape in time. After this scene, the stage eventually returns to the initial setting, enabling the audience to see the living room again. However, the furniture has disappeared, as though the stage were now featuring a parallel world. The start of this sequence (with the colourful flowers) is particularly tender. It seems to reveal a child's imaginary world, protective and reassuring. This tenderness is also to be found in the sense of relaxation; after the horror of the rape, the world regains its full potentiality (potentiality expressed through the showing of a poetic world). The scene takes the spectator back to a world of imagination, of representations. Yet, we have seen that the tragic too reveals a world of unlimited possibilities. To unveil the tragic is also to show the 'sea of potential'. This sequence thus appears both tragic and poetic. Is this a scene of both veiling and unveiling? That is the hypothesis defended by Daniel Sack:

> Could one not say that the mechanism at the end of *Purgatorio* is both a veiling and an unveiling at once? Certainly the machine veils the stage through its progressive blinding of the eyes/lens: it veils the actual image of the representational. At the same time, in the many tendrils of differentiation peeling outward one sees a form unveiling its potentiality. (2015: 177)

The tenderness of the scene is to be found in the way the stage shows many potentialities in a poetic way; the empty living room, for instance, looks like a parallel world ready to give the possibility for any situation to emerge. Nothing is yet imposed; everything has yet to happen. The scene is tender as the relaxation seems to enable the real to 'take' any direction. Something tender is usually something that has been stretched. The poetic showing of the world allows this sea of potential to be contained. Veiling and unveiling are thus complexly entangled to reveal the tragic world as a world of potentialities.

In *Le Metope del Partenone*, tenderness intervenes in a different way. It does not occur after a climax, after a particularly violently tragic scene but, instead, doubles the tragic, 'softens' it. In other words, the world seen in this performance is one of a tender tragic. It has been said earlier that the perception of the tragic may bring a certain form of fatalism, and that this fatalism may lead to a 'feeling of contentment' (Scheler 1965: 9). By acknowledging the tragic, 'a certain reconciliation takes place' (Scheler 1965: 9). Similarly, Schopenhauer stated in *The World as Will and Representation* that the tragic leads to resignation (2018). *Le Metope del Partenone* shows a series of deaths; it is indeed shocking at first. Yet, it gradually becomes more bearable; not because the violence becomes banal, but because the spectators may end up accepting to spectate these deaths. When I went to see the show, there was a certain atmosphere of benevolence. It reminded me of what occurs when we witness an accident in the streets or in a more intimate sphere; everyone suddenly seems to care for one another and only one thing matters: making sure that everyone is as safe as possible. It was particularly striking during the terrorist attacks in Paris in November 2015. Time seemed to have stopped, and the preoccupations of everyday life were simply gone. In front of death, humility prevails. In *Le Metope del Partenone*, performed a few days after the terrorist attacks,[66] this tenderness was, I think, felt very strongly. Perhaps it was because the show was intervening a few days after the horror, and was therefore a relaxed moment, similar to the one in *Purgatorio*, as though the attacks may have stretched our perception, making the staged violence gentler. Of course, some spectators may have been even more horrified, knowing what happened in the streets of Paris a few days before. Yet this reaction was imperceptible when I attended the performance. There was a certain sense of caring among the spectators. After all, it was only theatre, and the real physical violence that had been experienced a few days beforehand was somehow highlighting the fact that as shocking as it may be, the performance was not featuring real blood nor was it displaying real deaths. Alexandra Moreira da Silva, lecturer at the Sorbonne Nouvelle, told her class (in which I was then a student) in 2015 that Castellucci called this violence *douce* ('tender').

Moreover, this tender violence also seemed to be related to the lack of address from the actors. Each time a character died, the actor was slowly and solemnly getting up and leaving the space (which is also a recurrent motif in Lauwers' productions). Violence on stage can be unbearable to witness if it is directly addressed to the audience, or, rather, if this violence is perceived by the spectators as being *against* them. However, violence on stage can be apprehended in a completely different way if it appears indifferent towards the audience. And violence did seem indifferent towards the spectators in Le Metope. The characters died in front of us; the rescuers tried unsuccessfully to save them a few feet from us and yet, none of the actors ever acknowledged the spectators' presence. Our own incapacity to act was therefore underlined. The whole play seemed to tell us that the world is what it is and there is nothing we can do to change this. That is what made this tragic violence tender; it showed us that violence is unrelated to us. If someone had shouted during this performance, the infuriated exclamation *What have we done to you? Why have you made us suffer like this?*, this would have suddenly appeared very much self-centred. Besides the fact that the spectators were free to leave – some of them did – the performance was to some extent demonstrating that violence does not happen against us. It just happens. And that may already offer some appeasement.

To conclude this final chapter, I want to discuss the extent to which some contemporary shows may be defined as 'tragic performances', in opposition to 'tragedies'. To better understand this distinction, the difference between the tragic event and the tragic – as non-event – explained by Rosset, is useful. As seen previously, the tragic, for Rosset, is not an interpretation of the world. To understand his claim, one must differentiate between the tragic and the tragic event. Commonly, a tragic event refers to a situation in which a conflict occurs between individual freedom and superior forces, often resulting in death. This may refer to the situation of tragic heroes in tragedies and, by extension, to any event in the world that we may identify as 'tragic' as Marc Escola pointed out in his introduction to *Le Tragique* (2002). A violent hurricane or a deadly car crash on the motorway is thus typically defined as a tragic event. The tragic event, in this sense, emerges when individuals face something larger than themselves. These great forces can take various shapes: nature (in the case of the hurricane), gods, morals, social determinism and so on. Yet, they all have something in common: they instil a sense of fate in the observer of the tragic event. The tragic event is perceived as soon as the subject apprehends the outcome of an accident as the last stage of a structured series of unfortunate actions. By inserting meaning in a series of random actions, the idea of fate will appear. Escola argues:

> An *event* [fait divers] becomes tragic as soon as we consider it as the last term of a structure that pre-exists it [...], by putting it in relation to a transcendence external to its immediate causes [...]; to say that such an event is 'tragic', is to turn it into a sign with an uncertain content, in which chance seems to have found meaning. (2002: 12)[67]

Through the tragic event, the subject considers the outcome as retrospectively predictable. However, according to Rosset, the subject does not perceive the tragic event; he only believes that he does. In this sense, Rosset considers that the tragic event is an interpretation of the world, a human vision projected whenever the world fails to make sense and disturbs one's organized sense of reality. It is a means to comfort ourselves by putting order (destiny) where chaos manifested itself, in the way religion, science or myths already do. The tragic event is in fact intellectually created in order to flee the brutal discovery of the tragic. To experience the tragic event enables one to give spatial and temporal frames to a particularly chaotic moment; hence enabling one to rule out the possibility of facing the tragic. The tragic event is therefore created when the unpredictability of the real has been violently experienced. It addresses the frightening uncertainty of the world by claiming that what occurred is rare and extra-ordinary. Yet the tragic event is only an intellectual construction, as it remains irreconcilable with the notion of chance. Rosset explains:

> There is indeed [...] an insurmountable antinomy between notions of chance and of modification: if what exists is essentially due to chance, it means that what exists cannot be modified by any hazards, any 'events' (since no events, in the sense of something irrupting exceptionally in a field of chance, could ever happen). (2004: 23–4)[68]

Since the real, for Rosset, occurs necessarily by chance, the notion of event constitutes a contradiction. He continues: '*Nothing* can modify *nothing*. The real is precisely nothing – i.e. nothing that is stable, nothing that is constituted, nothing that is engraved' (2014: 24).[69] For Rosset, the tragic event and the tragic are antinomic. The tragic event is a projection or interpretation; the tragic, on the contrary, originates from a manifestation of the world as it appears before any interpretation. The tragic is experienced in a naked perception of the real. To perceive the tragic means, in this sense, to perceive without doubles. The tragic would thus be perceived when one feels that nothing can be changed; that one remains powerless before this superior force that is in fact not gods, not fate, but *only* indeterminism; randomness, chaos. Thus, to perceive the tragic is to perceive the 'non-event'.

In many ways, to witness a performance by some contemporary directors can lead to experience the real as non-event. To some extent, these shows manifest a different vision of representation, with a different relationship to the real. They aim to return to this very chaos, trying to unveil the spectator's perception of the world, rather than organizing it. It is true that their performances are rehearsed, and the actions on stage, anticipated. However, the stage appears as a space, inserted into the 'real world', where the tragic is discovered; the stage uncovers reality instead of covering it up. Their performances are anti-tragedies (anti-Aristotelian tragedies), in the sense that they are not representing tragic destinies. A short story developed by French writer Pascal Quignard in *La nuit sexuelle* (2007: 161–8) sheds some light on the fundamental difference between tragedies and what I have named 'tragic performances'. 'L'origine de la peinture' recounts the birth of painting, and explains it through the *desiderium* to see the absence. One started to paint when one started to be drawn towards doubles; painting is the expression of a desire to perceive what one cannot perceive. Quignard explains that the first painter was thus a young woman with a *desiderium* syndrome (161). He quotes Cicero in *Tusculum*, IV: '*Desiderium est libido videndi ejus qui non adsit*': desire is the libido to see someone who is not here (161). The young woman draws the contour of her lover, whose shadow is projected on the wall, illuminated by the flickering flame of a candle. He has been called to war; by sketching his outline, she does not express her desire for him, but rather desire for his absence. She does not desire his return; she desires this 'nothing'. 'She has the appetite for seeing the absent,' argues Quignard (162).⁷⁰ This story was first recounted by Pliny the Elder in *Naturalis Historia*, in which he refers to Callirhoe (believed to be born around 700 BCE), daughter of Greek potter Dibutades, who has decided to draw the contour of her lover's shadow with charcoal.

In fact, many paintings from the eighteenth and nineteenth centuries feature this scene: *Dibutade ou l'Origine de la peinture*, by Jean-Baptiste Regnault in 1786; *The Corinthian Maid*, by Joseph Wright of Derby in 1782–4; *Die Erfindung der Malerei*, by Eduard Daege in 1832; *L'Origine de la peinture*, by Anne-Louis Girodet-Trioson in 1829. On this painting by Suvée, Callirhoe appears to be ignoring her lover to rather focus all her attention on the drawing. She does not create a copy of the real; instead, she creates a representation, she engraves in the real an image that does not reflect a man but her own desire. A similar desire is expressed in tragedies as defined by Aristotle. Tragedies represent a certain vision of the world, organized and timeless. Like Callirhoe who flees the tragic (her lover going to war) by reinventing her own reality, tragedies flee the tragic by remodelling the real. In *Poetics*, Aristotle defines tragedy as 'a unified action, whole and complete, possessing a beginning, middle parts and an end' (1996: 38). Like the tragic event, tragedy is an organization of the real into a meaningful whole. The real is organized by the *mimesis*. Mimesis is not a pure reproduction of reality, but an organization of the world. Tragedies may therefore be seen as an attempt to put order into a chaotic world; to organize the tragic as I described it. On the contrary, tragic performances aim to display this initial chaos. In this sense, the spectators witnessing tragic performances become the tragic heroes: it is them who are now facing the tragic. It is them who are now experiencing theatre as a philosophical and existential practice. As Nietzsche noted, real tragedies (that I termed tragic performances) are not Aristotelian. The tragic in

**Figure 1** Joseph-Benoît Suvée, *The Invention of the Art of Drawing* (1791)

theatre no longer translates into a story: 'The word tragic which, after its very laborious enunciation, "produces" silence. Nothing to say at the end, more than the power of not saying anything. Empty sky, [. . .] or rather, emptied sky,'[71] states Romeo Castellucci in *Les dix mots de Romeo Castellucci* (Darge 2015a). Tragic performances aim to empty the stage from representations. Spectators are not simply invited to witness the tragic; they are invited to *experience* it. Some lucky spectators may even experience a catharsis *of* the tragic.

Spectatorship becomes a sea of possibilities.

# Conclusion

'If reality is inconceivable, then we must forge inconceivable concepts,'[1] argues Hegel (Escola 2002: 23). By exploring shows from a few contemporary directors, along with several concepts developed by Clément Rosset, Gilles Deleuze, Giorgio Agamben and Viktor Shklovsky, I hope I have raised interest in understanding theatre as a philosophical practice for us, spectators. Shows by contemporary artists can sometimes leave us startled, frustrated, having this strange feeling that we missed out, that we did not release the full potential of what was being done in front of us. This is not to say that the shows explored in this book are all brilliant and the directors are all geniuses. It is up to you, reader, to decide what you make of these performances and of these theatre makers. The ambition, here, was instead to discuss the possibilities of spectatorship, and to demonstrate how exciting and rewarding being a free spectator can be. By a free spectator, I mean a spectator who is aware of perceptual opportunities. This book is certainly not aiming to tell you how to perceive theatre; it only explains that you *can* perceive. In France, in particular, politicians have educated many audiences to have a certain understanding of theatre and its social purpose. Therefore, re-affirming this simple truth (there are as many perceptions as they are spectators) seems important.

The directors mentioned here use strategies to defeat their spectators' expectations and processes of recognition in order to make them face the real. Perhaps it is by better knowing about these ambitions that we may more willingly open our field of perception when coming to such performances. To unlearn, we probably need to know ahead of time that we are indeed invited to unlearn, and that we can. By exploring how our perception of the stage works, we may understand how to perceive more freely. As quoted in the introduction, Egginton concluded his essay *How the World Became a Stage* by stating that 'knowing how our spatiality works [. . .] can facilitate the effort to work effectively within it, and, if so desired, to effectuate change' (2003: 168). I hope this book has offered a new set of keys to understand our perception of the real and of the tragic in contemporary theatre.

Chapter 1 explored debates around contemporary theatre in France and questioned why the country is both welcoming of innovative forms and a place of radical rejections and miscomprehensions between the audience and the artists. The factors are political, cultural and situational. These shows are often funded with public money. A long tradition of French cultural policy has undoubtedly empowered French audiences. Theatre has been used, from the 1930s onwards, to circulate the French repertoire and to educate citizens. These ambitious cultural policies have shaped expectations on what kind of plays should be funded. It became apparent, in 2005 in Avignon, that innovative theatre does not make the cut. Other reasons have been explored, such as the relationship of power between the stage and the audience, and the fact that the theatres where these shows are performed are often used for more traditional forms. Spectators are invited to experience strong (and sometimes physical) emotions while sitting quietly and obediently in dark theatres. It is important to note, however, that all directors aim to shock their audience. Vienne, for instance, has explained that she does not create her shows to shock, but to serve the community. That does not prevent her productions from shocking, but it does at least clarify that not all directors are deliberately trying to put their audience in an uncomfortable position.

To better understand the aesthetics on stage that fuel frustration, Chapter 2 has explored the various strategies that aim to challenge the spectators' perception and make them experience the real: the world as it appears to them. Everyday perception is based on processes of recognition, thus having these processes challenged can be very particularly uneasy. The experience of a non-recognition is necessarily disturbing – strategies are used on stage to trigger it, such as the duration of an action until the exhaustion of its signs, the showing of the obscene on stage, the use of puppets, the mixing of representations that come from radically different registers and the presence of children and animals. These strategies have been analysed alongside philosophical concepts, such as Deleuze's concept of repetition, Shklovsky's concept of defamiliarization and States's phenomenological eye. Clear examples from various productions were given to exemplify the arguments. Overall, this chapter has offered alternative approaches to contemporary theatre that are first and foremost spectator focused.

To offer an alternative discourse that considers both audiences' and directors' frustrations, Chapter 3 has celebrated spectatorship as a philosophical practice. These productions offer the opportunity to explore and question our everyday perception of the world. They can be the opportunity for us to explore our perception as a playground, where we experience an encounter with the world. I redefined the experience of the real as an experience of the tragic. Following Rosset's philosophy, these two kinds of perception are indeed significantly alike insofar as they both aim to get rid of human interpretations projected onto the world. However, the tragic does display something unique: it shows a chaotic world, undetermined and cruel. While the real, in Rosset's philosophy, refers more to an approach to the world free from any intellectual interpretations, the tragic qualifies a view of the world as being indifferent to us, upon which humans have absolutely no control. It seems, in this sense, that the perception of the tragic is a consequence of the perception of the real. The perception of the tragic (as a philosophical concept) in theatrical spectatorship has not been widely discussed. Antonin Artaud is perhaps one of the few who did explore this matter. I therefore ended the reflection by revisiting these shows as tragic performances and by considering the spectators themselves to be the tragic heroes. These shows often do not offer an experience *of* the real but an experience *in* the real. In tragic performances, spectators are not invited to witness the tragic; they are invited to experience it. By asking the subject to abandon any forms of interpretation, the tragic offers a relatively ineffable perception that can lead to various emotions, from fear to appeasement. Adopting such a perception is not obvious;

in his reflections on the tragic Max Scheler claims that some people are 'blind, or half blind' to the tragic (1965: 3; 18). The tragic aims to 'return' to a naked perception, yet this perception is paradoxically far from being naturally experienced. Is the perception of the tragic a perception truly free from cultural representations, or is it just a peculiar intellectual projection? The question remains open and could be subject to further work.

In *Postdramatic Theatre*, Lehmann writes that 'even spectators who are convinced of the artistic integrity and the quality of such theatre often lack the conceptual tools to articulate their perception' (2006: 19). New conceptual tools can be found, and I have offered a few. As you will have seen, these are my own tools, which I developed over the years to better appreciate my experience as a contemporary spectator. I hope you found them inspiring; we all have the ability to come up with our own framework. But some experiences should probably be left to the unintelligible.

# Notes

## Preface

1 'Je connais un état hors de l'esprit, de la conscience, de l'être, et qui n'a plus ni paroles ni lettres, mais où l'on entre par les cris et par les coups. Et ce ne sont plus des sons ou des sens qui sortent, plus des paroles, mais des corps.' Unless otherwise indicated, all translations from the French in the text are from me. All original quotes are in endnotes for consultation.

## Introduction

1 'La réalité première de l'objet scénique est d'abord celle que lui donne le système de la scène, puisqu'elle lui donne sens' (Kowzan 1992).
2 In some ways, this is similar to what Sartre said in *L'être et le Néant*: 'S'il y a un Autre, quel qu'il soit, où qu'il soit, quels que soient ses rapports avec moi... J'ai un dehors, j'ai une nature; ma chute originelle c'est l'existence de l'autre' (Sartre 1943: 321). However, I will not pursue this further as my approach remains rather different. Sartre was mainly referring to other human beings (others' perceptions frustrating the subject's one, thus the famous quote 'L'enfer c'est les autres'), and his perspective was very much related to the question of human liberty and free will, which are themes that are not directly explored in this book.
3 'est un théâtre qui exige un évènement scénique qui serait, à tel point, [...] pure présentification du théâtre qu'il effacerait toute idée de reproduction, de répétition du réel'.
4 '[C'est] l'idée que le théâtre doit abolir la représentation et devenir une monstration'.
5 In her inspiring book *Le fantôme ou le théâtre qui doute* (1997), Monique Borie, in her own way, explores these paradoxes. She argues, for instance, that presence on stage is like a ghost: by seeing it, one paradoxically sees its absence.

6 'Depuis Bob Wilson, Pina Bausch et Kantor, il n'y a plus à faire ces catégories. Je m'étonne qu'en 2021 on se pose encore cette question'.
7 '*C'est du réel contre la réalité.* [...]C'est d'abord une énergie inconnue, une énergie de l'inconnu'
8 To see some pictures, visit: https://www.festival-automne.com/en/edition-2015/romeo-castellucci-le-metope-del-partenone.
9 I keep the literal English translation of 'double' (*Le Réel et son double* has been translated by Chris Turner into *The Real and Its Double*).
10 Some authors have, of course, developed theories of the real that remain more dominant than Rosset's. For instance, Žižek and Lacan argue that the real has nothing to do with objective empirical reality (which is similar to Rosset's approach). However, for Rosset, and contrary to Lacan and Žižek, the real is strictly non-representational, even though it cannot be experienced without a complex entanglement between its apparition and its representation. This study choses to focus on Rosset's philosophy mainly because of its playful approach to experiences, as explained further in the introduction.
11 'C'est comme cela, c'est tout, c'est incroyable mais cela est et il n'y a rien à chercher d'autre'.
12 As explained by Carole Talon-Hugon in *Avignon 2005, Le conflit des héritages*, and as described in an article for *Le Monde*, by Rosita Boisseau. See https://www.lemonde.fr/culture/article/2005/07/09/l-histoire-des-larmes-le-corps-selon-jan-fabre-laisse-avignon-perplexe_671258_3246.html.
13 'là où il y a un chemin, on peut toujours trouver une volonté' (Rosset 2004: 11). This seems to be a deliberate and inversion of the English idiom 'where there is a will there is a way'.
14 For more details on this, see 'recognition and the image of thought' in the great book by Daniel Koczy, *Beckett, Deleuze and Performance, A Thousand Failures and A Thousand Inventions*.
15 Yet, in *La philosophie tragique*, his very first essay, Rosset tends to refer to the tragic as 'la vraie connaissance' while personifying it into the ultimate truth; 'Vous saurez enfin, et pour toujours, cette vérité, ce mystère, cette joie : tout est mensonge; seul existe, seul vaut, seul vit, le Tragique!'; 'le tragique est ce qui, d'aucune manière que ce soit, ne peut être surmonté, mais qui ne peut être qu'adoré'. This is problematic insofar as he will argue later that the world cannot ever be objectively perceived.

16  It would be interesting to explore to what extent this relates to instincts. Something is *known* through the senses with the instinct of survival for instance.
17  See Catherine Bouko in *Théâtre et reception, le spectateur postdramatique*: 'Les horizons d'attente du spectateur sont questionnés: habitués à des signes qui renvoient vers le monde extrascénique, il se trouve confronté à des formes mystérieuses qui ne renvoient à rien d'autre qu'à elles-mêmes. Les codes dramatiques qu'il maitrise ne permettent pas au spectateur d'aborder ce langage scénique. Il est alors contraint de les abandonner et de s'ouvrir à d'autres modes de perception'.
18  It is interesting to note, however, that during a meeting in 2012 with Christian Schiaretti, former director of the TNP (public theatre in Villeurbanne), he argued that '90% of [his] audience is made of teachers, students, and retirees'.
19  This comparison is also made by Daniel Johnston in *Theatre and Phenomenology: Manual Philosophy*.

# Chapter I

1  'Pour tous, le festival de 2005 a marqué une rupture avec la tradition fondée par Jean Vilar. La cour d'honneur n'a pas accueilli comme spectacle emblématique la représentation d'un grand texte, ancien ou contemporain, œuvre d'un grand auteur, réalisé par un grand metteur en scène'
2  'pas de théâtre cette année à Avignon'
3  'Le théâtre n'existe pas, il y a des théâtres, et je cherche le mien'
4  Among the most famous examples is la querelle des Anciens et des Modernes that took place throughout the seventeenth century and perdured until Romanticism. This quarrel questioned the common assumption that writers had to imitate ancient authors (and addressed literature as well as theatre). Another famous example is la bataille d'Hernani, which erupted in 1830, following performances of Hugo's innovative play Hernani at the Comédie-Française. Two theatrical generations – one inspired by Classicism, the other by Romantism – passionately fought against each other then

5 'Mais qu'est-ce qu'on vous a fait? Pourquoi vous nous faites souffrir comme ça depuis une heure et demie?' The official festival is named the 'in' and is organized and funded by various public institutions, such as the French state and the city of Avignon. Only shows from the 'in' can perform in the Cour d'honneur of the Palais des Papes. The 'off' is composed by self-funded theatre companies (although some of them receive public funding) that perform in all sorts of places (streets, private theatres, schools, etc.).
6 'Devenue cri de ralliement des opposants, cette formule dit le refus et l'incompréhension d'une expérience esthétique qui, selon ses promoteurs, devrait être celle de la souffrance'
7 'sous le choc mais passif, face à un spectacle asséné, sans respiration ni ouverture à la réflexion'
8 'subi[ssaient] des électrochocs à jet continu'
9 'un public s'estimant, sans doute à tort, puni et innocent'
10 'celui de la provocation et du mépris'
11 'un mensonge institutionnalisé, revendiqué et imposé cyniquement à un public finalement pris en otage par ces véritables attentats à la vérité, à l'intelligence, à la modestie, à l'humilité, à la dignité tout simplement'
12 'Un seul spectateur se lève en cours de représentation et hurle "c'est nul à chier" avant de partir. Qu'est-ce qui fait que quelqu'un se sente aussi important, aussi sûr de lui pour s'adresser dans l'instant même à toute une audience?'
13 'Sur place, on eut surtout l'impression d'un grand point d'interrogation devant les spectacles de Jan Fabre, artiste invité, Castellucci, Py, Peyret, Decorte, Abramovic'
14 'un débat qui n'a pas lieu d'être'
15 's'abimer[ont] dans la contemplation de ses *qualia*. Cela signifie qu['ils seront] *indifférents à l'objet représenté*'
16 'Il ne fait pas de doute que Jan Fabre inonde de véritable sang le plateau de la scène de Je suis sang, et que les acteurs urinent vraiment dans Histoire des larmes. Ces spectacles développent donc des stratégies d'intéressement qui contreviennent à l'impératif kantien de désintéressement. [...] L'opposition entre les camps est donc nette : c'est celle de la distanciation contre l'implication, du désintéressement contre la participation empathique, des émotions esthétiques contre les émotions de la vie.'

17 'La beauté plastique ne masque pas le déficit de sens'
18 'faibles sur le plan artistique [...] sans méditation et sans véritable réflexion'
19 'l'esthétique formelle finissait par lasse[r]'
20 'Si on prend ce mot-là, "faire une expérience", on a une sorte de pivot, qui nous permet de mettre ensemble des choses qui ne peuvent pas être mises ensemble. Ce festival a été d'une incroyable densité, on ne peut pas repérer une école, une tendance...'
21 'Pourquoi après tout, le drame serait-il nécessairement à la base du théâtre ?'
22 This opposition has often been embodied by two directors' vision: Artaud's and Brecht's.
23 See the report of the meeting in *Le Cas Avignon*, 17–41.
24 There is some small history of this in the theatre; for instance, Ibsen providing an alternative ending to *A Doll's House* where Nora stays.
25 'Les gens qui ne comprennent pas croient qu'on les provoque. Rien n'a changé depuis 25 ans que je travaille. C'est triste; la stupidité est toujours prête à surgir'
26 'plus une fonction d'intermédiaire entre le public et le travail, qu'une fonction de destruction du travail en déclarant que c'est "raté"'
27 'l'art sans peuple, autiste et heureux de l'être'
28 The recent attacks against Fabre during the #Metoo movement made his persona even more ambiguous in the eye of the public. Fabre's creative process has been strongly criticized. Some of his actors (mainly actresses) have accused him of sexual harassment during rehearsals.
29 'le guide de lui-même et déambulant devant ses productions pour montrer à un cercle de groupies tétanisées l'exposition qui montre tout ce qu'un génie peut montrer des abîmes de sa personnalité, pas grand-chose'
30 'une imposture boursouflée de son importance'
31 I am referring to the spectator who expressed his discontent during *Frère&Soeur* by Monnier (as mentioned previously).
32 See Badiou (2013) and Badiou (2014).
33 'Je suis donc arrivé quelque peu inquiet, voire convaincu qu'il s'agissait d'une provocation stérile [...] C'était magnifique. J'ai dû m'avouer vaincu : il faut savoir s'incliner devant la puissance du théâtre. J'étais venu avec des idées toutes faites, des opinions mal fondées, qui ont été vaincues et annulées par la représentation.'

34 'Quand je lis que le théâtre c'est le théâtre grec, que ça a toujours été comme ça, un texte, des acteurs, j'ai envie de rappeler qu'il y a eu aussi la commedia dell'arte, le kabuki, pleins de formes différentes... Cette manière qu'on a en France [...] de faire preuve globalement d'une paresse intellectuelle, me fait un peu honte. Il y a un manque de générosité dans la compréhension des formes et surtout lorsqu'elles arrivent de façon déroutante et qu'elles ne sont pas 'clés en main.'

35 See for instance Ubersfeld (1996a and 1996b).

36 Two authors appeared particularly open to discuss the spectator's emotional response to the actions on stage: Luk Van Den Dries, in *Corpus*, L'Arche, 2005, on Jan Fabre's theatre; and Nicholas Ridout and Joe Kelleher in *The Theatre of Societas Raffaello Sanzio*, Routledge, 2007, on Romeo Castellucci's theatre.

37 'un art officiel qui s'offre un peu de scandale avec beaucoup de subventions'

38 'mensonge institutionalisé'

39 'Ces abstraites brutalités, ces cruautés LVMH disent au mieux la violence du crack et du gang, mais nullement les choses de la Cité, disons le chômage, l'identité, la religion, la frontière'

40 'antinomique du social'

41 'Reste une question. Si l'on cesse de prendre pour une évidence l'idée d'un impact social des arts, au nom de quelles vertus l'Etat doit-il garantir les conditions économiques de leur épanouissement ? Si l'on ne se contente pas de songer au bénéfice économique que la présence des arts procure aux centres urbains en attirant les entreprises et les activités dont les personnels sont sensibles à leurs agréments, qu'est-ce qui justifie le soutien public de la vie artistique ?'

42 'Le rôle de l'Etat dans la protection du théâtre doit être réformé et amplifié. Il ne faut certes pas supprimer la Comédie-Française. Il faut la dédoubler : avoir d'un côté un théâtre purement consacré au répertoire, un théâtre-musée, administré avec toute l'autorité et la continuité nécessaires, par un homme que cette tâche passionne [...] d'un autre côté, un théâtre national réservé à la création d'œuvres nouvelles, de haute littérature.'

43 'Finalement, les Centres dramatiques nationaux apparaissent comme l'outil complément à un apprentissage livresque du théâtre [...] Faire

connaître à un public neuf des pièces reconnues : telle est bien l'ambition de la décentralisation. De ce point de vue, la décentralisation théâtrale contribue à une appropriation du patrimoine culturel français, au même titre que l'enseignement des collèges et des lycées qui, parallèlement, se développe massivement.'

44 'Le sens est donné par l'Etat: priorité aux œuvres du patrimoine national d'abord, étranger ensuite. La marge de manœuvre apparaît par conséquent comme très limitée'

45 'un quart au plus pourront être des œuvres contemporaines à créer et une au moins sera une œuvre française classique. Les œuvres dramatiques françaises constituent les deux tiers du répertoire'

46 '[Il faut présenter] des spectacles dramatiques de langue française, et en particulier les oeuvres classiques du répertoire français'

47 'mission ne présente aucune présentation d'auteurs contemporains, encore moins de créations'

48 It may include, for instance, plays by Molière, Racine, Marivaux, Beaumarchais, Corneille, Musset or Shakespeare.

49 'la politique culturelle n'est plus, vive le soutien public à l'économie de la vie artistique!'

50 'intérêt public [et de] s'efforcer de diffuser des œuvres théâtrales de haut niveau [...] rechercher l'audience d'un vaste public et la conquête de nouveaux spectateurs' in 'Arrêté du 23 février 1995 fixant le contrat type de décentralisation dramatique', see: https://www.legifrance.gouv.fr/affichTexte.do?cidTexte=JORFTEXT000000350888&categorieLien=id.

51 'Grâce à ces aides massives, le théâtre public a largement supplanté le théâtre privé, dont les établissements sont concentrés à Paris'

52 Here is, for instance, the requirement to get funding from the DRAC (*Direction régionale des affaires culturelles*): 'Les Directions Régionales des Affaires Culturelles (DRAC) accordent cette aide dans le but de distinguer un *projet de création* et de soutenir une *prise de risque* de la part de jeunes artistes ou de donner les moyens à une équipe ou à un artiste confirmé d'entreprendre une production *ambitieuse* dans le domaine de l'écriture dramatique, du cirque, des arts de la rue, de la marionnette ou de la danse'. My italics.

53 'On reprocha l'absence de textes ; à quoi l'on rétorqua qu'il y en avait pourtant. On regretta le temps heureux des classiques ; à quoi l'on

répondit que ce genre de regrets témoignait d'un conservatisme immobile. Le Figaro fit de Jean Vilar, fondateur en 1947 du festival d'Avignon, son égérie, cinquante ans après avoir mené, sans relâche, une bataille pour le faire trébucher.'

54 'grandir et se moderniser'
55 'À Montpellier, les gens aimaient avoir leur petit théâtre de province, leurs œuvres classiques qui les rassuraient, même s'ils s'endormaient dans leur fauteuil'
56 'J'ai pensé que la société de cette ville serait plus réceptive. Je propose un théâtre contemporain mais le public a été plus habitué à Molière, à Shakespeare. Je crois que c'est une belle mission, mais que je ne vais pas continuer'
57 'Qu'est-il advenu du dialogue, où sont passés les échanges d'idées et la collaboration avec les partenaires qui soutiennent ce lieu public?'
58 'Je ne suis pas gêné par les langues, même si l'ouverture vers l'Espagne et le Portugal me paraît limitée et un peu exclusive, mais je regrette qu'en tant que grand théâtre de province, on n'ait plus aucun répertoire, comme dans toutes les autres grandes villes'
59 'C'est d'abord [l'expérience] d'une immobilisation. S'asseoir au théâtre, c'est se trouver en état d'impossibilité de mouvement, pendant une durée assez longue, puisque l'on ne peut pas se déplacer, faire de bruit, et surtout, puisqu'il est totalement interdit de parler avec son entourage, contrairement à ce qui se passe par exemple devant un écran de télévision, dont on a beaucoup dit que c'était un inducteur de passivité, mais du point de vue strictement comportemental c'est faux: devant la vidéo on bouge et on parle. Cette situation de neutralisation motrice est contraire aussi aux pratiques spontanées des publics populaires, des adolescents, des enfants: nous en avons tous souffert.'
60 'Les comédiens et joueurs de toute sorte qui ont pris d'assaut les théâtres, mais par l'entrée des artistes, sont très exactement des expérimentateurs contemporains de nouvelles figures de liberté. Ce sont des acteurs du monde d'aujourd'hui. Les spectateurs, en revanche, qui font sagement la queue devant les guichets de location, sont à mon avis dans une situation plus critique. Il me semble que les choix esthétiques et politiques qui régissent les théâtres contemporains ne pourront pas longtemps éviter de se déterminer par rapport à ce profond divorce.'

61 'd'un côté quelqu'un qui agit, de l'autre, quelqu'un qui regarde. A partir de là, se dégage un troisième espace qui sépare la tribune du plateau, tel un voile transparent, tendu entre les deux côtés et qu'on ne peut percer'
62 Annabelle Chambon, during a private conversation in Lyon, in November 2017. She was only referring to his shows; this must be distinguished from his performance art.

# Chapter II

1 'Penser, seulement penser, sans utiliser. […] Penser, c'est désirer le nouveau'
2 See the full interview here (in French): https://www.youtube.com/watch?v=wiqTr2-ebxQ
3 'Wilson, Bausch et Kantor ont permis un développement de notre acuité perceptive et ont permis des déplacements perceptifs qui font qu'on apprend à entendre des choses qu'on nous a désappris à entendre, qu'on nous apprend à voir des choses qu'on nous a désappris à regarder […] J'essaye de déplier dans l'espace l'expérience du temps. Je ne sais pas comment décrire cette langue-là, mais c'est une dissection de la perception. Révéler la construction culturelle de la perception'
4 'Le théâtre n'est pas quelque chose qu'il faut reconnaître. "Moi-je-vais-au-théâtre-pour-reconnaître-Shakespeare-mes-études-ce-que-j'ai-fait": ce n'est pas comme ça. C'est un voyage dans l'inconnu, vers l'inconnu. On ne peut pas calculer ces conjonctions des éléments du possible.'
5 'Ils viennent pour reconnaître ce qu'ils connaissent déjà et pour être intellectuellement consolés. Cela devrait s'arrêter avec l'école où l'on reconnaît ce qu'on désire voir. Ce type de consolation produit de l'inertie, un marécage d'eaux mortes pour la pensée, alors que l'expérience théâtrale doit être un voyage, un chemin vers l'inconnu. C'est une aventure.'
6 'La distinction que vous venez de faire entre ces deux attitudes au théâtre se retrouve également dans le travail des critiques dramatiques. Il y a ceux qui acceptent de mettre des mots sur l'inconnu, et ceux qui refusent paresseusement, en dénonçant les "élucubrations faussement avant-gardistes, vraiment prétentieuses et stupides" […]. De tels jugements à

l'emporte-pièce expriment la peur de ne pas reconnaître et d'identifier ce que l'on voit – d'où la référence (sans fondement) aux avant-gardes.'

7  'Il y a là une médiocrité scandaleuse qui rend les gens paresseux'
8  'la beauté plastique ne masque pas le déficit de sens'
9  'L'Histoire des larmes se piège parfois dans son jeu d'accessoires pour finir par s'en servir comme alibi. La beauté plastique ne suffit pas toujours à muscler le sens d'une image, aussi saisissante soit-elle. [. . .] Même si la célébration du corps dans sa crudité et sa vérité est évidemment au cœur de la pièce, son propos explose au point de se perdre de vue.'
10 'votre interprétation doit être plus ludique, comme lors d'une improvisation, rapide et légère. Sinon les gens croiront que nous voulons faire passer un message intellectuel et leur asséner des vérités'
11 'Les horizons d'attente du spectateur sont questionnés: habitués à des signes qui renvoient vers le monde extrascénique, il se trouve confronté à des formes mystérieuses qui ne renvoient à rien d'autre qu'à elles-mêmes. Les codes dramatiques qu'il maitrise ne permettent pas au spectateur d'aborder ce langage scénique. Il est alors contraint de les abandonner et de s'ouvrir à d'autres modes de perception.'
12 'Il a un effet ensorcelant, il absorbe la perception et nous force à nous fondre dans l'image'
13 This is also where Artaud's theories encounter their own limits: even tough he was advocating for a a-cultural theatre, his considerations are mainly related to Western theatre and are therefore, partly cultural considerations.
14 'Je connais un état hors de l'esprit, de la conscience, de l'être, et qui n'a plus ni paroles ni lettres, mais où l'on entre par les cris et par les coups. Et ce ne sont plus des sons ou des sens qui sortent, plus des paroles, mais des corps'
15 The drunk man is also an important figure in *Le Réel, traité de l'idiotie*, by Clément Rosset, as he is the man who can see the real without doubles, who experiences a certain lucidity, unreachable to others.
16 See http://www.ccnr.fr/p/fr/jan-fabre-teaching.
17 'Je ne fais pas un spectacle sur l'amour. Mais l'amour est important durant le processus de création. Mes meilleurs spectacles sont l'ouvrage d'acteurs qui s'aimaient'
18 'Le son de son corps qui s'écrase sur un plancher en bois n'est ni plus ni moins celui d'un corps quelconque qui s'écrase sur un plancher en bois'

19 'le corps tout entier doit se sentir ému et convaincu par tout ce qui s'agite autour de lui'
20 'plus de ralentir, c'est d'être dans le réel'
21 'Une telle coïncidence entre le réel et sa représentation a pour conséquence de priver l'intéressé du temps généralement nécessaire à la prise en considération de ce qui lui arrive: d'où une situation d'urgence qui refuse tout délai et interdit toute délibération.'
22 'La conscience tend à envisager le corps fatalement comme un résidu obscène, ob-scaena, c'est-à-dire en marge de la scène comme lieu d'observation. Peut-être que le corps doit-il, dans la vie quotidienne, demeurer à l'écart de l'espace de la conscience. Le théâtre est là justement pour faire de cette régularité une exception, pour réussir à la rendre problématique.'
23 The interview can be found here: https://youtu.be/OHGs4ZAA6f0?t=207
24 'La trahison des images'
25 'C'est l'homme qu'il faut maintenant chasser du théâtre: son insupportable perpétuel penchant à l'autoportrait. Au théâtre il faut être des animaux. Interroger en l'écartelant dans l'espace, non notre humanité – mais notre pantinitude. Voir la parole sortir en volute des bouches de bois et s'en étonner. S'étonner de ce ruban matériel qu'on souffle.'
26 'Je suis un véritable animaliste parce que je ne confonds pas les hommes avec les animaux. Je ne leur prête pas de sentiments semblables aux miens ni un visage expressif comme le mien. Je ne leur donne pas de nom. Je ne crois pas aux larmes humaines de Dumbo. […] Avoir un animal sur scène, c'est comme une vengeance parce que l'animal revient vivant, muet, sans aucune expression humaine; il est là, splendide, occupant le centre des planches; mais un animal sur scène c'est aussi une sorte de prière sans parole, une forme de pardon.'
27 'c'est la froide indifférence qui est de toute beauté'
28 'become 'seigneur[s] de la scène'
29 'L'animal est plus impressionnant d'envergure parce qu'il ne tente justement rien, parce qu'il respecte tout à fait et malgré lui, l'aliénation de la scène'
30 'L'animal entre en scène pour apporter un peu de ce qui lui appartient: un peu de ce monde, de cette réalité et de ce temps'
31 'l'enfance, dans le sens d' "en-fance", c'est-à-dire de condition de celui qui se trouve en dehors du langage'

## Chapter III

1. See for instance the article by John O'Mahony in *The Guardian*, 19 April 2011, https://www.theguardian.com/stage/2011/apr/19/romeo-castellucci-concept-face-son and the article by Luk Van Den Dries, 'Artaud and Fabre', 2011, https://www.academia.edu/31110681/Artaud_and_Fabre_2011.
2. 'Le corps n'est plus une chair habitée par l'esprit, mais une simple ossature. […] les mouvements mécaniques, répétés en série, de formes se résumant à un squelette. Aucune individualité ne se dégage de ces mouvements. […] Aucun moi n'habite encore ce corps, seule subsiste l'expérience du vide de l'ossature.'
3. 'un mécanisme figé', 'un temps immobile'
4. 'l'on se donne la vie humaine comme une grande ligne entre deux extrémités. L'une est à gauche, l'autre est à droite. C'est un mythe de symétrie, un mythe spatial, de même que la pendule est entre les deux candélabres dans une garniture de cheminée. Mais la vie, c'est le temps. Le temps ne peut pas être étalé dans l'espace. […] le passé n'est pas un futur à l'envers ou le futur un passé à l'endroit. Le passé et le futur ne sont pas d'un côté et de l'autre du présent. Je vis dans un présent continuel. Gare aux mythes de symétrie!'
5. 'the *passage* entre l'état vivant et l'état mort'
6. 'cru, non digéré, indigeste'
7. 'lorsque la réalité se présente de manière visiblement incohérente et désordonnée, à l'état de pure et arbitraire contiguïté'
8. 'Philosophes tragiques, dont le but était de dissoudre l'ordre apparent pour retrouver le chaos enterré par Anaxagore […] La philosophie devient ainsi un acte destructeur et catastrophique: la pensée ici en œuvre a pour propos de défaire, de détruire, de dissoudre – de manière générale, de priver l'homme de tout ce dont celui-ci s'est intellectuellement muni à titre de provision et de remède en cas de malheur. Tout comme le vaisseau par lequel Antonin Artaud, au début du Théâtre et son double, symbolise le théâtre, elle apporte aux hommes non la guérison, mais la peste.'
9. 'non, l'amour humain n'est pas, la grandeur humaine n'est pas […] L'homme tragique se découvre soudain sans amour, sans grandeur et sans vie: et voilà la situation dont il ne pourra jamais donner d'interprétation,

devant laquelle il aura perpétuellement l'étonnement, la surprise de l'enfant à qui, pour la première fois, on a refusé un jouet. Si sa stupéfaction cesse, il n'est plus tragique.'

10 'L'homme de la croyance préfère vider les tombeaux de leurs chairs pourrissantes, désespérément informes, pour les remplir d'images corporelles, sublimes, épurées, faites pour conforter et informer – c'est-à-dire fixer- nos émotions, nos craintes et nos désirs.'

11 'La tragédie s'accompagne souvent d'une transgression, qui est une manière de couper les liens; mais aussi une façon de montrer, par la même occasion, un détachement – au sens plein- vis-à-vis du monde. Le monde n'importe plus [...]. Il n'est pas méprisable; il devient indifférent.'

12 Szondi compares the two principles Dionysian and Apollonian developed by Nietzsche to the concepts of Will and Representation as discussed by Schopenhauer.

13 'L'animal en scène se trouve pleinement à son aise, parce qu'il n'est pas perfectible. Ce dont il est sûr, c'est de son propre corps; il n'est pas sûr, en revanche, de toute l'étrangeté de l'atmosphère qui l'entoure. [...] L'indifférence, oui. C'est la froide indifférence qui est de toute vraie beauté.'

14 'Le problème est d'être pèlerin dans la matière. La matière est l'ultime réalité. [...] C'est, donc, un théâtre des éléments. Les éléments ne sont que ce qu'il y a de plus purement communicable, comme la plus petite communication possible. C'est ce qui m'intéresse: communiquer le moins possible. Et le plus petit degré de communication possible se trouve dans la surface de la matière. Dans ce sens-là, et paradoxalement, c'est un théâtre superficiel, fait de surface, parce que c'est un théâtre qui recherche l'émotion.'

15 'Je suis définitivement en dehors de l'éthique; je suis dans un no man's land, dans la condition, errante, erronée, de celui qui vient à la recherche d'une chose dont, en réalité, il ne sait rien: ni le nom ni l'entité [...] Une forme est une forme seulement si c'est avec indifférence qu'elle traverse notre humanité. Une forme est une forme seulement si son inhumanité émeut notre humanité.'

16 'Quand tu es devant une œuvre d'art, tu as la sensation d'être regardé par l'œuvre et pas le contraire. Ton regard ne se pose pas sur un objet, tu deviens plutôt l'objet de l'œuvre. Tu as la sensation d'être nu, découvert,

comme un voleur, tu te sens sans protection, touché au plus profond de ton intimité. Tu es soudain dans l'œuvre et pas devant. J'ai éprouvé cette sensation devant les Rothko de la Tate, devant Mulholland Drive de David Lynch, d'être dépouillé, écorché. Tu es dans la condition de l'animal débusqué au fond de sa tanière.'

17  'Il y a donc toute une économie du regard, une circulation, un courant du regard, qui est capable, je crois, de transporter le spectateur sur le plateau. [...] On est vraiment – littéralement- transporté dans la représentation: on est là.'

18  To some extent, Sartre describes shame in a similar way in *L'Etre et le Néant*. However, he mainly relates it to the sudden visualization of other humans' judgement, whereas the nature of the shame described here does not involve the acknowledgement of others.

19  'Harmonie + Dissonance = Accord tragique'

20  'langage pré-alphabétique'

21  'antinomique du social'

22  'Je voudrais réagir à une remarque de George Banu selon laquelle ces pièces nous renverraient à notre solitude. J'ai souvent pensé ces derniers jours aux tableaux de Rothko, de Fautrier, de Bacon, à une solitude primordiale. Du coup, ça remettrait en cause une idée assez convenue sur le théâtre qui devrait créer de la communauté'

23  'Nous, artistes, ne sommes pas contre quelque chose (le groupe...) mais répondons à un besoin intérieur de nous adresser directement à l'individu. Cela appelle une autre dramaturgie, d'autres images, d'autres états ou sensations, et c'est pourquoi les réactions actuelles correspondent à une incompréhension de cela'

24  Toute la valeur de l'œuvre provient de cette force occulte, transcendante et mystérieuse'

25  I was told so during a private conversation with Cédric Charron and Annabelle Chambon, on 30 November 2017, in Lyon.

26  'Fabre observe ses acteurs et travaille avec eux comme un biologiste. Il est fasciné par la structure du corps, l'implantation des membres, le fonctionnement des organes. Sa technique de mise en scène tient de la dissection: il examine les articulations, analyse chaque mouvement jusque dans les moindres fibres. Mais il est aussi le biologiste qui veut savoir comment les êtres vivants se développent, se reproduisent et meurent. Cette évolution cyclique l'intrigue et est source intarissable d'inspiration'

27 'Les instincts sont cachés sous une épaisse couche de civilisation'
28 See the video they did together 'The Problem', 2001; https://www.youtube.com/watch?v=0kLESYLo9-s. The connections between Sloterdijk's philosophy and Fabre's theatre are made by Villeneuve-Soutoul (2013).
29 'La compréhension d'un langage oublié. Ce langage [que] nous portons tous en nous, mais [que] nous refoulons, parce qu'il contient l'anarchie de la nature. Ce langage relève d'une logique différente de notre logique de société civilisée. Ce langage est plus proche de l'essence des choses et témoigne d'empathie à l'égard de la vie. (…) C'est un langage d'intensité, d'instinct, d'intuition.'
30 In the documentary *Jan Fabre Beyond the Artist*, in *Jan Fabre, the Box*, 2015.
31 'Il s'agit d'un moment de transgression. Le corps veut pour un instant s'extraire de son exclusion. Il veut faire partie du grand courant, il veut se noyer dans une forme de continuité dans laquelle il se sent lié à l'énergie de la vie. Il veut briser toutes les barrières. L'expérience est d'une violence inouïe. On perd tout contrôle'
32 'On la voit changer. Ses yeux, son visage, son corps, ses cheveux, on les voit changer. C'est une sorte d'extase. La ligne de démarcation est très fine et il faut faire attention. Les bons acteurs, qui ont su développer leur cruauté personnelle, savent aussi comment retrouver leur équilibre à un moment donné, avant de péter les plombs. C'est évidemment un chemin difficile, tant sur le plan mental que physique'
33 'C'est difficile à décrire. […] Pour moi, c'est une sensation d'abandon complet, un état d'authenticité que l'on ne peut expliquer'
34 'Sur mes scènes, ce retour aux racines fait des acteurs, des danseurs, presque des dieux grecs. En effet, mes pièces se construisent de sorte qu'elles deviennent des structures contre lesquelles ils doivent combattre, pour perdre ou gagner. Dans ce cadre, ils sont très près de l'idée d'une tragédie grecque'
35 'Le guerrier de la beauté a peut-être assez de liberté pour comprendre qu'il n'est pas totalement libre, mais avec la liberté dont il dispose, il s'oppose à sa finitude. Il aspire à être un dieu. Le guerrier est mortel, tel est son sort. Mais il prétend aussi ne pas l'être et là est son péché. C'est l'essence de ma tragédie'

36 'Il existe une tradition complètement oubliée, effacée, surannée du théâtre occidental qui est celle du théâtre prétragique. Et elle est surannée parce que c'est un théâtre lié à la matière et à l'effroi de la matière. Il est lié plutôt à une présence ou une puissance de genre féminin, sans aucun doute. [...] L'art dans le théâtre prétragique avait ce lien privilégié avec la mère par rapport au corps engendré et au corps recomposé pour la sépulture. On sort de la sphère linguistique'

37 The English translation is from Carolina Melis, Valentina Valentini and Ric Allsopp, quoted in Ridout (2006: 111).

38 'Contre Aristote, [Walter] Benjamin pensait que la tragédie manquait la catharsis. La comédie permet cet immense éclat de rire qui va résoudre la tension nerveuse et hystérique, biologique et sociale qui s'est accumulée dans la tragédie. Ce rire permet la catharsis de la tragédie, et non dans la tragédie. C'est une libération "de" la tragédie elle-même, et non "dans" la tragédie. Cette vision est tout à fait anti-aristotélicienne.'

39 'une tension en permanence ouverte, ouverte vers l'inconnu, ouverte vers l'ouvert même. C'est l'ouverture même'

40 'Examinons, par exemple, le cas d'une mort accidentelle: je me promène dans la rue, au pied d'un immeuble en construction; un maçon fait un faux pas sur son échafaudage, tombe de 20 mètres à mes pieds et se tue. La nausée me monte à la gorge, mais tandis qu'on emporte le corps sur une civière et que je contemple la mare de sang sur laquelle on répand du sable, je m'aperçois que je suis plongé dans une horreur intellectuelle et non sous le coup d'un bouleversement physiologique'

41 'nous nous révélons pour la première fois absolument incapables de trouver une solution, de vaincre l'obstacle qui s'est dressé devant nous. Pour la première fois, nous sommes arrêtés, nous ne pouvons parvenir à continuer dans la voie sur laquelle nous étions engagés [...] Nous sommes véritablement pris au piège: impossible de chercher à reculer pour passer plus à droite ou plus à gauche, nous sommes condamnés à ne plus bouger'

42 'Ce n'est plus cet ouvrier seulement qui est mort, mais c'est tout le reste des humains, mais c'est nous-mêmes [...] Soudain, ce n'est plus une vie, c'est la vie qui meurt! Nous découvrons que la mort insurmontable d'un être humain condamne la vie d'une façon irrémédiable'

43 'l'idée de la mort [...] qui apparaît vers l'âge de quatre ans'; 'la découverte intuitive de la mort, la découverte tragique'

44 'Je sais que je mourrai, mais je ne le crois pas'
45 'Je le sais, mais je n'en suis pas intimement persuadé. Si j'en étais persuadé, tout à fait certain, je ne pourrais plus vivre'
46 'Le tragique, ce n'est pas ce cadavre que l'on emporte, c'est l'idée que ce tas de chairs sanguinolentes est le même que celui qui est tombé il y a un instant'
47 'A la fin, deux voiturettes aspirantes viennent nettoyer tout ce sang, tous ces restes de chair humaine. La vie continue. *Qu'avons-nous vu?*'
48 'Le processus iconique appelle un "temps d'arrêt" lors duquel la perception demeure au niveau de la priméité et est délivrée de toute recherche de sens. La pensée iconique est fragile et éphémère; elle ne peut être atteinte qu'en de rares instants et requiert une attitude ouverte de la part du spectateur: ce dernier doit accepter d'abandonner ses repères (dramatiques) pour aborder ce langage scénique. S'il s'oppose au flottement, il ne pourra pas atteindre ce type de réception.'
49 'dès qu'elle est intellectualisée, la pensée iconique disparaît et est relayée par le processus de dramatisation'
50 'Ce nouveau théâtre-pragma se sert des paraboles pour ses communications. […] ce qui est dit est trop intime pour l'être sur un ton journalistique et de vulgarisation. La parabole a un aspect extrêmement simplifié, ce qui explique que bon nombre de gens – scandalisés par un symbolisme aussi décadent- s'en vont dégoûtés par trop de simplicité. Ils font bien de nous mépriser, parce qu'ils s'attendent à une langue pleine de doubles sens poétiques, dont ils ont envie de déchiffrer la "complexité", grâce à leur culture humaniste. Eh bien, ici, celui qui est cultivé et celui qui ne l'est pas ont exactement les mêmes possibilités […] parce que c'est un théâtre qui transcende complètement la culture.'
51 'Le théâtre qui essaie de produire la résolution est inacceptable. Il me donne l'impression d'être encore à l'école. C'est même pire, parce que ce type de théâtre voudrait nous faire croire qu'il dit la vérité. Même Brecht est tombé dans ce travers et cette prétention dogmatiques. Il est beaucoup plus juste pour le théâtre de laisser passer une inquiétude.'
52 'asséner des vérités'
53 'Il est important de se tromper et de se méfier des solutions toutes faites. En tant que metteure en scène, je ne prétends pas être Dieu, et je ne veux pas que les spectateurs m'imaginent ainsi'.

54 'Il n'y a pas de mystère dans les choses, mais il y a un mystère des choses. Inutile de les creuser pour leur arracher un secret qui n'existe pas; c'est à leur surface, à la lisière de leur existence, qu'elles sont incompréhensibles.'

55 'Je suis dans un no man's land, dans la condition, errante, erronée, de celui qui vient à la recherche d'une chose dont, en réalité, il ne sait rien: ni le nom ni l'entité, mais seulement (et si on a vraiment beaucoup de chance) la lueur féerique de sa forme.'

56 'Je suis un chasseur de formes. [...] La sensation, face à chaque découverte d'une forme, est une vague, une secousse [...]. Une forme est une forme seulement si c'est avec indifférence qu'elle traverse notre humanité. Une forme est une forme seulement si son inhumanité émeut notre humanité.'

57 'non, l'amour humain n'est pas, la grandeur humaine n'est pas, la vie – entendons la vie telle que nous ne pouvons manquer de l'imaginer lorsque nous sommes joyeux, la vie toujours existante et toujours jeune – la vie *n'est pas*'

58 'le tragique, c'est d'abord ce qui nous permet de vivre, ce qui est le plus chevillé au corps de l'homme, c'est l'instinct de vie par excellence, puisque aussi bien, sans tragique, nous ne pourrions pas vivre: nous n'estimerons pas qu'il vaut la peine de vivre, si la voie tragique nous était bouchée.'

59 'a désappris de marcher et de parler et est sur le point de s'envoler à travers les airs, en dansant'

60 'En tant qu'être humain je suis déjà mort, socialement mort depuis des années. C'est le souffle de mon œuvre qui me fait vivre. Je vois mon œuvre artistique comme une préparation à la mort. Je vois la mort comme un champ d'énergie positive. En acceptant la mort et en lui laissant une place centrale, vous voyiez la vie différemment.'

61 'c'est une grâce de l'instant, qui n'est pas divine dans son origine, ni dans son objectif. C'est une ivresse'

62 'Nous admirons ces danseurs et en ressentons une fierté d'exister, parce que nous savons, par leur allégresse tragique, qu'ils savent que l'allégresse n'est pas pour l'homme [...] nous les aimons parce qu'ils ont, au moment de leur danse, la révélation aigüe, beaucoup plus aigüe que dans les autres moments de leur existence, qu'ils sont éphémères et mortels, que leurs pères sont morts, qu'eux-mêmes vont vieillir, que peut-être l'amie avec laquelle ils dansent en ce moment périra demain d'un accident. Notre

fête, c'est la révélation subite du tragique: c'est le voile du bonheur qui se déchire… et voilà pourquoi nous sommes si joyeux!'

63 'Je défends surtout la vulnérabilité du corps. Simplement, je rappelle qu'on vit toujours dans un état post mortem, ou pour le dire autrement, que pour rester vivant, il faut avoir conscience qu'on ne fait que revenir à la vie. Le moindre mouvement que nous faisons est une joie. Cette joie est une réjouissance.'

64 'Nous fûmes quelque temps tangiblement immergés dans ce bleu nocturne, une expérience "totale". Il me semblait que mon corps, le mouvement et les choses autour de moi étaient intensément reliés. Et Merleau-Ponty, qui disait que nous ne faisons pas que regarder les choses, mais que les choses nous regardent aussi, me revint à l'esprit. Jusqu'à ce que, la lumière devenant trop vive, tout se désagrège.'

65 'Il n'y a pas de fête le matin. Les matinées sont tout juste bonnes pour les messes, ou à la rigueur pour les conférences scientifiques, les meetings politiques: pour les "petites" fêtes. Ce ne sont pas pour elles que nous revêtons nos plus beaux habits, nos véritables "habits du soir", nous, les hommes tragiques. Nous les réservons pour nos fêtes à nous, celles qui célèbrent le culte du mystère de l'homme et de la vie, et qui ont lieu invariablement le soir, quand toutes les lumières des hommes se sont éteintes.'

66 The terrorist attacks occurred on the 13th of November 2015 and the show was displayed from the 23rd to the 29th. See https://www.festival-automne.com/en/edition-2015/romeo-castellucci-le-metope-del-partenone

67 'Un fait divers devient tragique dès lors que l'on considère l'événement comme le dernier terme d'une structure qui lui préexiste […], en le mettant en relation avec une transcendance extérieure à ses causes immédiates […]; dire d'un tel accident qu'il est "tragique", c'est en faire un signe au contenu incertain, dans lequel le hasard semble se mettre à signifier'

68 'Il y a en effet […] une antinomie insurmontable entre les notions de hasard et de modification: si ce qui existe est essentiellement hasard, il s'ensuit que ce qui existe ne peut être modifié par aucun aléa, aucun "événement" (dans la mesure où aucun "événement", au sens d'un quelque chose faisant irruption et exception dans un champ de hasard, ne saurait jamais se produire).'

69 '*Rien* ne peut modifier *rien*. Or le réel n'est rien – c'est-à-dire rien de stable, rien de constitué, rien d'arrêté'
70 'Elle a l'appétit de voir absent'
71 'Le mot tragique qui, au terme de son énonciation très laborieuse, "produit" le silence. Rien à dire à la fin, si ce n'est dire la puissance du ne pas dire. Ciel vide, […] ou plutôt, vidé'

# Conclusion

1 'Si la réalité est inconcevable, il nous faut forger des concepts inconcevables'

# Works cited

Agamben, Giorgio (2007) *Profanations*, trans. Jeff Fort, Zone Books.
Aristotle (1996) *Poetics*, Penguin Classics.
Artaud, Antonin (1970) *The Theatre and Its Double*, trans. Victor Corti, Calder.
Artaud, Antonin (2004) *Suppôts et supplications*, in Antonin Artaud, *Œuvres*, Quarto Gallimard.
Aurelius, Marcus (2006) *Meditations*, Penguin Classics.
Auslander, Philip (1999) *Liveness, Performance in a mediatized culture*, Routledge.
Badiou, Alain (2013) *Éloge du théâtre*, Flammarion.
Badiou, Alain (2014) *Rhapsodie pour le théâtre: Court traité philosophique*, PUF.
Banu, George, dir. (2005) 'Romeo Castellucci, la permanence du risque', in *L'épreuve du risque*, Alternatives théâtrales 85–86, Festival d'Avignon.
Banu, George and Bruno Tackels, eds (2005) *Le Cas Avignon 2005, Regards Critiques*, L'entretemps.
Barraband, Mathilde (2020) 'Incroyable García', *COnTEXTES*, 26.
Bataille, Georges (1988) *Inner Experience*, trans. Leslie Anne Boldt, State University of New York Press.
Bergson, Henri (2003) *Time and Free Will an Essay on the Immediate Data of Consciousness*, Dover Publications.
Bernard Barbeau, Geneviève, Marty Laforest and Jessica Rioux-Turcotte (2020) 'De l'art et de la religion, ou quand les internautes commentent l'affaire Golgotha picnic', *COnTEXTES*, 26.
Borges, Jorge Luis (2000) 'Pierre Menard, Author of the Quixote', in *Fictions*, trans. Andrew Hurley, 33–43, Penguin Classics.
Borie, Monique (1997) *Le Fantôme ou le théâtre qui doute*, Acte Sud.
Bost, Bernadette (2009) 'Le théâtre de Rodrigo García: un autoportrait à la dynamite', *Recherches & Travaux*, 75: 103–10.
Bouko, Catherine (2010) *Théâtre et réception, Le spectateur postdramatique*, P.I.E. Peter Lang.
Brillaud, Jérôme (2010) 'If You Please! Theater, Verisimilitude, and Freedom in the Letter to d'Alembert', in Christie McDonald and Stanley Hoffman (eds), *Rousseau and Freedom*, 77–91, Cambridge University Press.

Caemerbeke, Pascale (2015) 'Quand la subversion nourrit la norme. *La chambre d'Isabella* de Jan Lauwers', *Essais*, 7: 96–108.
Cage, John (2013) *A Composer's Confessions*, Allia.
Callery, Dymphna (2005) *Through the Body: A Practical Guide to Physical Theatre. Exploration and Exercises in Devising, Mask-Work, Play, Complicité and Total Theatre*, Nick Hern Books.
Cassiers, Guy and Romeo Castellucci (2012) *Europe, le regard des artistes*, Editions Universitaires d'Avignon.
Castellucci, Claudia, Romeo Castellucci, Chiara Guidi, Joe Kelleher and Nicholas Ridout (2007) *The Theatre of Societas Raffaello Sanzio*, Routledge.
Castellucci, Romeo (2000) 'The Animal Being on Stage', *Performance Research*, 5 (2): 23–8, https://doi.org/10.1080/13528165.2000.10871727.
Castellucci, Romeo and Claudia Castellucci (2001) *Les Pèlerins de la matière*, Les Solitaires intempestifs.
Conroy, Colette (2010) *Theatre and the Body*, Theatre&.
Corrigan, Robert W., ed. (1965), *Tragedy, Vision and Form*, Chandler Publishing Company.
Cull, Laura (2012a) *Theatres of Immanence, Deleuze and the Ethics of Performance*, Palgrave Macmillan.
Cull, Laura (2012b) 'Performance as Philosophy: Responding to the Problem of "Application"', in *Theatre Research International*, vol. 37, 20–7, Cambridge University Press.
Cull, Laura and Alice Lagaay (2014) *Encounters in Performance Philosophy*, Palgrave Macmillan.
Danan, Joseph and Catherine Naugrette, eds (2018), *Les nouveaux matériaux du théâtre*, Presses Sorbonne Nouvelle.
De Beauvoir, Simone (1954) *Les Mandarins*, Gallimard.
Debray, Régis (2005) *Sur le pont d'Avignon*, Flammarion.
Degaine, André (2000) *Histoire du Théâtre Dessinée*, Nizet.
De Greef, Hugo and Jan Hoet (1994) *Jan Fabre, le guerrier de la beauté*, L'Arche.
Deleuze, Gilles (2006) *Difference and Repetition*, trans. Paul Patton, Bloomsbury.
Deleuze, Gilles and Félix Guattari (1994) *What is Philosophy?* Columbia Press.
Delhalle, Nancy, Aline Dethise and Romeo Castellucci (2012) *Le théâtre et ses publics: la création partagée*, les Solitaires Intempestifs.

Derrida, Jacques (1967) *Writing and Difference*, The University of Chicago Press.
Derrida, Jacques (2008) *The Animal that Therefore I Am*, trans. David Wills, Fordham University Press.
de Villeneuve-Soutoul, Monique (2013) 'Ambivalence de la métamorphose et paradoxes d'une poéthique du monstrueux', in Marianne Beauviche and Luk Van Den Dries (eds), *Jan Fabre, Esthétique du Paradoxe*, L'Harmattan.
Diderot, Denis (1975), *Discours de la poésie dramatique*, Larousse.
Didi-Huberman, Georges (1992) *Ce que nous voyons, ce qui nous regarde*, Les Editions de minuit.
Dobson, Julia (2013) 'Troubling matters: Mannequins, Murder and Gisèle Vienne's "corps troublants"', in Maggie Allison and Imogen Long (eds), *Women Matter / 'Femmes Matière: French and Francophone Women and the Material World'*, Peter Lang.
Dupont, Florence (2007) *Aristote ou le vampire du théâtre occidental*, Flammarion.
Egginton, William (2003) *How the World Became a Stage, Presence, theatricality and the question of modernity*, State University of New York Press.
Escola, Marc (2002) *Le Tragique*, Flammarion.
Foucault, Michel (1995) *Discipline and Punish*, trans. Alan Sheridan, Vintage Books.
Gallagher-Ross, Anna (2017) 'Uncanny Landscapes', Interview with Gisèle Vienne, *Theater*, 47 (2): 35–45.
Goetschel, Pascale (2004) *Renouveau et décentralisation du théâtre*, PUF.
Gravier, Jean-François (1947) *Paris et le désert français*, Flammarion.
Guénoun, Denis (2005), 'Une crise de la condition spectatrice?' in *Actions et acteurs*, Belin.
Guénoun, Denis (2014), 'The Face and the Profile', in L. Cull Ó Maoilearca and L. Lagaay (eds), *Encounters in Performance Philosophy*, 87–104, Palgrave Macmillan.
Gumbrecht, Hans Ulrich (2004) *Production of Presence, What Meaning cannot Convey*, Stanford University Press.
Gunn, Daniel (Spring 1984) 'Making Art Strange: A commentary on Defamiliarization', *The Georgia Review*, 38 (1): 25–33.
Jankélévitch, Vladimir (1994) *Penser la mort?* Liana Levi.
Johnson, Derek (2007) 'Fan-tagonism: Factions, Institutions, and Constitutive Hegemonies of Fandom', in Jonathan Gray, CornelSandvoss and C. Lee

Harrington (eds), *Fandom: Identities and Communities in a Mediated World*, New York University Press.
Johnston, Daniel (2017) *Theatre and Phenomenology: Manual Philosophy*, Red Globe Press.
Jolly, Geneviève (2006) 'Le rire insupportable de Rodrigo García', *Recherches & Travaux*, 47–61.
Koczy, Daniel (2018) *Beckett, Deleuze and Performance, A Thousand Failures and A Thousand Inventions*, Palgrave Macmillan.
Kowzan, Tadeusz (1992) *Sémiologie du théâtre*, Nathan.
Krasner, David and David Saltz, eds (2006), *Staging Philosophy: Intersections of Performance, Theater and Philosophy*, University of Michigan Press.
Lauwers, Jan (2010) '"Most Questions are More Interesting that their Answers", in Jan Lauwers in conversation with Jérôme Sans', *Contemporary Theatre Review*, 20 (4): 449–54.
Lavalette, Chloé (2020) 'Rodrigo García et la "crise de la culture": contextualisations critiques', *COnTEXTES*, 26.
Lehmann, Hans-Thies (2006) *Postdramatic Theatre*, Routledge.
Looseley, David L. (1995) *The Politics of Fun*, Berg.
McAuley, Gay (1999) *Space in Performance, Making Meaning in the Theatre*, University of Michigan.
Merleau-Ponty, Maurice (1960) *L'œil et l'esprit*, Gallimard.
Merleau-Ponty, Maurice (1994) 'Corpus', in Juliet Flower MacCannell and Laura Zakarin (eds), *Thinking Bodies*, Stanford University Press.
Miquel, Jean-Pierre (1997) *Propos sur la tragédie*, Actes Sud.
Nancy, Jean Luc (1994) *The Birth of Presence*, Stanford University Press.
Neveux, Olivier (2013) *Politiques du spectateur*, La découverte.
Nietzsche, Friedrich (1911) *The Twilight of the Idols*, trans. Anthony M. Ludovici, Oscar Levy.
Nietzsche, Friedrich (1956) *The Birth of Tragedy & Genealogy of Morals*, trans. Francis Golffing. Anchor Books.
Noiriel, Gérard (2009) *Histoire Théâtre Politique*, Agone.
Orozco, Lourdes (2013) *Theatre & Animals*, Theatre&, Palgrave Macmillan.
Orozco, Lourdes (2015) 'There and Not There: Looking at Animals in Contemporary Theatre', in Lourdes Orozco and Jennifer Parker-Starbuck (eds), *Performing Animality, Animal in Performance Practices*, Palgrave Macmillan.
Palazzolo, Claudia (2020) *Rave, dystopie du populaire*, Recherches en danse.

Peyton Jones, Jeremy (2011) 'Accommodating the Threat of the Machine: The Act of Repetition in Live Performance', in *Third Colloquium of the Society for Minimalist Music*, University of Wolverhampton.

Quignard, Pascal (2007) *La nuit sexuelle*, Flammarion.

Power, Cormac (2008) *Presence in Play: A Critique of Theories of Presence in the Theatre*, Flammarion.

Rancière, Jacques (2011) *The Emancipated Spectator*, trans. Gregory Elliott, Verso.

Reynolds, Bryan (2017) *Intermedial Theater: Performance Philosophy, Transversal Poetics, and the Future of Affect*, Palgrave Macmillan.

Ridout, Nicholas (2006) *Stage Fright, Animals and Other Theatrical Problems*, Cambridge University Press.

Ridout, Nicholas and Joe Kelleher (2006) *Contemporary Theatres in Europe: A Critical Companion*, Routledge.

Ridout, Nicholas and Joe Kelleher (2007) *The Theatre of Societas Raffaello Sanzio*, Routledge.

Rosset, Clément (1988) *Le Principe de cruauté*, Les Editions de Minuit.

Rosset, Clément (2004) *Le Réel, traité de l'idiotie*, Les Editions de Minuit.

Rosset, Clément (2012a) *Tropiques*, Les Editions de Minuit.

Rosset, Clément (2012b) *L'invisible*, Les Editions de Minuit.

Rosset, Clément (2013) *Logique du Pire*, PUF.

Rosset, Clément (2014) *La philosophie tragique*, PUF, Quadrige.

Sack, Daniel (2015) *After Live, Possibility, Potentiality, and the Future of Performance*, University of Michigan Press.

Sanchez, José A. (2014) *Practising the Real on the Contemporary Stage*, Intellect.

Sarrazac, Jean-Pierre (2000) *Critique du théâtre. De l'utopie au désenchantement*, Circé.

Sartre, Jean-Paul (1943) *L'être et le néant*, Gallimard.

Scheller, Max (1965) 'On the Tragic', in Robert W. Corrigan (ed.), *Tragedy, Vision and Form*, Chandler Publishing Company.

Schopenhauer, Arthur (2018) *The World as Will and Representation*, Cambridge University Press.

Schopenhauer, Arthur (2000) *The World as Will and Representation*, Dover Publications Inc.

Schuermann, Eva (2019) *Seeing as Practice. Philosophical Investigations into the Relation Between Sight and Insight*, Palgrave Macmillan.

Scott, Suzanne (May 2018) 'Towards a Theory of Producer/Fan Trolling', *Journal of Audience & Reception Studies*, 15 (1): 143–59.

Semenowicz, Dorota (2021) 'Playing Slaughter: On Staging Animal Deaths and Entangling Art with Life', *Contemporary Theatre Review*, 31 (4): 422–37.

Shklovsky, Viktor (2015) 'Art, as Device', *Poetics Today*, 36 (3): 151–74.

Sofia, Gabriele (2018) 'Blasphème, Sacré et Politique: quelques réflexions sur *Golgotha Picnic*', *Revista Brasileira de Estudios da Presença*, 8 (2): 348–63.

Stalpaert, Christel, Frederik Le Roy and Sigrid Bousset, eds (2007) *No Beauty for Me Where Human Life is Rare*, Academia Press and International Theatre & Film Books.

States, Bert (1987) *Great Reckonings in Little Rooms: On the Phenomenology of Theater*, University of California Press.

Szondi, Peter (2002) *An Essay on the Tragic*, trans. Paul Fleming, Stanford University Press.

Tackels, Bruno (2005) *Les Castellucci. Écrivains de plateau*, Les Solitaires Intempestifs.

Tackels, Bruno (2007) *Rodrigo García*, Les Solitaires Intempestifs.

Talon-Hugon, Carole (June 2006) *Avignon 2005, le conflit des héritages*, Du théâtre, Hors- série n°16.

Turk, Edward Baron (2011a) 'Avignon 2010: Celebrating the Body -Singular and Collective', *The French Review*, 85 (1): 30–41.

Turk, Edward Baron (2011b) *French Theatre Today: The View from New York, Paris, and Avignon*, University Press of Iowa.

Twitchin, Mischa (2016) *The Theatre of Death – The Uncanny Mimesis*, Palgrave Macmillan.

Ubersfeld, Anne (1996a) *Les termes clés de l'analyse du théâtre*, Editions du Seuil.

Ubersfeld, Anne (1996b) *Lire le théâtre II, l'école du spectateur*, Belin.

Urfalino, Philippe (2011) *L'invention de la politique culturelle*, Pluriel.

Van Den Dries, Luk (2005) *Corpus Jan Fabre, observations sur un processus de création*, L'Arche.

Van Den Dries, Luk (2006) 'Lust for Life. Images of the Body in the Work of Jan Fabre', *Discourses on Dance*, 3 (2): 33–43.

Van Den Dries, Luk and Marianne Beauviche, eds (2013) *Jan Fabre, Esthétique du Paradoxe*, L'Harmattan.

Yalom Irvin, D. (2016) *When Nietzsche Wept*, Harper Perennial Modern Classics.

Zola, Émile (1881) *Le naturalisme au théâtre*, Charpentier.

# Newspaper Articles And Videos

Boisseau, Rosita (2005) 'Le corps selon Jan Fabre laisse Avignon perplexe', *Le Monde*, 9 July, https://www.lemonde.fr/culture/article/2005/07/09/l-histoire-des-larmes-le-corps-selon-jan-fabre-laisse-avignon-perplexe_671258_3246.html (accessed 4 December 2022).

Bouchez, Emmanuelle (2018) 'The Sea Within', *Télérama*, n° 3570: 75.

Capron, Stéphane (2016) 'Rodrigo García quitte Montpellier et ne demandera pas de renouvellement de son mandat: il s'explique', *SceneWeb*, 7 October, http://www.sceneweb.fr/rodrigo-garcia-quitte-montpellier-et-ne-demandera-pas-de-renouvellement-de-son-mandat-il-sexplique/ (accessed 4 December 2022).

Castellucci, Romeo (2015) 'Festival d'automne: les dix mots de Romeo Castellucci', *Le Monde*, 4 September, https://www.theatregaronne.com/sites/default/files/pdf/le_monde_les_10_mots_de_romeo.pdf (accessed 4 December 2022).

Chrisafis, Angelique (2011) 'France and the Arts: A New Revolution', *The Guardian*, 24 March, https://www.theguardian.com/world/2011/mar/24/france-arts-revolution (accessed 4 December 2022).

Darge, Fabienne (2015a) 'Les 10 mots de Romeo Castellucci', *Le Monde*, 28 August, https://www.lemonde.fr/scenes/article/2015/09/04/festival-d-automne-les-dix-mots-de-romeo-castellucci_4746247_1654999.html (accessed 4 December 2022).

Darge, Fabienne (2015b) 'Castellucci, de sang et d'os', *Le Monde*, 24 November, https://www.lemonde.fr/scenes/article/2015/11/25/castellucci-de-sang-et-d-os_4816842_1654999.html (accessed 4 December 2022).

Darge, Fabienne and Brigitte Salino (2005) '2005, l'année de toutes les polémiques, l'année de tous les paradoxes', *Le Monde*, 27 July, https://www.lemonde.fr/culture/article/2005/07/27/avignon-2005-l-annee-detoutes-les-polemiques-et-de-tous-les-paradoxes_675755_3246.html (accessed 4 December 2022).

De Baecque, Antoine and René Solis (2005) 'La querelle d'Avignon joue en prolongation', *Libération*, 26 November, https://www.liberation.fr/evenement/2005/11/26/la-querelle-d-avignon-joue-en-prolongation_539771 (accessed 4 December 2022).

García, Rodrigo (2014) open letter in *Télérama*, 6 June, http://www.telerama.fr/scenes/lettre-rodrigo-garcia-intermittents,113422.php (accessed 4 December 2022).

Herzberg, Nathaniel, Rosita Boisseau, Fabienne Darge and Brigitte Salino (2005) 'Une partie du public et des critiques contestent la direction prise à Avignon', *Le Monde*, 23 July, https://www.lemonde.fr/culture/article/2005/07/23/une-partie-du-public-et-des-critiques-contestent-la-direction-prise-a-avignon_674982_3246.html (accessed 4 December 2022).

*La gazette de Montpellier*, http://www.lagazettedemontpellier.fr/.

Mereuze, Didier (2005) 'Festival d'Avignon 2005', *La Croix*, 25 July, http://www.la-croix.com/Archives/2005-07-25/Festival-d-Avignon-2005-_NP_-2005-07-25-241163 (accessed 4 December 2022).

Pascaud, Fabienne (2021) interview with Gisèle Vienne, https://youtu.be/wiqTr2-ebxQ (accessed 4 December 2022).

Salino, Brigitte (2005) 'Avignon, un début de festival noir, très noir', *Le Monde*, 14 July, https://www.lemonde.fr/culture/article/2005/07/14/un-debut-de-festival-noir-tres-noir_672437_3246.html (accessed 4 December 2022).

Salino, Brigitte (2015) 'Rodrigo García pousse le homard à bout', *Le Monde*, 8 Avril, https://www.lemonde.fr/culture/article/2015/04/08/rodrigo-garcia-pousse-le-homard-a-bout_4611501_3246.html (accessed 4 December 2022).

Van Den Dries, Luk (2011) *Artaud and Fabre*, Academia, https://www.academia.edu/31110681/Artaud_and_Fabre_2011.

Vidal, Nicolas (2015) 'Rodrigo García, un avant-gardiste controversé', *El País*, quoted by *Putsch*, 17 April, https://putsch.media/20150417/culture/actualites/rodrigo-garcia-un-avant-gardiste-controverse/ (accessed 4 December 2022).

# Index

Abramović, Marina   12, 32, 34, 81–2
accident   17–18, 111, 139–40, 159, 163, 165
Agamben, Giorgio   25, 89, 92–3, 142, 171
anti-perception   23–4
anxiety   138, 148, 155
apocalypse   145–6, 161
Aristotle   113–14, 137–8, 155, 167
Artaud, Antonin   12, 16, 35, 47–8, 55–6, 69, 95, 109–12, 121–3, 129–30, 136–8, 143–7, 151, 173
aura   117, 130–3
Aurelius, Marcus   2, 6

Bausch, Pina   11, 57, 65, 75
Bergson, Henri   124
Brecht, Berthold   55, 122, 148

Cage, John   82
Camus, Albert   62
cancel culture   39
capitalism   92
Castellucci, Romeo   5, 8–10, 12–13, 15–17, 32, 34, 51–2, 56, 61, 65–6, 75, 77–8, 98–106, 108, 117–21, 125–7, 136–8, 141–53, 161, 163, 169
catharsis   91, 130, 136, 138, 156, 169
chaos   88, 112, 118, 124, 145–6, 148–9, 154–6, 165–7
Cicero   166
conscience   69, 72
controversy   3, 35, 49, 72, 96–7
critics   9, 10, 31, 33, 37, 40–3, 66–8
cruelty   12, 56, 69, 109–10, 112, 121, 125, 132, 144–5

dance   11, 35, 54, 66, 78, 88, 134, 158–9
death   13, 17, 73, 93–5, 104, 110–11, 130, 134, 137, 139–41, 144–5, 158, 160–1, 163–4
de Beauvoir, Simone   160
Debord, Guy   136
decentralization   46–8
defamiliarization   25, 85–6, 101, 107, 173
Deleuze, Gilles   21–3, 25, 61–2, 65, 73–4, 85, 106, 145, 171, 173
Derrida, Jacques   102–3, 125, 144
difference   25, 73–6, 101, 114, 124–5, 144–5
Dionysian   91, 115, 116, 156
dissonance   94, 116, 123–5, 155
domestication   55, 98, 129
Don Quixote   63, 74
double   3–5, 14, 18, 23, 77, 105, 128, 142, 144, 148–9, 154, 166
duration   3, 12, 35, 65, 72, 76, 84–5, 107, 124, 150, 172

empathy   2, 43, 66, 110, 129
endurance arts   11, 55
epiphany   63, 69
Eros   133–4, 158
essence   114, 129, 135, 142

Fabre, Jan   1, 3, 5, 8–10, 12–14, 21, 32, 34–7, 40, 42, 45, 49, 52, 56, 66–73, 75–7, 79–80, 83–4, 89–93, 99, 108, 125–36, 149, 158–60
Foucault, Michel   53, 55, 128
fourth wall   55–6, 72
Freud, Sigmund   19

García, Rodrigo   5, 8–10, 12–13, 40–1, 49–50, 52, 87–8, 94–7, 99, 104, 108, 126
genesis   145, 161
genius   89–90, 126
God   93, 104, 134–5, 144, 149, 157–8, 164, 166
Greek tragedies   115, 134–5

Hamlet   116
Hegel   171

iconoclasm   141–3
iconography   41
idiocy, idiotic   17–19, 40, 75, 77, 81, 97, 149, 157
illusion   8, 14, 72, 101, 108, 111, 145
improvisation   67–8
indetermination   154–6, 161, 166
indifference   102, 114, 117–18, 152
insignificance   111–12, 128, 152–3
instinct   70, 115, 128–9, 133, 155
interpretation   5, 24, 38, 69, 81, 109, 111, 113, 116, 118, 137, 146, 149, 152–3, 164–6, 173
intuition   124, 129

Kantor, Tadeusz   11, 14, 57, 65, 96

language   23, 50, 65, 68, 105–6, 118, 122, 125, 127, 129, 136–7, 143–8
Lauwers, Jan   5, 7–11, 13–14, 32, 49, 72, 75, 108, 125–6, 148, 163
Lehmann, Hans-Thies   5–7, 11, 14, 37, 72, 82, 109, 174
love   71, 75, 113, 153, 167

manifestation   14, 166
matter   10, 29, 117–18, 137, 151–2
Merleau-Ponty, Maurice   28, 160
Miller, Arthur   154
mimesis   128, 138, 142, 167

naked body   35, 41, 67, 87, 92, 102, 119
Nancy, Jean-Luc   6, 22, 70, 145, 159
narration, narrative   11, 32, 36–8, 78, 107, 123
Nietzsche   115–16, 123, 126, 155–6, 167
non-recognition   64, 68–9, 107, 120–1, 172

obscene   9, 31, 71–2, 86–8, 92, 95, 107, 172
Ostermeier, Thomas   4, 32

painting   35–6, 68, 90, 126, 166–7
phenomenology   63–4, 147, 173
physical effort   1, 72, 77, 84
physical exhaustion   12, 135–6
physical theatre   11, 35, 55, 59
plague   112, 129–30, 138
primitive   69, 84, 115, 127–30, 132, 143
profanation   25, 89, 92–3, 142, 146
psychological theatre   12, 35
puppet   10–11, 14, 19, 95–6, 107, 173

Rancière, Jacques   27, 50, 55–6
rebirth   156, 161
recognition   3–4, 8, 19, 21–2, 24, 27, 59, 61–6, 68–9, 72, 74–6, 85–6, 92, 106–8, 115, 120–1, 124, 134, 171–2
rehearsal   1, 12–13, 67, 136
repetition   3, 6, 25, 72–6, 107, 110–12, 139, 145, 150, 153, 173
revelation   15, 108, 113, 115, 125, 140–1, 146, 153, 159
ritual   69, 78–9, 90–1
Rosset, Clément   8, 17–21, 23–5, 73, 77, 80, 111–13, 123–5, 137, 139–41, 145, 149, 151–3, 155–7, 159, 161, 164–6, 171, 173

Scheller, Max   116
Schelling   113–15
Schopenhauer   115, 163
semiology, semiotics   26, 43, 63, 67, 107, 147
sensations   23, 27, 110, 126, 136
senses, sensory experience   23, 25, 27, 36, 75, 78, 86, 151
sex   2, 67, 86, 97, 122
Shklovsky, Viktor   25, 62–3, 85–6, 101, 106–7, 171, 173
signifiant, signifier   20, 80
silence   82, 116, 169
simplicity   95, 146–51, 157
States, Bert   63–4, 147, 173
sublime   113, 115
suicide   144

Thanatos   133, 134, 158
theatre of cruelty   12, 56, 69–70, 109–10, 144, 151
theatricality   4–6, 24, 42
tragic event   164–7
tragic hero   114–16, 135, 164, 167, 173

tragic joy   155, 158–9
tragic pleasure   122–3
tragic trap   112, 121, 123, 140
training   25, 70–1, 77, 84, 91–2, 97, 129, 132–4, 136
transcendence, transcendental forces   69, 126–7, 151–2, 165

uncanny valley   96
unfamiliar   36–7, 85, 101, 107, 132, 136, 148
unveiling   24, 121, 146, 162

Vienne, Gisèle   5, 8–11, 13–14, 32, 65, 70, 75, 78–9, 83, 95–6, 108, 110, 149, 172
Vilar, Jean   31, 49, 51
violence   34, 38, 45, 53, 97, 103–4, 108, 110, 116, 118, 121, 163–4

warriors of beauty   89, 130–2, 135

Zola   32, 34, 51

www.ingramcontent.com/pod-product-compliance
Lightning Source LLC
Chambersburg PA
CBHW052113300426
44116CB00010B/1648